FROM CORUNNA
TO WATERLOO

THE NAPOLEONIC LIBRARY

Other books in the series include:

1815: THE RETURN OF NAPOLEON
Paul Britten Austin

ON THE FIELDS OF GLORY
The Battlefields of the 1815 Campaign
Andrew Uffindell and Michael Corum

LIFE IN NAPOLEON'S ARMY
The Memoirs of Captain Elzéar Blaze
Introduction by Philip Haythornthwaite

THE MEMOIRS OF BARON VON MÜFFLING
A Prussian Officer in the Napoleonic Wars
Baron von Müffling

WATERLOO LECTURES
A Study of the Campaign of 1815
Colonel Charles Chesney

WATERLOO LETTERS
A Collection of Accounts From Survivors of the
Campaign of 1815
Edited by Major-General H. T. Siborne

www.frontline-books.com/napoleoniclibrary

FROM CORUNNA TO WATERLOO

THE LETTERS AND JOURNALS OF TWO NAPOLEONIC HUSSARS

MAJOR EDWIN GRIFFITH AND
CAPTAIN FREDERICK PHILIPS
15TH (KING'S) HUSSARS
1801–1816

Edited by Gareth Glover

Frontline Books

From Corunna to Waterloo

A Greenhill Book

First published in 2007 by Greenhill Books, Lionel Leventhal Limited
www.greenhillbooks.com

This edition published in 2015 by

Frontline Books
an imprint of Pen & Sword Books Ltd,
47 Church Street, Barnsley, S. Yorkshire, S70 2AS
For more information on our books, please visit
www.frontline-books.com, email info@frontline-books.com
or write to us at the above address.

ISBN: 978-1-84832-844-0

CIP data records for this title are available from the British Library

Printed and bound by CPI Group (UK) Ltd, Croydon, CR0 4YY

CONTENTS

PREFACE

'One line on the spot is worth half a page of recollections'

These words, written on the front page of Major Edwin Griffith's daily journal for the year 1813, sum up entirely my reason for writing this book.

A number of memoirs have already been published over the last century or so, by men who served in what is now commonly termed the Napoleonic wars, describing the wartime exploits of just some of the thousands of men who took part in those protracted wars; a number of these memoirs are, however, deeply flawed. The clamour by Victorian audiences to read of the valiant exploits of their forebears; and the harsh economic realities of life after the wars for many of the returning men, led to a profusion of publications describing these events. Some were written soon after the events they describe and seek to give a relatively truthful view of their experiences and thus are of use in our search for the facts. However, too many of these hugely entertaining books were written and published well in excess of forty years after the events they purport to describe and must be treated very cautiously indeed. Not only had time and age muddled memories, but incidents became confused scenes and occasionally these transformed their complete interpretation of events; but there is also evidence of the insidious effect of the publication of the first great histories of these wars, including Napier's history of the Peninsula War and other popular productions, which can be seen to have subtly influenced those journals and memoirs. It should also be borne in mind that, because so many of these memoirs were printed during this particular period, to ensure success in the cut-throat world of print, their memoirs had to be very entertaining indeed! This factor should not be underestimated; it is no coincidence that many of the most famous memoirs, with their masterful descriptions of battle, some of which have become some of the great literary masterpieces of military history, appeared during this very period. This is not to say that the incidents described were not real memories, but it is certain that many embellished their version of events and undoubtedly some completely invented memories or acquired the

Preface

memories of others, claiming them as their own. These distortions can sometimes affect our understanding of these momentous events; for at best some are guilty of bending the truth; at worst some completely distort facts and mislead. Some others are extremely poor regurgitations of these very histories that had started to appear, giving no insight into the actual life and sufferings of the writer and his colleagues, and thus are completely worthless.

To anyone wishing to study and understand how these wars were fought, how the men truly viewed things as they occurred and how they survived the harsh rigours of interminable marching with few provisions and little shelter only to face almost certain death or severe mutilation in battle as their prize, then such journals written with so much hindsight are often a terrible thing.

In such circumstances the discovery of a mass of letters written home from Spain and France and daily diaries full of entries made on the spot and with great immediacy, with no other aim than to entertain themselves and their friends, provide a vital source of information on life as a soldier in Wellington's army and a very valuable aid to our greater understanding of the military history of this period.

Gareth Glover

INTRODUCTION

I had been aware for many years that a short selection of letters written by Major Edwin Griffith 15th Hussars while in Spain and France had been published in *The National Library of Wales Journal* by Mr Norman Tucker of Colwyn Bay, a local historian of some renown. A couple of years ago, I decided to check with the Flintshire Record Office, based at The Old Rectory in Hawarden and the home of the original letters, whether this was the full extent of the documents they had relating to this officer. I was surprised and intrigued when I received the answer that the published letters formed a mere fraction of the archive, as there existed a voluminous correspondence sent to his family and a number of journals besides, not only from Edwin Griffith but also from his nephew Frederick Philips also of the 15th Hussars.

Having obtained photocopies of some of the journals, it was obvious from a cursory examination that they were clearly written contemporaneously with events and they proved to be fascinating and instructive. The letters proved a little more difficult to read, the paper being fragile, the ink fading, and the writing especially difficult, as the shortage of writing paper and the expense of postage meant that the sheets had been written on both horizontally and vertically. Indeed the parlous state of the papers forced me to photograph digitally hundreds of individual pages and to transcribe them painstakingly from the resultant prints, a very tiresome and laborious task. Comparing the originals with the transcribed versions of the few letters as published, I must state that I found a few errors in the reading of the texts by Mr Tucker, but more seriously, I have discovered that at some stage an unfortunate error has occurred which means that various sections of different letters have been badly muddled, either in transcription or in printing. Therefore the printed versions in this book are at times markedly at variance with those published by Mr Tucker in *The National Library of Wales Journal*, but I have checked the originals thoroughly to ensure my version is certainly correct.

The learned reader well may be aware that there are already some published accounts from the 15th Hussars during the Napoleonic wars, namely Captain

Introduction

Alexander Gordon's journal and Adjutant Charles Jones' diary relating to the Corunna campaign, Joseph Thackwell's journal of Spain and Waterloo, and Assistant Surgeon William Gibney's journal which mostly relates to Waterloo, and therefore will wonder if there is need for another memoir of this regiment to be published. The answer is undoubtedly a resounding yes. Edwin Griffith and Frederick Philips proceeded to Spain with the Army under Sir John Moore in 1808, both writing a number of letters, and Edwin further wrote a full journal of the Corunna campaign. Since the regiment was effectively operated in wings, Edwin often serving in a wing separated from Gordon, their experiences were markedly different and thus this journal helps to complete the story of the regiment's part in the Corunna campaign.

The letters from the regiment while in England prior to the Corunna campaign, when they were often spread across vast tracts of England in small detachments to quell electoral riots or to act as customs officers, are often intriguing. Occasionally these duties were suspended so that they could act as a bodyguard to the royal family, or to escort huge shipments of treasure. Those from the Midlands between 1809 and 1812, where they policed the civil disruption and economic unrest caused by industrialisation, high taxation and the shortage of grain, are again very interesting in regard to the cavalry's domestic role as Britain's police force.

The journals and letters of the 1813–14 campaign, when the regiment rejoined Wellington's army in Spain, are virtually unique with regard to the regiment, as they provide a very valuable addition to our knowledge of the actions of this regiment in Spain and southern France, including their valiant part in the battles of Vitoria and Orthes, where Edwin actually commanded the regiment. The only previously published diaries of the regiment during this period, being Thackwell's and the anonymous 'Jottings from my sabretasch',* which are very limited in their extent. Their journals and letters in Belgium during the Waterloo campaign further advance our knowledge of the regiment in this famous campaign.

These young officers seem to have had strong family ties, spending as much

---

* Some claim this work is that of a Sergeant William Tale; however, I have been unable to establish this as fact as there is no mention of a Sergeant Tale at Waterloo nor in the Military General Service Roll. Indeed my own research to date offers up a more likely candidate. We do know a little about this person from his jottings. His Christian name was William, he served at Sahagun, Vitoria, Orthes, Toulouse and Waterloo; he served at Waterloo as a troop sergeant major and served for twelve years after Waterloo before retiring. By a process of simple elimination, from the six troop sergeant major's present at Waterloo, only one appears to match the criteria, and that is Troop Sergeant Major William Dawes. There is however no question as to the veracity of the memoirs but as there is some doubt to his identity I have simply referred to him throughout as William.

Introduction

time together on campaign as duty allowed and both wrote regularly to maintain links with those left at home. Their letters were clearly only intended for the eyes of their family and friends and are therefore of great value, as they indicate their true feelings at that very moment regarding events and the conditions they endured, indeed they often also contain strong criticism of those around them, particularly those in command, the conduct of operations and the Spanish!

My intention within this book is to publish as much of the original text of the letters of Edwin Griffith and Frederick Philips as possible and merely to interject short passages to aid the flow of the story for the general reader. For those who require a more detailed analysis, I have included a number of footnotes, which I hope will be of interest, but I trust they do not detract from the fine story that our two correspondents have to tell. I have not altered the letters in any significant way, but I have altered the often phonetic spelling of place names and persons to the usual modern spelling to aid identification and I have written words out in full where the constant use of apostrophes can irritate and greatly disrupt the flow. In the few letters where I have omitted a portion of text, this is purely because it is of a particularly social nature and of no significance to us now, but I have kept such omissions to an absolute minimum; in the opposite situation, where a word is omitted in the original to make a sentence read correctly or I have been unable to read the original word and have been forced to guess, then the inserted words are identified by square brackets according to convention.

It has been a great privilege to work on the correspondence of Edwin Griffith and Frederick Philips and to get to know them so intimately. I am glad to say that the resultant body of work was well worth all the effort involved and forms an important new body of material regarding many aspects of the role of Wellington's light cavalry.

HISTORICAL BACKGROUND

Edwin Griffith, the thirteenth child of Thomas Griffith and Henrietta Maria Clarke of Rhual in Flintshire, North Wales, was born on 15 January 1786, by which time seven of his older siblings were already dead. As with many younger sons of the landed gentry at this time, Edwin would have faced the choice of the clergy or the army for a profession. His decision was probably swayed by the success of his brother Watkin, a major in the 29th Light Dragoons in India; and his uncle on his mother's side, one Lieutenant-General Sir Alured Clarke, who had served with distinction in America and India, soon to become colonel of the 7th Regiment of Foot and later still a field marshal; and whose positive influence could certainly be exerted to help Edwin's career. His father's service as a captain with the Flintshire yeomanry would also have given Edwin some experience of a martial life. Thomas Griffith had been appointed as captain of the Mold Volunteer cavalry in 1797 and when a second troop was raised at Hawarden in 1803 he was confirmed captain commandant, a post he retained until he resigned due to ill health in June 1811.*

Edwin was subsequently entered for the army at the tender age of 14 as a cornet in the 25th Light Dragoons on 31 May 1800.† It is unclear why this regiment was chosen, as there is no clear family connection, indeed it is likely that Edwin never served with the regiment, as it was quite normal practise at this time to enrol young children in a regiment if a vacancy came available, well before they took up army duties, to gain years of seniority on the army list. The Duke of York had introduced reforms to stop the enrolment of children under the age of 16, but these rules were yet to be universally followed. The date of Edwin's commission is also significant; in late 1799 the light cavalry regiments

---

* I must thank Philip Haythornthwaite for bringing this information to my attention. He is mentioned in Bryn Owen's paper Yeomanry Cavalry in Flintshire 1797–1838, published in the *Bulletin of the Military Historical Society*, vol. XV p. 131 (1975).
† The Army records at the National Archives state 31 May 1800, but Wylly has 17 February 1799 on the basis of the Army List of 1801.

had all been ordered to expand their numbers from nine troops to ten troops each, thereby creating the requirement for an additional cornet per regiment; it is likely that this was the position that Thomas Griffith bought for his son.

It is actually more likely that Edwin commenced his army career in February 1801,[*] having exchanged into the 15th Light Dragoons on 15 January 1801, his 15th birthday. Again there are no clear family connections to this regiment; although there had been a Lieutenant John Griffith in Elliot's Light Horse, a predecessor of the 15th Light Dragoons, between 1759 and 1762, the family link has not been proven. Edwin was to see out the entire war in the 15th; his rise through the ranks of the regiment was steady and he gained the rank of major on 5 November 1812.[†]

He was joined in the regiment on 13 October 1808[‡] by his nephew Frederick Charles Philips, son of Edwin's eldest sister Henrietta Maria, as a cornet fresh from graduating at the Royal Military College. He was also to enjoy steady promotions, becoming a Captain by 16 April 1812.

Both served in the Corunna campaigns, much of the 1813–14 campaign in Spain and Portugal and the Waterloo campaign.

The Rhual Connection

Throughout all of their letters, it is clear that these young men held a strong affinity to the family seat at Rhual, near Mold, in North Wales, but there is a constant thread of discussion regarding the problems of the cost of its upkeep.

It is unclear from the records as to the original date of the house, but it certainly existed in the 1520s as it is mentioned in the diaries of John Leland, who noted that 'Robert Edwards, a gentleman, dwelleth at Rhual on the north side of the Alen yn Moldsdale having plenty of wood and goodly meadow by Alenside'.

This original house has largely disappeared, as a descendant, Evan Edwards, had the house rebuilt in 1634, although some thick stone walls in the current property would indicate that at least part of the original house was incorporated within the new. Rhual Hall was rebuilt in brick rather than local stone and had a grand staircase installed; indeed it was the admiration of the local gentry. The house seems to have survived the ravages of the Civil War by the very deft political machinations of the Edwards family; initially siding with the King; they successfully changed sides in 1644 when the tide appeared to be changing, and aided the parliamentarian siege of nearby Hawarden castle.

---

[*] Evidence at Rhual bears out a January transfer date and that Edwin proceeded to join the regiment in the February; however Wylly states the exchange was dated 15 June 1801.

[†] The Army list and Wylly confirm this date; however Mr Tucker states 5 November 1811; but this seems to be a typographical error.

[‡] I have followed the army records but Wylly states 18 October.

Historical Background

However, the male line failed in 1700 and the house passed to the elder daughter Mary who was married to one Walter Griffith, Edwin's great grand father, and from this time on the house became the headquarters and heart of the Griffith's family and their descendants. Rhual has remained in the same family, with one short break which will be explained in due course, until the present day; however, the residing family has changed surname on three occasions in total when the male line has failed and the house has passed through the female side. This last occurred in 1921 to the present name Heaton; the house is now home to Major and Mrs Basil Heaton, who continue to care for the beautiful Jacobean house, fine landscaped park and gardens and the splendid family heirlooms within.

ACKNOWLEDGEMENTS

I must start by thanking sincerely Major and Mrs Basil Heaton for so gracefully allowing me to work on the Rhual papers and publish the resulting work. I must also thank them for kindly inviting me into their beautiful home to view the numerous artefacts of the Griffith family still housed within its walls. It was very moving to handle the very writing cases which they had taken with them to Spain, France and Belgium and to view Edwin's writing still etched into the panes of glass. It was also a privilege to meet Major Heaton, a hero of the Second World War, whom I met on the eve of his visit to Normandy for the sixtieth anniversary of the landings, in which he played such a significant part, being one of the first to land on Gold Beach on 6 June 1944.

I must also thank all the staff at the Flintshire Record Office, for their patience and understanding during all my various requests and queries regarding the Rhual papers and the local area in Georgian times; particularly Mr Paul Mason and Miss Elizabeth Pettit the archivists, particularly the latter who patiently sat with me while I carried out the laborious task of digitally photographing a vast number of the documents which were too frail to withstand photocopying, so that I could work on them at my leisure.

With any such book, one also has to seek the learned help of a great many people, too many to list individually, but to all I offer my sincere thanks for the time and effort they gave up willingly to help me answer the myriad of questions thrown up by the letters and journals.

I wish to particularly thank Philip Haythornthwaite who kindly read the manuscript and suggested a number of improvements to the work.

Finally I must thank my devoted wife Mary and my children Sarah and Michael, for putting up with me and my hogging of the computer for so many nights!

NOTE ON SPELLING

The letters have been transcribed from the original sources as accurately as possible. Clearly, the manuscript material is subject to the idiosyncracies of early nineteenth-century spelling: Edwin Griffith especially uses spellings now defunct, and these have been retained. Examples include:

cloathes
clokes
story (for storey)
stile (for style)
staid (for stayed)
shewed (for showed)
chuse (for choose)

He also often has plurals ending in '-ys' where modern spelling has '-ies', and regularly uses ''s' for the plurals such as 'Mainwaring's' or 'balcony's'. The word 'eat' is found with a past meaning, i.e., instead of 'ate'. Words ending in -ic often have a final k, e.g., garlick, politick, etc. Terminations in -our often coexist with -or, e.g., honor and honour are found. Occasional uses of non-standard spellings (such as chaco for shako) are marked by [*sic*], but in general the usage has been followed without comment provided that the meaning is clear.

Letters written in haste are sometimes unpolished; lacunae in the text are marked by text in square brackets [ ]. Often names are in abbreviated form and the missing elements are also supplied in square brackets.

MAP

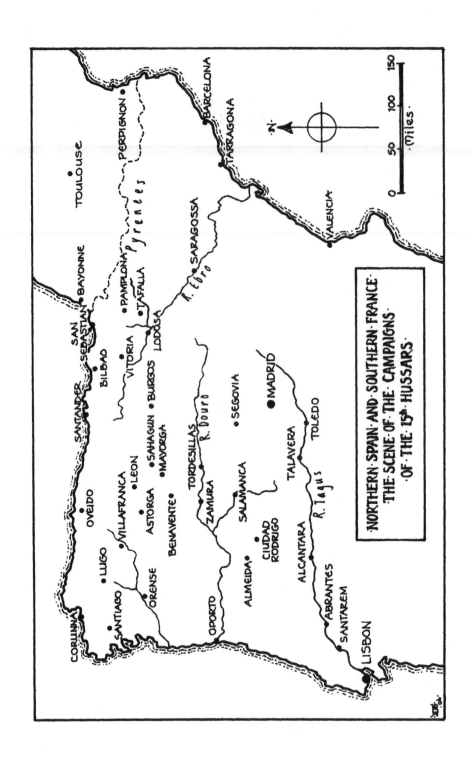

NORTHERN·SPAIN·AND·SOUTHERN·FRANCE·
·THE·SCENE·OF·THE·CAMPAIGNS·
·OF·THE·15th·HUSSARS·

Chapter 1

HOME SERVICE

Edwin Griffith spent the short chilly winter days of early February 1801 with his mother Henrietta, preparing his uniform and equipment for his 'great adventure'. For Edwin was now a cornet in the 15th (King's) Light Dragoons, his father Thomas having arranged his exchange from the 25th Light Dragoons on the day of his fifteenth birthday. Edwin had nominally served with the 25th since His Majesty King George III had graciously granted him a cornetcy (by purchase) on 31 May 1800, but he probably never saw the regiment. This was not of concern to him, for it was quite normal for the landed gentry to purchase a junior commission for their siblings to gain seniority while absent still playing in the nursery.

The cost of a commission as cornet was not an inconsequential sum, for his father would have paid at least the official price of £735. The Duke of York, in his reforming zeal as commander-in-chief, had ordered that young men must be sixteen years of age before they could become a cornet, but it was to be a few years more before this reform really took effect.

The exchange to the 15th had major advantages; being the king's own regiment there was a greater possibility of royal recognition and promotion; and having duly entered his sixteenth year, it was time to take up arms and begin his military life in earnest. The cost of kitting out a cavalry officer would have been astronomical; a fine charger and its saddlery, full dress and undress uniforms, a curved light cavalry sword and accoutrements all cost a pretty penny, and it was difficult to maintain the life of a cavalry officer without a private income. Indeed, a board of officers was assembled in 1806 to enquire into the 'expense attending the equipment of a subaltern officer' on first joining the 15th Hussars and concluded that the cost of two horses, their uniform, arms and appointments amounted to some £458. However, this was far from the total cost, as the board added that it was 'almost absolutely necessary' to employ a private servant and to provide an allowance 'to support himself in that situation as an officer and gentleman'; and this did not include the cost of purchase. Indeed it is clear that an initial outlay of close to £1,000 was required to set up a young man as a cornet in the cavalry and he would require a further £500 per annum to maintain his lifestyle.

Edwin's uniform would have consisted of a short tight-fitting jacket in dark blue, laced across the front with twenty bars of silver braid, (the regulations also called for scale epaulettes and wings but it is uncertain whether the 15th wore these), buff breeches and long black boots, all topped by a 'Tarleton' helmet with a black fur crest and a distinctive all scarlet plume and turban, a regimental distinction.

When all was ready, Edwin proceeded to join his regiment, with all his equipment in a great trunk, presumably by mail coach; but one of his final acts was to scratch a message on the window pane near the top of the stairs at home as a permanent reminder of the momentous day; it is still there today etched in the glass.

Edwin Griffith left this for to join the 15th Drags.
At Dorchester on Monday 16 day of February 1801.

The 15th Light Dragoons, who had originally been raised in 1759 as Colonel Elliott's Regiment of Light Dragoons, had an excellent reputation; they served in the Seven Years War, particularly distinguishing themselves at the battle of Emsdorff in 1760; and in the Dutch campaign of the Duke of York in 1793, where they again distinguished themselves, particularly at Villiers en Couche in 1794. Having returned from a second foray into Holland in 1799, the regiment had returned to home duties, which generally meant policing the towns and aiding the revenue men. Indeed five troops of the regiment were stationed in Dorchester on Edwin's arrival, with a detachment at Poole on the preventive service,* a troop at Shaftesbury, two at Trowbridge and one at Wells. Edwin would have slowly settled into the life of a soldier, learning his duties, practising his riding and sword drill and learning how to act like an officer. But the regiment was not to lie idle for long; on 28 March they received orders to hold themselves at a moment's notice to march to Somerset to quell some serious riots. Indeed they shortly marched to Taunton and the neighbouring towns with two troops sent as far as Bodmin and Launceston. In that April HRH the Duke of Cumberland†

---

* The adjutant's diary for 23 January reads, 'Received letter from the Comptroller at Poole informing of the party under Sergeant Kitson having seized 500 tubs of spirits etc.' Wylly (1908) p. 133.

† Lieutenant General HRH Ernest August, Duke of Cumberland, became a field marshal in 1813. He had commanded the Hanoverian cavalry in Holland in 1793–4 and lost his left eye and was severely wounded in the right arm at Tournay. He was renowned for his bravery following an incident seven months after his wounding, when he lifted a French dragoon bodily out of his saddle and carried him a prisoner into the British lines. He commanded home districts throughout the war but in 1806 and again in 1813 he commanded the Hanoverian troops in expeditions into northern Europe. His affinity with the Hanoverians led to George IV leaving him as Governor of the German Kingdom

became colonel of the regiment vice Lord Dorchester* and orders arrived to augment the regiment's establishment to 101 men and horses per troop.

The regiment was on the move again in August and spread across the country from Winchester to Stevenage. They moved again in early October to the Guildford–Basingstoke area. Presumably Edwin's early days would have been hectic and disconcerting; however, by the November when his first surviving letter home was written, it is clear that he had settled in well, and he evidently did not have a great deal of time to sit writing although he certainly had time to develop an eye for the local ladies. He starts with an apology for his tardiness in writing to his sister Charlotte and mentions having received news from his brother-in-law Morgan of Golden Grove in Flintshire.

Guildford Barracks, 4 November 1801

With love and repentance dearest sister I trembling write to you. I assure you I never was so astonished at your not having heard from me since July, as I *positively* wrote to you in the beginning of September and have been waiting for you to answer it ever since, but however misfortune will happen in the best regulated families, and that has been the case here, but now we are settled (I hope) for some time our correspondence may go on more regularly than ere.

Pleasant quarters as far as I've seen and I like it much, by some good fortune or other I have got acquainted with several very pleasant girls, which you perhaps know make any place pleasant. To me Mr Fulham has left a card for me with my mother, I intend calling upon him in a day or two when I will give you a history of the family (which I hear is rather a quisical [*sic*] one) but no matter for that, if they are civil, are they any kind of relatives to the Captain? Lynch† has left us and gone to Basingstoke for which I am very sorry as he is as perfectly good natured pleasant a creature as ever was, he and I often talk of *old combemere*‡ and its charming inhabitants, the cottage, skiff *Brankillen, Cheddar cheese* etc etc are common topics for conversation, . . .

---

until the accession of Queen Victoria, when, as the kingdom could not pass to a woman, he became King Ernest I of Hanover. He died in Hanover in 1851.

* Colonel Guy Carleton, Lord Dorchester, had originally joined the army as an ensign in 1742. He had spent much of his career in America and served at the capture of Quebec and later became governor of the province. Ceding the Colonelcy of the 15th to the Duke of Cumberland, he became colonel of the 4th Dragoons but died in 1808 at the ripe age of eighty-four.

† Captain Lynch Cotton became major in 1805 and transferred to the 17th Light Dragoons in 1806. With them he soon sailed to India, where unfortunately he died in 1809.

‡ Combemere Abbey was the home of the Cotton family.

I received this morning a long letter from *Morgan** giving me an account of everything in his part of the world which I shall answer soon, some of you will of course write the moment you can after another nephew or niece makes its appearance, the fifteenth shall fire a foie de joy on the occasion. We hear the reduction is immediately† to take place thank goodness I am out of the way of it as I think I shall never get into a Regiment I like so well as this again.

We are to be reviewed by the Duke of York in the course of a fortnight. I am one of the officers fixed upon to do the sword exercise in speed before HRH, glorious fun;‡ I think I shall astonish his weak mind for men.

The Duke of Cumberland asked me the other day where my uncle§ was, I said on a visit to my friends in Wales, he then asked me if we were a large family and how many sisters I had. I told him. I had, he thinks *Four*,¶ they are I dare say nice girls, are they not; till he put that question to me I got on very well but I did not exactly know how to answer that but I did. I told him you were and that I loved you all very much, he smiled and said I was a happy fellow which I really think I was so I shall conclude with wishing to always.

Ever yours, Edwin

The peace having been declared, the government looked to reduce its army budget dramatically; the regiment was forced to discharge 325 men in May and in late June another 132 went, including Joseph Thackwell** to the half-pay list. In August 1802 the regiment moved to Worcester, with troops detached to Gloucester, Hereford, Bewdley and Kidderminster. However, the peace was

---

* Morgan was his brother-in-law, being married to Edwin's second surviving sister, Louisa, who lived at Golden Grove.

† The preliminaries for the Peace of Amiens which ended the revolutionary wars were signed in October 1801 but were not ratified until March 1802. Plans were obviously put in place immediately for a reduction of the army and the 15th were not exempt. Being one of the more senior cornets (thanks to the seniority gained during his appointment to the 25th Light Dragoons), Edwin was sure of avoiding being placed on half pay.

‡ Wylly states that the Prince of Wales and Duke of York witnessed another exhibition of the sword exercise at speed in May 1802.

§ Colonel Sir Alured Clarke, 7th Foot.

¶ His four surviving sisters were Henrietta Maria (born 1770), Louisa (1773), Charlotte (1778) and Carolina (1778). He also had an elder brother Watkin (1774).

** Lieutenant Joseph Thackwell eventually rose to colonel of the regiment in 1837 but soon transferred to the 3rd Dragoons. He was severely wounded at Waterloo, losing his left arm but this did not prevent him actively serving in India with the 3rd. He then became a lieutenant general and Inspector General of the Cavalry in 1854 but died in 1859. His memoirs were published by Wylly.

clearly not going to last as there was bad faith on both sides, Napoleon having used the period of peace to re-arm and the British to strengthen their hold on their newly acquired dominions around the world, particularly Malta and the West Indies. With the renewal of the war, the regiment was moved down to the Kent coast to help protect the country against invasion and an order was given to augment each troop to seventy-five men, which was quickly increased in the July to eighty-five, each. The troops were stationed at Margate, Ramsgate, Deal and Dover. Edwin wrote to Charlotte that he was temporarily adjutant for the regiment, that he had dined with Lord Keith* and was candid enough to admit he was deeply in love.

Ramsgate, March 3rd 1803[†]

Your letter my dearest Chat's came just in time to prevent a huge says that I felt beginning at all your larginess [*sic*]. Pray don't be so long again, [for] all your good advice came [just] in the nick of time for I was going to dine at Lord Keith's the very day I received it, . . . to say nothing of my being overhead and ears with Miss Bentinck. I really never was so far gone in my life before.

I like Lord Keith very much indeed. He is so affable in his manner and so very entertaining in his conversation; he threatened giving a fete onboard his ship in the Downs as soon as this fine weather settles, which you will know will be famous fair . . .

Our adjutant[‡] is gone to give evidence on some trial at the Gloucester assizes and Colonel Anson[§] has appointed me to act till his return, so you must be very *proud* of so long a letter, as between giving and sending out orders, drilling, answering letters, making out the states and entering of the different troops and *divers* other duties, I have not much time to eat my meal or pay visits.

---

* Admiral George Keith Elphinstone had become a wealthy man from the prize money for commanding the expedition that captured the Cape of Good Hope from the Dutch in 1795. He aided the capture of Ceylon in 1796 and landed the British army in Egypt in 1801. He commanded in the North Sea from 1803–7, his fleet being based at the Downs. He was on board HMS *Bellerophon* when Napoleon surrendered in 1815 and died in 1823.

† Wylly says that the regiment marched to Ramsgate on 24 May but this letter clearly shows that the regiment was already there in early March.

‡ Lieutenant James Gibson was adjutant at this time. He became a captain in the 69th Foot in 1806 and transferred to 4th Garrison Battalion in 1811. He went on half pay in 1816 and retired from the service in 1832.

§ Lieutenant Colonel George Anson transferred to the 16th Light Dragoons in 1805 and was made a major general in 1810. He became colonel of the 23rd Light Dragoons in 1814, colonel of 4th Dragoon Guards in 1827 and full general in 1837. He died as Governor of Chelsea Hospital in 1846.

To the delight of everybody in the regt, Master Lynch made his appearance at Deal (where his troop is) on Friday last,* I long much to see him you may be sure, but have not had time to ride over. I will write as soon as I have. Till then adieu, I am so drowsy that I cannot read this over but I know it's a famous polisher my next shall be an improvement upon it, with a 1,000 loves to you all,

Believe me ever your most attached and affectionate Edwin

The regiment remained on the south coast for the next year, and there was little excitement or good news apart from Edwin's successful purchase of a lieutenancy in the regiment dated 17 March† and therefore little incentive to write home; however, bad news prompted a letter from Edwin; it was news of the death of his elder brother in India. Major Watkin Griffith was killed outright, being struck by a cannonball at Laswaree on 1 November 1803 while commanding the 29th Light Dragoons.‡ News of this loss would have taken fully six months to reach the family in Wales and Edwin wrote to console them.

Ramsgate, April 20th 1804

Since the arrival of this melancholy news I have not ventured to address a line of condolence to my dearest Charlotte and Caroline, being well convinced that every moment they can snatch from grief will be much better employed in the care and consolation of our dearest father and mother, than in the perusal of a stupid letter of mine. I rather expected to have heard from Rhual today. You may easily conceive how anxious I am to hear constantly, therefore pray my dear girls don't omit writing whenever you feel yourselves equal to the task, if it is but two lines, or perhaps Emily would be kind enough when you have other things to do.

How fortunate you were in having so kind and affectionate a friend with you to support you under your first affliction as Emily, in no one instance are the caresses and attentions of a friend so warmly acceptable as when the mind labours under that peculiar sort of distress; fifty times a

---

* Captain Cotton had been placed on half pay during the Peace of Amiens; he returned to the regiment with its augmentation in 1803.

† This step in rank would have cost an additional £262, but his pay rose from eight to nine shillings per day.

‡ War being declared by the British against the Maharatta armies in 1803, General Gerard Lake's forces attacked from the north while General Arthur Wellesley, later to become the Duke of Wellington, attacked from the south. Lake's force encountered a major force at the village of Laswaree but fell on them immediately. The action was very fierce and Watkin Griffith was killed when leading the only cavalry regiment with Lake's force in a charge to rout the enemy.

day have I been going to apply for leave of absence to share them, and as often recollected it was impossible to get it, but even if I had a chance of succeeding it could only be for so short a time *at present* as to make it not worth the journey. . .

I hope my mother got one from me this morning, you must not expect longer letters yet for I assure you I find it a very difficult matter. Let me beseech you both before I conclude to endeavour to keep up your spirits as much as possible, and to bear our misfortune with resignation and calmness, it is not only essential on your own account but will necessarily contribute vastly to the restoration of composure and happiness to our dearly beloved father and mother who will regain all your care.

Adieu my very dear girls, my best love and kindest wishes ever attend you and do not forget to write one who is and always will be yours with the truest affection, and sincerity.

Edwin Griffith

The regiment eventually marched from the Kentish coast and while passing through London was reviewed by HRH the Duke of York on Wimbledon Common on 12 June 1804. The regiment then marched into Hampshire, having three troops stationed at Winchester, three at Southampton and two at Romsey. In August the regiment was ordered to recruit a further two troops, returning the regiment to the level of ten troops of eighty-five men and horses each. Edwin was not in good spirits; he had lost his horse, presumably to illness, but was grateful to his uncle for providing a sum towards the purchase of a replacement.

Southampton, Thursday October 11th 1804

It is late in the day and I don't feel at all in a communicative humour but as I have got a frank I'm determined it shall go if I write but ten lines, to return through you my kindest thanks to my very dear and good uncle for his most acceptable present towards the purchase of a charger to replace the lost Mercury. Horses are very scarce now and I fear it will be some time before I meet with one that suits my purpose and never shall I possess such a one as him again.

I heard of you yesterday or the day before through Hayman,* I am never to get acquainted I believe with Louisa for each time Lynch & I have bent our steps that way we have met him [Hayman] just going out & he always turns us back with him. I will make one more attempt some day soon & then I shall be able to give you a descriptive act of the family . . . was acquainted with Mr Wilbraham's daughters but not with him, if ever

---

* Probably John Hayman, paymaster for the recruiting district.

you meet with them at the Chester Assembly you will admire the eldest I'm sure for I did. Bye the by I never either directly or indirectly in the letter you wrote the day you left Downing. Excuse this hasty scrawl & with best love to all in which my uncle is most particularly included. I remain most affectionately

Yours E. G.

In November 1804, a detachment of over 260 officers and men was sent to escort from Plymouth to London the treasure taken from the three Spanish plate-ships captured on 5 October by Captain Graham Moore's* squadron, despite war not having been formally declared against Spain. Edwin next wrote home from Oxford where he had evidently met up with his father; it seems that he was due some leave and an active military life was evidently causing him to lose weight.

Oxford, Dec 4th 1804†

Better late than never, said a letter from my dear Chat's when it landed safe & sound on my breakfast table a few days before I left Southampton too. Exactly three calendar months after date, which was Downing‡ Aug the 20th & it made it's appearance on the 20 something of November, this is most unaccountable, so very clear was the direction, but I suppose like myself he was indisposed and chose to perform his journey by short stages; I hope we shall be something less on ours, though we get on confoundedly. Now it is a week tomorrow since we left Southampton & rode yet 70 miles; I have no idea when or what time we shall reach you, so shall only petition that a mutton chop or something that can be speedily prepared may be kept in readiness all next week.

I am rather bony, pale & lean, but never in better health, so I beg not to be treated as a patient at home in any way whatsoever, but exactly as if nothing had been the matter, and I shall do infinitely better. We have been parading this magnificent City all morning; receiving the colledges [*sic*] &c, & calling on Brooke & Charles Shipley;§ the latter of whom has promised us his company to dinner, he is looking very well, & made many enquiries after you all. It has got so I can write no longer to the dear Shanklins, my

---

* Brother of Sir John Moore.

† Wylly states that the regiment was still stationed in Hampshire at this time; Edwin's letter indicates that his movement was with at least part of the regiment: was he involved in the escort of the treasure?

‡ Downing, Flintshire, is five miles north-west of Holywell.

§ Possibly Lieutenant Colonel Charles Shipley, Royal Artillery.

dad is excessively well, sleeps two or three hours every evening which is saying enough.

With much love to yourself mam & Carro.

I remain ever most affectionately yours EG

With my mothers good will I'll get into the blue room the first night it will be pleasanter than moving there afterwards.

In March 1805 the regiment was ordered to recruit to 106 men per troop; the total establishment now being one colonel, two lieutenant colonels, two majors, ten captains, twenty lieutenants, ten cornets, one adjutant, one surgeon, two assistant surgeons, one paymaster, one veterinary surgeon, ten quartermasters, two staff-sergeants, fifty sergeants, fifty corporals, ten trumpeters, 950 rank-and-file and 1,062 horses. In June Edwin was able to purchase the rank of captain in the regiment and thus took command of E troop.*

In July the regiment moved to Weymouth, and the regiment camped at the nearby village of Radipole. Here they joined the 1st Hussars King's German Legion† and three brigades of horse and field artillery, while in barracks in Weymouth itself were the 1st and 2nd Dragoons KGL. With nearly 8,000 infantry, additional foot artillery and a few companies of riflemen also encamped near the sea, there were around 11,000 troops in the area. Their colonel, the Duke of Cumberland commanded this force and the cavalry, including the 15th, were brigaded under the command of Brigadier General Slade.‡ The royal family were at Weymouth at the time to enjoy the bathing and frequently visited the camps. The troops were exercised daily in outpost work, advance and rear guards and a number of field days were held throughout this summer. In later years the light cavalry of the KGL were acknowledged to be the best in the British Army and this training would certainly have been very beneficial to the 15th. The camp broke up in the September and the 15th moved into the barracks in the town

---

* Army records state that he became a captain on 27 June 1805 by purchase; this step in rank would have cost a massive £1,785 and his pay duly rose to fourteen shillings and seven pence per day. It seems very likely that he received financial help from his uncle for this, the most expensive jump in rank.

† The KGL was raised in 1803 from foreign volunteers. Initially recruitment was slow but with Napoleon's occupation of Hanover the number of German recruits increased rapidly. They were uniformed and treated as an integral part of the British army and gained an excellent reputation in the field. At its height it consisted of ten battalions of infantry, five cavalry regiments and six batteries of artillery. Following the wars it became the core of the new army of Hanover.

‡ Brigadier General John Slade was on the staff and an equerry to the Duke of Cumberland. He commanded the hussar brigade in the Corunna campaign and commanded a cavalry brigade throughout the Peninsular War.

vacated by the dragoons of the legion. Edwin wrote home just before Christmas and clearly missed his family; he mentions Rico going home to his mother for the holidays; this was the family name for his nephew Frederick Philips, who was then studying at Great Marlow.

Radipole Barracks, Dec. 24th [1805]

My dearest Chats,

I am hard run for time but am determined to scribble a few lines in answer to yours. Which I would have done by return of post according to your desire, if there had not been a letter on the road from me. I have had a fright about my long promised leave, in consequence of another captain having had his extended, & have written to Cumberland himself about it, backed by one to my uncle, and I dare say I shall not hear anything more about it till the day before I set out. I proposed stopping one day at Bath, as I have numerous friends there old & new, so if I can do anything for any of you write me word directly, & you know I am to be depended upon.

Tomorrow I partake of a grand feast at Mr Charles Buxton's to meet a parcel of stupid people that I neither know or care about, but as my thoughts will be with you I fear I shall be very distant and as stupid as the rest of them. The dear Morgan's are I find with you & will remain I hope till I come; it will be some time I fear before 'mirth & joy' resume their reign among you all, but comfort & hapinness [*sic*] are ever to be found at Rhual & I would give anything to be there. I got a long letter from sister yesterday, written in good spirits. I am delighted she is prevailed upon to have the dear Rico to her. If there is not a letter coming I beseech you to write by return of post & send me a good account of all; I wrote to Louisa a few days ago, before I knew they had come to Rhual & directed to G[olden] G[rove]. It is no loss if she never gets it as it was only to request to hear from her; give her my best love also to him and all the fire side; excuse great haste and believe me my very dearest Chats.

Ever your most affectionate Edwin

Wednesday night, I have just received a letter from the Duke, saying, he has not forgot my claim to leave of absence & acceding to his permission I shall receive direction to that affect in the course of a few days, how absolutely stupid of him, as if he could not as well have said what day I might go.

Life at Weymouth was clearly relatively mundane, Edwin's letters home indicate that there were regular parades and inspections of the men and horses, but there was clearly plenty of time not only to study, but to socialise and particularly to court the young ladies, something that seems to have been a popular activity for Edwin. His next letter talks of his poor brother Watkin and his love for India and his unrequited love for a Miss Thompson. He tells of the compliments paid him by the Duke of Cumberland and his hopes for advancement in the regiment. It is clear that there were strong hopes for peace, which Edwin was glad of as he wished to travel to improve his French and German.

Radipole Barracks, 31 January 1806

I have been flirting away with Lady George Murray* and her charming daughters on the esplanade tiles, I am so cold I can hardly use my fingers but I this day determined to apprise you my 'dearest Chats' that I have not cut the correspondence for good & will write you yet. You will be deservedly disappointed, & because I have no further occasion for the subject of gussets and gloves to fill my letters with, you expect an agreeable one 'now,' not really.

I live such a sober steady life, that I am become perfectly stupefied, to give you an idea of it, I get up in the morning precisely at eight, attire myself in my gaudy trappings, and go to my beautiful chestnuts† turn out for their walking exercise, after that I go to the mess room and read the papers, from thence my own room where I find breakfast ready set out, play a pretty good part there as you may remember & from that till twelve I invariably (when possible) devote to my studies. At twelve I go round & inspect every table, and all my troop appointments, see that the rooms &c are clean & that the cooks have got everything for the men's dinners, at one I mount my Pegasus & take lessons in the school until its time to dress for the evening parade. This lasts till four o'clock, from then till five (the present hour) I generally if unmolested write letters or something; find a good dinner in the mess room at five, go round stables at seven, drink tea at nine & go to bed at ten.

The Duke paid us another visit last week for a few days, I am happy that at last the kick up about Anson is settled amicably;‡ his Highness was so condescending and came forward before us all in so open & handsome a manner to explain his conduct that we could not but make every concession; very 'gracious to me' I waited upon him at the lodge on the

---

* Lieutenant Colonel George Murray was serving with the expedition to northern Germany under Lord Cathcart. He was to become quartermaster general under Moore and Wellington in Spain. He was sent to Canada in 1814 and therefore missed the Waterloo campaign, despite the pleas for his re-call by Wellington. He eventually became a lieutenant general and colonel of the 42nd Regiment.

† All of the horses of the regiment had to be chestnut in colour.

‡ The actual reason for the public disagreement between the Duke of Cumberland and Lieutenant Colonel George Anson is unclear, but it caused Anson to transfer to the 16th Light Dragoons on 12 December 1805.

day he went with my report as Captain of the Day & found him alone; after enquiring very tenderly after my health, he said he was very happy at finding that I & few others had had nothing, to do with late unfortunate occurrences, that as I was a very young man & a very promising young man, he strongly recommended me to continue the same line of conduct & wished others would imitate the example, a sense and easy advancement to future promotion. So high flown accomplishment & so little expected I never before had made me, I was for a moment 'accablee de hock'* but soon found utterance for my thanks in a neat and appropriate speech, bowed & returned.

Wallace† who I mentioned in my last has this moment been in my room; he is the son of Sir Thomas & the Lady Wallace. Went very young into the company's service‡ & is now a Captain in the 12th Native infantry, but getting three years leave of absence for his health; he very laudably enters the King's service rather than remain, he was as usual all that time idle; his numerous anecdotes of poor Watkin are interesting in the extreme to me you may suppose; he says that he was so attached to the country & the sport & of it, that he is convinced he would not have returned to England for 20 years, if ever, but to return again to India. Have you heard that Miss Thompson is married? William says she was engaged (at least her affections were) to a Mr Law before Watkin proposed to her, & a few months before he left India married him. He speaks of her as does everybody in the most flattering manner possible, he knows her & her husband intimately; Mr Law is a civilian in Colombo, has made a large fortune, & (will soon) he thinks come to this country. Wallace is at present in our dear good uncle's regiment and will not be gazetted to this till he has received a certain quota of men, amounting to the difference of exchange between cavalry and infantry;§ his services here are therefore voluntary.

---

* This is poor French but reads 'overwhelmed by hock': could he mean the wine?

† George Thomas William Wallace had been appointed in the 7th Foot in November 1805 and succeeded in transferring to the 15th Hussars as a lieutenant on 6 February 1806. He again transferred as a lieutenant in the 17th Light Dragoons in 1808 and retired from the service in March 1809.

‡ The East India Company maintained their own native troops.

§ 'Recruiting by purchase' whereby an officer gained his rank by the successful recruitment of a number of men, had been experimented with a few times during the wars. This statement seems to indicate that Wallace was allowed to transfer from the infantry at the same rank having recruited a number of men to the value of the difference of the cost of the ranks in each service; this was perhaps a local agreement, rather than standard practice in the army. It is not known how many men he had to recruit but the difference in purchase price of a lieutenancy in the cavalry in comparison with that of the infantry was £447.

Since the much to be lamented Billy Potters dead & Fox Secretary of State for the foreign department.* I think we may soon & reasonably look for peace, and for the first time in my life I wish for it; we have now no chance of being sent abroad, & war will only serve to confine us to our regiments at home, should there be one. I most certainly will make every interest for at least a year's leave of absence from the British islands to learn German and perfect myself in French and from what my uncle once said to me, I know he would give me every assistance.

I expect in a very few days to get a step by Graham,† all his courtship has at length proved unavailing & the Duke has forbid his ever putting on the regimentals of the 15th again, he had better at first have stuck to my old text which I have so often occasion to repeat 'put not thy trust in Princes, or in any child of man' &c. He it must be all owed is incorrigible & I have long ceased to feel for, or pity him; for his wife (I entertain far different sentiments & ever shall) she expects to be brought to bed very soon now, and if she has not a litter I shall be surprised for I never saw a woman near so large in all the course of my practise as the girl is. I shall drink a bumper on the 1st, I thought of you all at Downing on the 22nd, had it not been for the cursed news we've had I should have been with you from about a week before that time to March, it was half promised me, but this knocked all on the head, adieu chere Chats. I have avoided mentioning shirts, you must be so sick of the name, 1,000 loves to all from your affectionate

I don't remember whether I wrote to you or Cony last, if to you pray use your utmost endeavours to assure her. I have heard very lately from Louisa; she says Edward‡ talks & thinks of nothing but ships & sailors, since the holding up of a finger would make him change his profession, what a neat.

I received a large & fishy letter from sister, forwarded by Mr Williams the day before yesterday, which I will soon answer.

5 o'clock the Friday morning, collecting the trumpeter for old post so I have only to say that I am in high health and beauty and hope you all are the same. The frost is gone, I don't remember ever reaching February

---

* 'Billy Potter' was a nickname for William Pitt who died 23 January 1806. With his death the government failed, leading to the formation of the misleadingly titled 'Ministry of All Talents', which included Charles Fox as Secretary of State for Foreign Affairs.

† Although given the rank of captain in the army on 27 June 1805, he could only become a captain in the regiment when a vacancy occurred. Captain Henry Charles Graham was appointed to the 26th Foot as a captain on 8 March 1806 and thus Edwin became a captain in the regiment.

‡ His nephew, Edward Morgan.

before without seeing one single flake of snow which is now the case, the *Medusa* frigate* from the East Indies put in here a few days ago for five minutes and told us that we had been confoundedly beat in that quarter and that poor old Marquis Cornwallis is no more!† Sad work.

Encore me fois adieu.

The regiment still remained at Weymouth and life became tedious owing to its monotonous routine. Indeed, a regimental order of 17 February 1806 can be quoted as a perfect example of this.

> The commanding officer has observed that in some of the rooms the men have amused themselves with throwing herring-guts against the ceiling. If any such irregularity is again observed, the rooms will be fresh whitewashed at the expense of the men occupying them.

The practice of 'picketing' was also abolished at this time; this consisted of the offender being tied up by the wrists with his feet just resting on two sharp pegs, rather than holding a court martial for the men; however, evidence exists that it still existed unofficially in 1810.

Edwin wrote again while still at Weymouth: he was still hoping for leave to go home. He had clearly formed an acquaintance with all the young ladies of society and there was obviously little other news apart from the elections and the dismal foreign news.

Weymouth, October 30th 1806

I have for several days intended writing to you my dearest Chats of communicating my sorrows, then I read a letter from Cony imparting yours & as it is sorrow of the same nature we may finely sympathise with each other; you are mourning the departure of our dear uncle‡ and I of our life and soul. The divine Anna left us on Sunday, & God knows when we shall see her again as he is coming in for Newark, & in consequence

---

* The *Medusa* was a 32-gun frigate that had participated in Captain Graham's capture of the Spanish treasure ships.

† Major General Charles, Earl Cornwallis was persuaded to go to India as Governor General and Commander in Chief, replacing Richard Wellesley, Arthur Wellesley's elder brother; however, he deteriorated rapidly in health and died three months after his arrival in 1805. The bad news from the East Indies was that of the near disastrous retreat of General Monson's force in early 1805. This fortunately did not lead to any further reverses in India.

‡ Sir Alured Clarke sailed with the expedition that captured the Cape of Good Hope in 1806.

may be absent from his brigade as much as he pleases after the meeting of Parliament; she really is an irreparable loss & I had no idea we could so all do without her till taught by sad experience; I don't think I ever enjoyed myself more than I have these last three months, my party was a most fishy one, it consisted of Lady Ath the two Miss Methuen's, Miss Manners & the two lady Paulette's & we invariably kept together at everything going on such as balls, plays, dejeunes &c &c, the latter are the most delightful girls I know without exception, quite a second edition of the Cunliffes. They & the Rich's are the only people here now that I care about & I sigh for the day that I shall step into the mail for the spot 'my soul holds most dear', bye the by I have faithfully promised the general to meet him at the Abbey for some shooting; I wish you would not continue a visit there, otherwise I shall not think of it. How decidedly I am counting my chickens before they are hatched, for all their movement it is quite uncertain whether I shall get leave or no.

The Duke has been with us some time & stays about a fortnight before, towards the end of which I will attack him, not without the most sanguine hopes of success either, for he happens to be in high good humour, & has more than once expressed his satisfaction at the state, & condition of my troop. One thing you may reply upon, that if I can only gain leave from the 19th to the 1st I am determined to be at Downing on the 22nd of January.

Pray write me all the electioning goings on, I think if it was all fair play Sir Edward would come in, but expect to hear that Wm Shipley has got it; we are to have fine fun here on Monday & Tuesday, there are only eight candidates, five of them with wooden legs, which has been the subject of much wit, & we allow to be much the most proper persons to approve the sitting members. Think of your having read that ridiculous paragraph from Weymouth, there is not one word of truth in it; the poor Master Bolton who they made open the ball is upwards of seventy, he has been bothered with letters of congratulation ever since; Lady Anna & Miss M have both sprained ankles but not the same night; Lady Mary Blair who was classed amongst the dashing equipages drives a sort of garden chair machine close to the ground, with one horse, which very much resembles old Steady the year before he died, & the matches were all ginger; nobody knows how it got into the paper, but I strongly suspect the female sex had the principle hand in it.

When you write to Hester give her my best love & tell her to tell Lorna that Weymouth has been insufferable since her departure. This is a dreadful stupid epistle my dearest Charlotte but it is my misfortune in this as in many other instances only to be able to offer the will for the deed and to apprise you that I am ever

Your most affectionate Edwin

I leave this late after the post comes in today, Friday 7 o'clock a.m. I went out riding after I had written this far yesterday & met my friend Ernest who asked me to dinner at Hancock's lodge where I went but he was so deservedly in the dumps about the Prussians* that there was no good to be had of him. Just going to a field day. Adieu

In January 1807 for reasons unknown, the establishment was drastically cut to eighty-five men per troop and a corresponding reduction in officers, leading to well over one hundred men and officers being borne on the strength as supernumeraries. The regiment finally moved from Weymouth in January 1807 to Dorchester and while here an order for the regiment to be converted from Light Dragoons to Hussars was issued in March 1807, which required a completely new uniform. The jacket just reaching the waist was still blue and braided across the front with three rows of buttons and with scarlet collar and cuffs. The pelisse or hanging jacket worn over the left arm was of the same colour and trimmed all around and on the cuffs with black fur. The sash round the waist was of crimson silk with gold edging and white buckskin breeches and black knee boots; they also wore a black leather shako with a white plume. The shabraque was of blue cloth with scarlet edging and a white sheepskin saddle cover was worn. Weapons carried were to be a small carbine, pistols and a light cavalry sword. It was further ordered that the men would grow moustaches to complement the hussar uniform; however, it would seem that the order was not popular as the officers removed them when on leave and had to re-grow them on return. This failure to gain uniformity led to the order being cancelled. The introduction of the new uniform was a very costly business for the officers as they paid for their own equipment and their various tailors provided their own versions of the dress code, which forced Lieutenant Colonel Long,† who commanded at this time, to inform officers that a standard boot, spur, hat and feather had been lodged with the adjutant and they were to conform to this pattern immediately.

During this change, the standards and guidons of the regiment were lodged at the Duke of Cumberland's residence and it appears that the regiment did not carry a standard as hussars.

---

* Prussia's military reputation had been second to none since the days of Frederick the Great; but times had changed and following their declaration of war, Napoleon's army swiftly crushed the Prussian army at the joint battles of Jena–Auerstadt. Napoleon made the mistake of humiliating them politically; he was to rue this in 1813 when German nationalism raised the country against him. This contributed greatly to his final overthrow.

† Robert Ballard Long became a lieutenant colonel in the 15th in December 1805 having transferred from the 16th Light Dragoons. He served on the staff during the Corunna campaign and Walcheren, and commanded a brigade of cavalry in Spain. He eventually rose to the rank of lieutenant general in 1821 and died in 1825.

Home Service

In the June the regiment marched to Richmond and fired a *feu de joie* with pistols on the King's birthday and were then reviewed on Hounslow Heath on 20 July by the Prince of Wales and Duke of York. The regiment moved to Woodbridge barracks at the end of July where it was formed into a brigade under Lieutenant General Lord Paget,* consisting of the then existing hussar regiments, the 7th, 10th and 15th and two troops of horse artillery. Field days were held twice a week on Rushmere Heath near Ipswich, and the entire brigade, totalling nearly 2,000 men was inspected by the Duke of York on 5 October. The troops were then spread in cantonments across Essex until July 1808, when they moved to Romford, where they were reviewed again by the Prince of Wales and Duke of York on Wanstead flats on 19 August. During this period, the uniform was amended slightly with the introduction of a black fur busby with a scarlet bag and a white plume with a red tuft at the bottom to replace the shako. The regiment remained in the Romford area until the October; therefore Edwin's letter from Oxford in September must mean that he was there on leave, possibly visiting his father again.

13th September 1808, Oxford.

So you charge me to write directly do you madam? Charge me? Oh that I had my troop & you in the middle of the obelisk field, if I would not charge you up & down till you was too out of breath to speak I'll be hanged. Never did I hear anything better than your presuming to charge me!!!

Your letter, (we get our letters here at 7 in the morning) found me in the arms of 'Orpheus', I opened one eye & proceeded as far as 'a civil quiet man', when finding it was likely to be a polisher, I again resigned myself to the dominion of the drowsy God. At eight I roused & finished it, then I was very happy to find that what I had at first mistaken for a polisher turned out a devilish and entertaining letter, & that the mistake was to be imparted to the density of my brain, not yours dear Charlotte.

It contains quite a mass of news, none of which surprised me more than that ma-pin should be singled from the world by a man with 3 thousand a year! She is, as you observe, a very good humoured quality but on much too magnificent a scale of the opposite quality of beauty ever (I should have thought) to make a conquest of the heart of man, but there is no accounting for taste. I cannot help thinking of the lines 'A sixteenth heaven knows were sufficient for me'† &c I can easily imagine a person's

---

* Lieutenant General Henry William Paget, colonel of the 7th Hussars was renowned as an excellent commander of light cavalry. He later served at Waterloo as Lord Uxbridge and rose to be the first Marquis of Anglesey and field marshal. His letters have since been published by his descendant in 1961 as *One Leg*.

† A quote from a poem of Sir Thomas Moore entitled 'To the Large and Beautiful

falling in love with Anna Maria but if the Colonel Dashwood is the man who was in the Blues, and I never heard of any other, he is I should think old enough to be her father, & partakes a good deal of the nature of the turtle (not dove).

I have not been in town this fortnight, but the last time I was there I called upon the Wardles who in a very pleasant residence looking into St James's Park; I was not fortunate enough to find them at home & the servant told me they were to leave town the next day or the one after for some watering place. I hope your dose of bark had the desired effect upon my mother. I am going through a course of that article in consequence of symptoms of the return of the plagues & torments that I suffered this time last year. Tell sister that I return her many thanks for her letter from Denhall which passed through Lord Cooke with the greatest facility & arrived here in due time, as soon as I have a opportunity of speaking to Cumberland I will answer it & this I expect will happen soon, as he is coming down to introduce a new Lt Colonel to us (Grant*) I hate these new brooms.

God bless you my dearest Chats. Let me hear from you soon, & with best love to the breakfast table believe me your ever loving fraternity.

Edwin Griffith

Edwin had clearly settled comfortably into army life on home service and was now used to the regimental routines and the interminable politics of the mess. Officers of the regiment quite clearly vied to gain the notice of their colonel; when serving at home the only real chance of promotion was through the favour of senior officers, and royal ones were even better.

It is at this point that Edwin's nephew Frederick Charles Philips, known

---

Miss . . .'; the verse reads:

> If ever, by Fortune's indulgent decree
> > To me such a ticket should roll
> A sixteenth, Heaven knows! were sufficient for me;
> > For what could I do with the whole?

* Lieutenant Colonel Colquhoun Grant was appointed to the 15th from the 72nd Foot on 25 August 1808, but clearly did not join until later. He had been wounded with the 72nd at the recapture of the Cape of Good Hope and was wounded again at Sahagun when commanding the 15th. He became ADC to the Prince Regent in 1811. He again commanded the 15th in the 1813 campaign in Spain and then the hussar brigade until wounded at Vitoria. He commanded the 5th Cavalry Brigade at Waterloo and had five horses killed or wounded beneath him. He rose to colonel of the 12th Lancers in 1825 then the 15th again in 1827. In 1831 he was elected MP for Queensborough and died in 1836.

This officer should not be confused with the Colquhoun Grant who acted as a reconnaissance officer behind enemy lines for Wellington and was immortalised as *The First Respectable Spy* by Jock Haswell in 1969.

affectionately to the family as 'Rico', enters the story. Born in 1793, Frederick was only seven years younger than his uncle Edwin; he had attended the junior department of the Royal Military College which had just been established at Great Marlow under Major General Le Marchant* and General Jarry from which he graduated. He was then sent to Eton but it is clear that the £400 a year fees were a great burden to his mother† and by 13 October 1808 he had been forced to leave Eton and was appointed as a cornet in the 15th Hussars.

There is no hint in this last letter from Edwin that he had the remotest idea of the changes that were suddenly going to affect him and Frederick; for just ten days after this letter was written, orders arrived for the regiment to prepare for foreign service.

---

* Major General John Gaspard Le Marchant did much to modernise the army in his short career; he proposed and set up the first college for the military training of young British army officers, the forerunner of Sandhurst. He was called back to active service in Spain and was killed at the head of a magnificently successful charge at the battle of Salamanca in 1812. General Francois Jarry was a Frenchman by birth although he had served on the staff of the Prussian army of Frederick the Great. He had become the first governor of the military school in Berlin and an excellent reputation as a staff officer; indeed he was the ideal man to help Le Marchant set up the British equivalent ten years later. He died of old age in 1807.

† Letter from Henrietta Philips dated Rhual, 7 December 1807, D/HE/536. This clearly states that she would put him into Eton for a term and see if she could maintain the fees; obviously she was unable to sustain these costs and he was duly entered into the army some ten months later.

Chapter 2

DEEP INTO SPAIN

The British army had enjoyed its first successful land campaign against Napoleon's forces, when General Arthur Wellesley* had succeeded in driving the French from Portugal in 1808. However, the government had ordered out more senior but less capable commanders as the size of the force in Portugal increased; and, immediately following victory at the battle of Vimiero, he was superseded twice in quick succession and the advance was halted. A peace treaty was soon signed at Cintra, allowing the French forces to be repatriated to France in British ships. Britain in time-honoured tradition won the war only to lose the peace.

Following publication of the details of the Convention of Cintra, a great outcry arose in the country and the commanders, including Wellesley, were summarily ordered home to answer for their actions, leaving General Sir John Moore† in command of the forces in Portugal. The government was very keen for the army to support the fledgling uprising in Spain now that Portugal appeared secure and Moore organised his troops to advance towards Salamanca where they could cooperate with the Spanish armies against Napoleon's troops. Reinforcements were promised to Moore for this advance into Spain and a force totalling some 15,000 men was organised under General Baird‡ to land in northern Spain and form a junction with Moore's army. The hussar brigade commanded by General Sir John Slade, consisting of the 7th, 10th and 15th Hussars, was ordered on this service.

Orders to prepare to march, with eight troops of eighty-five men each, were received on 23 September 1808. This would have been a period of great

---

* Lieutenant General Arthur Wellesley, of course, later became the Duke of Wellington.
† Lieutenant General Sir John Moore had previously enjoyed a distinguished career in Corsica, Holland and Egypt and is credited with the birth of light infantry training in the British army. He was to be killed famously while commanding his army at the battle of Corunna in 1809.
‡ General Sir David Baird had previously enjoyed great success in India and Egypt. The Corunna campaign was destined to be his last period of active service.

43

confusion and changes in the regiment, men and horses would be switched between troops so that the cream of the regiment would go on service. Edwin commanded E troop which was one of those selected to go; it became the right troop of Major Leitch's* squadron, Captain Gordon† commanding the left troop.‡ Ensign Frederick Philips joined the regiment from Eton just before embarkation and was attached to Captain Gordon's troop and sailed with him on the transport *Rodney* of 300 tons. The regiment began their march in four divisions to Portsmouth for embarkation on 20 October with twenty-seven officers, seven quartermasters, thirty-six sergeants, thirty-two corporals, eight trumpeters, 642 privates and 682 horses proceeding by easy stages. The regiment arrived at Portsmouth and embarked immediately between 28 and 30 October in twenty-six transports which eventually sailed in a convoy under the protection of HMS *Endymion* a 40-gun frigate commanded by Captain Capel.§ During stormy weather in the Channel ten transports including the headquarters ship the *Lord Nelson*, became separated from the convoy and had to be escorted to Corunna by the *Nonpareil* schooner of fourteen guns.

Edwin wrote a journal of the voyage and Corunna campaign, which he then edited on his return to Britain when stationed at Romford in Essex in May 1809, entitled *'Journal of my proceedings during the campaign in Spain in the winter of 1808–9 with observations on the dispositions, manners &c of the people of that Country.'* It is uncertain why Edwin chose to rewrite the journal directly on his return when the

---

* Captain Walter Nathaniel Leitch became a major in the 72nd Foot in July 1809 and rose to the rank of lieutenant colonel in the same regiment. He retired by the sale of his commission in 1818.

† Captain Alexander Gordon had originally served in the 15th Light Dragoons but gained his captaincy by purchase in the 3rd West India Regiment, but remained on their books only two weeks before transferring back to the 15th Hussars on 3 March 1808. He transferred to the 60th Foot in 1811 and retired by the sale of his commission in late 1811 and died at Ellon in Aberdeenshire 21 March 1873. His journal of the Corunna campaign was published in 1913 as *The Journal of a Cavalry Officer in the Corunna Campaign*.

‡ The squadrons were organised as follows for the 1809 campaign:
   Right Squadron commanded by Major Forrester, *Right Troop* Captain Seelinger, *Left Troop* Captain Thackwell.
   Right Centre Squadron commanded by Captain Broadhurst; *Right troop* Captain Broadhurst, *Left Troop* Captain Dalrymple.
   Left Centre Squadron commanded by Captain Murray, *Right Troop* Captain Murray, *Left Troop* Captain Cochrane.
   Left Squadron commanded by Major Leitch, *Right Troop* Captain Griffith, *Left Troop* Captain Gordon.
   Captain Foskett appears to have been left behind in command of the two troops remaining in England.

§ The Honourable Sir Thomas Bladen Capel had been signal lieutenant to Nelson at the battle of the Nile and served at Trafalgar. He eventually rose to be a vice admiral.

memories were still very fresh, but from the form of layout he chose, it would appear that he may have had the idea of submitting it for publication. We are lucky enough to have the original journal written in Spain and the rewritten version in existence to compare. From this comparison it can be seen that the texts are virtually identical and that he had not made any major or significant changes; but he did remove some of the scenes written during the voyages from the second version, presumably as he felt these were irrelevant to the narrative. I have therefore chosen to publish the rewritten journal, but have added back into the text the 'missing' scenes from the original journal and a number of letters sent home by the two during the campaign. Edwin's journal begins as they prepare to embark:

The eight troops of the 15th Light Dragoons selected for service embarked at Portsmouth on the 28th and 29th of October 1808. Contrary winds detained us till Wednesday the 2nd of November, on which day the fleet got under weigh; it consisted of about 40 sail of ships including transports, victuallers &c, under convoy of the *Endymion* frigate, Capt Capel. I sailed in the *Lively*, a stout north country ship, of about 300 tons burthen, commanded by Captain Francis Wright; 27 troop horses besides my own three embarked in her, and had as roomy a stable as transports generally afford. We ran through the Needles with an easterly wind, were off the Start Point on Thursday morning, & lost sight of England the same evening.

The swell in the Channel being very great, I this day experienced the horrors of that disease called sea sickness; no words can describe so distressing a sensation and yet the seamen kept laughing and telling me all the time, *not to think about it* for it was *nothing at all*, although I found it quite impossible to follow their advice strictly, yet was I determined not to give way to the sickness. I staid upon deck almost all night and as soon as we were fairly *at sea* it went off and I enjoyed perfect health all the rest of the voyage. Nothing could be more favourable than our weather all Friday & Saturday; the close of the latter was a particularly delightful evening; a light breeze from the north west just sufficient to fill the sails set us on at the rate of about four knots an hour; the moon shone bright, & the fleet collected as near as they could in the wake of the convoy formed altogether a beautiful & interesting scene. I sat upon deck enjoying it till ten o'clock at which time I retired to my birth [*sic*], I slept till near five in the morning, when I was roused by the tossing of the vessel, and the noise she made in dashing through the water. The breeze had increased during the night to a *fresh gale*, and all hands were busily employed except the captain & myself. We were however soon up, & never shall I forget the scene that presented itself. All was hurry, noise, and confusion upon deck;

the sea was in a white foam, and breaking over us every moment, & the wind came in gusts which frequently laid the ship on her beam ends; our only consolation was having plenty of sea room and the sailors called it (like the sickness) *nothing at all*. In addition to these *little comforts* a cask of port wine that was secured in a corner of the cabin broke from its moorings by the rolling of the vessel, & in an instant destroyed all our crockery, (which for security's sake had been placed on the floor) and a stone bottle containing four gallons of lamp oil. The weight of the cask, & the violence with which it was sent from one side of the room to the other; rendered the securing it again a task of both danger & difficulty, which was much increased by the oil having made the floor as slippery as ice, and notwithstanding the stench, the confusion & the misery it occasioned I could not help laughing at the dance it led us round and round the cabin for some minutes. It continued to blow with violence till towards noon, when the wind abated, being fairly beat down by the rain; which for some hours fell thicker & heavier than ever I remember to have seen it before. By four in the evening it became a dead calm; the sea however ran literally *mountains high*, & not a ship of the fleet was to be seen. On Monday the weather was squally & unpleasant, & on Tuesday it grew worse; this day we were chased by a French privateer, but she did not like the preparations we made for fight, and after getting within gunshot of us, tacked, and we saw no more of her. This is only to be lamented for one reason, namely, that my account of the voyage would have been less insipid if I'd had the narration of a naval engagement to excite my powers of description; *barring* this I must confess the great satisfaction I felt on beholding an inclination on the part of Monsieur to decline the *combat*, as however gallantly our little crew might have behaved, I could not help thinking that it was on an element where the cavalry could not act without difficulty, & certainly not to advantage.* This event was however the cause of a serious alarm to me & to us all, the barrel of cartridges for the 3 pound carronades, was, after they had been loaded, were conveyed out of the rain to a cupboard under my berth; where they were left by the neglect or forgetfulness of the mate, till sometime after I had been in bed; when the wind blowing fresh & the master & all hands upon deck, this barrel of gunpowder played us the same trick that the port wine had the day before; I jumped up & secured it again as soon as I could, retired to my couch, & was just dropping to sleep when I heard something move underneath me, & looking out discovered a little rascal of a cabin boy, in the place with the

---

* Captain Gordon says that the *Endymion* frigate chased the privateer off, a more likely reason.

Deep into Spain

powder, holding in his hand a candle with a long snuff, & without candlestick or lanthern, that we were not all blown into the air I must ever consider as highly providential, but the danger past was soon forgotten. On the day week on which we sailed, we found ourselves within 20 miles of the Spanish shores and at twelve o'clock the weather having cleared, we made Cape Ortegal & at half past six the same evening came to anchor in the road of Corunna, where we found the *Endymion* and the greatest part of the fleet had arrived the day before. The coast as far as we could see on our approach is very bold, and the rocks projecting into the sea occasions a tremendous surf. On Thursday morning we warped into the inner harbour which is a very snug one, & has depth of water sufficient for very large ships to come within a stone's throw of the landing place.

We found the 7th and 10th Lt Dragoons had not finished disembarking* so we were forced to remain on board, and it was not until Monday the 14th of November that my troop got on shore & went into the barracks of St Lucia. During this period I only dined on shore once, preferring the provisions of the transports to the food that is given at a Spanish inn.

Being at length *established* on shore, I had time to look about me a little and make my observations on the place. Corunna is a large irregular built town; the citadel which stands high, commands a fine view of the harbour & the opposite shore; the streets are in general narrow, the principal ones are flagged, but they are universally filthy to the greatest degree; the houses have in general a gloomy appearance and are comfortless in the extreme; the walls of the rooms are bare, curtains & carpets are seldom to be seen, & fireplaces never. A few skins of beasts scattered about the floors add nothing to the comfort, but form a safe retreat for an inexhaustible establishment of fleas, with which the beds and every place swarm. But the natives themselves are the greatest objects of attraction; the men bustling along wrapped up in their cloaks and with great cocked hat on their heads; the women ill dressed & dirty looking; the squalid, meagre and dissatisfied countenance of both, soon convince the Englishman that he is among a different race of beings; the variety of strange noises too are fully equal to the variety of strange appearances; the habit all the people have of speaking as if they were in a violent passion; the braying of the mules & asses; the dreadful screams made by the wooden axletrees of the little carts which are never suffered to be greased; with the horrid *Arree-bo!* the drivers continually bellow at the oxen, make altogether an uproar in the streets

* The 7th, 10th and two horse artillery troops had sailed from Portsmouth in another convoy two days before.

that *may* be imagined but cannot be described. Having mentioned the screaming carts, I must inform the reader that they used originally to grease them, but a priest returning home in the dark with his head fuller of wine than devotion having been run over & killed by one of them, an act was immediately passed prohibiting the use on pain of forfeiting both cart and oxen; the consequence of which is that they utter a yell which may be distinctly heard a mile or more, and are a perfect pest to the community at large.

The theatre being open at this time, curiosity tempted me to go to it; I was here gratified by the sight of a *few tolerably* well dressed and pretty women, and also of seeing a fandango danced; this was performed by a lady & gentleman who threw themselves into all kinds of attitudes, (and the more indecent they were, the greater the applause) keeping time with their castanets. Castanets are small shells of wood fastened with a ribbon to the thumbs and played upon with the fingers; they are a simple and not unpleasing accompaniment to dancers when gracefully used. The theatre which is constructed much in the usual manner was tolerably shabby and badly lighted, the scenery miserable and the performers especially so. Of the merits or demerits of the piece I am ignorant, but a clown was the only character that excited the smallest degree of merriment or applause.

In my walks about Corunna I was frequently witness to extraordinary scenes, none of which afforded me greater amusement than seeing the women *abridging* the *retinue* of each others heads; one of them seats herself on the threshold of the house door in the sun, where her neighbour also extends herself, her head resting on the seated woman's lap, & in this office I have seen two women employed alternately for hours. In some parts of Spain I am informed they have monkeys trained to this business who are particularly dexterous in the art, but this is a *refinement* of luxury which has not yet reached the province of Galicia. There are many good shops in the principal streets, where you can procure everything you want, but no thanks to the natives as they are all kept by Italians or Germans who get their goods from England, France & Germany; the hardware almost all from England. The scarcity of glass in Spain is a great misfortune; none of the shops have glazed windows & very few of the houses; they are closed with shutters only, so you must either be exposed to all the inclemency's of the weather, or suffer a total deprivation of daylight.

Corunna stands on the side of a peninsula, upon the extremity of which is built the largest & handsomest lighthouse I ever saw; the walk from hence to the town is most delightful being on the ridge of a hill commanding beautiful & extensive prospects in each direction; a row of windmills here called to my recollection the exploits of that gallant knight Don Quixote, but my former wonder at his having the temerity to attack them at the same moment vanished, they not being above eight or ten feet high & with such little short insignificant sails that a person possessing half his spirit & resolution might with great ease vanquish a host of them. All the young Donna's used to parade here on an evening to inhale the fresh sea breezes. *I* also attended pretty generally in the hope of discovering a little of their boasted beauty but never failed meeting with disappointment. They are not very difficult to get acquainted with as I was invited to two *routs* [evening receptions] without having been introduced to either of the ladies who gave them, but this might have proceeded from kindness to us as strangers. These routs were more stupid if possible than an English one; the company sat in a formal row all round the room without seeming to know for what purpose they had assembled or how they were to get away again; there was no amusement, nor any refreshment; most of the ladies however spoke French and some of them were very chatty. They always asked a thousand questions about the Signoras Ingleses (English ladies) and if they were not remarkably handsome? To one young lady who asked me this question & who seemed to possess more vanity than the rest I ventured to reply 'that I had always esteemed them so *till* I had been at Corunna'. But she shook her head & said 'ah that won't do! We know what the English ladies are as well as you can tell us'. This was the *first* & *last* attempt I made at complimenting a Spanish lady at the expense of truth.

There are two inns at Corunna, the Leon D'Oro and the British Hotel; at the latter was a table d'hote where they professed cooking dinners in the *true* English style, and which they exemplified by boiling the meat, and *roasting* the fish; and for fear the cooking *alone* should not be sufficiently convincing that we were dining at a British Hotel they served the meat up first, and sent the *fish & dessert* in as a second course. The articles were all very bad of their kind; the bread in particular, here & throughout the province of Galicia is intolerable, owing in the first place to the softness of the mill stones which makes it very gritty, and in the second to the quantity of leaven used which makes it abominably sour; the wine is weak, acid and bitter and the misfortune is that they have nothing else to drink. Cheese, butter and milk are very scarce articles and what there is to be got is the produce of goats, sheep and I believe I may add of anything but cows. All these disagreeable circumstances and a great many more might be forgiven these miserable people if they would only be cleanlier, or more properly speaking when applied to them, somewhat less dirty wherever the appetite is concerned; but I really have seen enough in Spanish kitchens alone, to disgust me with the whole nation.

While recovering from their sea crossing at Corunna both managed to pen their first letters home from foreign soil. Frederick wrote to his mother Henrietta Maria Philips in Bath.

Corunna, November 11th 1808

My dearest mother,

I take up my pen with the greatest pleasure to inform you of our safe arrival at Corunna on Tuesday evening, after a very good passage considering the season which is generally reckoned the worst for voyages. We weighed anchor at Stokes Bay (which is about two or three miles out of Portsmouth harbour) on Wednesday the 3rd inst. about 1 o'clock and sailed with a fair wind all that day, Thursday Friday, and Saturday, but on Sunday morning about 3 o'clock the wind changed and began to blow most violently. Our ship rolled so amazingly that the master of the vessel said that he did not expect the masts would have stood, everything was in an uproar in the cabin and all over the deck, several of the men were thrown down and cut their legs very badly; but however it abated about 12 o'clock and there was almost a dead calm; the next day a fresh easterly breeze sprung up and brought us in as I told you. Edwin was not so fortunate as us; he was driven round Cape Prior a great way and did not arrive till Wednesday evening, fortunately however they received no damage and he is very well and in excellent spirits. I went ashore on Thursday to see the place which is something like a miserable Welsh village, it is certainly much larger, but to describe the filth and dirt that incommode the streets would be impossible. They are the most extraordinary set of *animals* I ever beheld and seem as if they had never seen a soldier in their lives, for the ladies very often stop us in the streets to look at our clothes. Yesterday as Edwin and I were walking in the street he was putting his handkerchief into his sabretash and a lady very well dressed came and put her hand into it to see what it was. They have a kind of cart with two wheels which they drive about the streets with oxen and make such a miserable creaking that you can hardly hear yourself speak as they pass by. Edwin and I walked up to the convent here yesterday and as we were there the physician which attends the nuns came out and opened the door so that we had a very long chat with them in French which most of them understood. There are a great number of catholicks here and numbers of chapels most of which are very handsome. Almost all the officers of the 15th dine every day at a kind of ordinary that there is here for the English,* they give us plenty of 'olla podridas' &c &c and plenty of

---

* The Hotel d'Ingleterra supplied 'British food' which was well received by the officers who constantly complained of the profuse use of garlic in Spanish cooking.

soup, fish and game and wine all for four pistrenes which is equal to 10d English money. We went to the play last night and the night before for which you pay one pistrene, the scenery and dresses were very good but the performance I cannot say much for; you may see the prompters head above the level of the stage and he reads the whole play quite loud enough for the audience to hear him, there was afterwards some very good dancing with castanets and it concluded about 11 o'clock. The night before last a Marquesa gave a very fine ball to which all the English had a general invitation but we did not go to it. Edwin and I are looking out for a mule to carry my baggage, as I have only one horse, I am afraid I shall have to pay a great deal for it as you can get nothing of the sort under five and twenty pounds and then very bad. There was a report yesterday that there had been a grand battle between the two armies, and the French defeated with great slaughter, but I cannot answer for the truth of it. They say also that Marshal Ney had been very dangerously wounded. We are to remain here about four or five [days] longer till Sir David Baird's army & all [have] marched.

If you direct to me 15th L.D. British Army, Spain, I should think it would reach me, but I am not certain, however you had better try. I have met with many of my old friends from Marlow here, amongst whom is Fitzclarence who is in the 10th L.D.* and in the same brigade as myself. I have not room for any more, so must conclude. Edwin joins me in best love to my grandmother & grandfather, Charlotte, Conny, Uncle and Aunt Morgan and *all* my friends when you write to, or see them. I suppose you are still in St James's Square, so I shall direct to you there. Is Sophy Boycott in Bath now? If she is pray remember me to her and Maria. I am afraid you will think this stupid letter hardly worth paying for, but you know I have not a *very bright* genius for letter writing. I remain my dearest mother your ever most dutiful affectionate son.

F C Philips

---

* Lieutenant George Fitzclarence 10th Hussars had been involved in a little scandal. Orders arriving for Fitzclarence to embark were received with glee by the young man and he had to be removed from Marlow in disgrace as 'his mind has been so bent on going on service that he has totally neglected his studies and made himself completely miserable'. His father had other ideas, however; he wrote to the Prince of Wales that 'George is too young to go on service particularly with light cavalry and at the same time he cannot with propriety remain in your regiment and not go on service'. A face-saving solution was found and he served as an extra aide-de-camp to Brigadier General Slade during the Corunna campaign. He eventually rose to the rank of lieutenant colonel in the 24th Dragoons then retired on half pay.

Edwin also found time to write to Frederick's mother, Henrietta, whom he always referred to as Harriett, which was received 30 December 1808 at her home at 5 Wood Street, Bath.

Corunna, November 13th 1808

My dearest Harriet,

Having just learnt that the *Sybille** frigate sails tomorrow for England, I take the opportunity of scribbling a few lines by her for the chance of your receiving them before a letter which Rico put into the post office yesterday; & as he most likely gave you a history of our proceedings for this last fortnight I shall content myself with assuring you that he & I are in perfect health, & very anxious to get away from this most wretched & filthy town. Nothing but the misery of a transport & the buffeting of a winters sea could at all reconcile me to it, but 'any port in a storm' they say; God knows *I* was thankful enough to find myself once more on terra firma; we weathered two *fresh gales,* the first of which dispersed the fleet, & drove *me* near two hundred miles out of our course; the *Rodney* had the good fortune to stick to the commodore, & most happy I was to find her on my arrival here last Wed'y evening, one of our ships was taken by a privateer but abandoned on the appearance of a ship of war;† the *Lively* was chivey'd by another but they stood off on our *shewing disposition for fight;* the head quarter ship, having on board Colonel Grant, the adjt. paymaster, & a capt. is still missing & great fears are entertained for her safety, as she was last seen upon a lee shore at the close of day & has not been heard of since.‡

I am sorry I cannot give you any information with regard to our future operations but we are all in the dark; it is not unlikely we may remain here a fortnight longer; a fine scramble the march will be whenever it happens; I have not been able to get Rico another horse that will suit him as a charger but have made a bargain that he is to give me a good mule to carry my baggage in exchange for one of my horses if I should be unsuccessful in my searches; you cannot think how the lad is admired by *his shipmates;* Gordon says he never saw such a disposition in his life, for that do what you will with him he was always good humoured & contented; he has

---

* *Sibylle* frigate, 38 guns, Captain Clotworthy.

† A transport carrying Cornet Samuel Jenkins with twenty men and horses was captured by a privateer and released on their parole awaiting exchange. The British authorities for reasons that are unclear refused to accept the parole and ordered Jenkins and the men to join the regiment on service. However, he seems to have been ordered on duties that avoided his presence at the fighting (see Frederick's letter of 13 December).

‡ The *Nelson* transport carrying Colonel Grant, Captain Murray, adjutant C Jones and Paymaster Henslow did arrive safely a few days later having survived storms and waterspouts.

found several Marlow friends here, Fitzclarence seems to be the favourite, & they are always together in the streets, at the opera &c &c. I shall be able to give you some account of Spain in my next I hope. At present I can only say that it appears some *century's* behind England in *everything*, the extreme poverty & wretchedness is past all description; & to give you some small idea of the *general appearance* of the natives I can only declare that the *most ludicrous* and *absurd figure* you ever saw dressed up for an English stage, male or female, might walk the streets of Corunna without being noticed *as at all odd or particular*, this I would forgive them if they were *cleanly* in their habitations, persons, &c, but I am sorry to say they are quite in *the opposite extreme*. The ladies have sallow complexions, bad legs & worse teeth; the men are equal in point of *beauty* with the addition of a discontented & suspicious look, & both dress very ill. So much for the Dons & Donnas at present. I *hope* they may *improve* upon acquaintance but *fear* I can *never like them*. I *live* on shore but *sleep* onboard my ship in preference to a lousy, filthy, buggy, Spanish bed which I must turn into as soon as she quits the harbour; I am writing this in the cabin, where two or three rude & boisterous Captains of the sea are making such a confounded noise that you must excuse all blunders.

I send a letter to Rhual by this same conveyance but closed it in such a hurry just before I came onboard, that I forgot to tell them to direct to '*Corunna*' & '*to be forwarded to the head quarters of the British army*'. I am also told that the English postage being paid there is necessary to insure their coming safe – will you give all these directions when you write to Rhual.

Pray let us hear from some of you *very often*, it will be our only comfort; & from never seeing an English *paper* everything in the news way will be highly acceptable. For the present adieu; my best love to the Morgans and Charlotte & believe me ever most affectionately yours.

EG

Edwin also wrote further details to his sister Charlotte.

Corunna, November 17th 1808

My dearest Chats

As the transport which brought us here returns tomorrow I shall charge the captain with two or three letters, which all go hopping &c as they now leave Rico and I at present; the Hussar Brigade consisting of the 7th, 10th & 15th under one Lord Paget* commenced their march yesterday, but as we only go

---

* Following the reorganisation of the army Paget actually commanded all the cavalry of the army, and Slade and Stewart officially commanded the Hussar Brigades.

one squadron per diem,* it will be some time before it comes to our turn. Any thing for a change, I hope to goodness that Spain will improve upon acquaintance and I had almost forgot to tell you that the name of my horse is Don Manuel Monkey, which amuses Rico & I much, goodness knows there is room for it.

I am billeted upon a merchant in the Rue Royale and you never saw anything so ridiculous as the figure I cut among them not understanding a word of Spanish; he has two or three daughters besides a wife, and we all sleep as it were in the same room, for the recesses where the beds stand are open to it, & we dress and undress in each others presence in the utmost sangfroid, the room that they open into is however very handsome & large; in the morning as soon as I am awake one of the handmaids presents herself with a large cup of chocolate & dry toast which I am forced to eat in bed as I cannot make them understand that I would rather dress first. As soon as I am dressed & sat down (as at this moment) to write a letter, they all collect round me, cram me with apples, dry'd fruit &c &c, and pull & tumble all my things about in such a way that I could with the greatest pleasure kick them down stairs. There are very few tolerably pretty women to be seen, & as they have all got teeth of any colour but white, I don't think there is much chance of my losing any heart to a Donna. I hope my mother will receive my letter giving an account of my voyage &c some days before you get this; I fear you must never expect any very long letters from me, having as you may guess my hands full of regimental business. Pray let us hear often from some of you & direct 'Corunna, Spain', 'to be forwarded to the Head qtrs of the British Army.' As we see no English papers here, all sorts of news will be acceptable. I am told that it is necessary the postage of English letters should be paid there; but my uncle to whom I write by this same conveyance will be better able to tell you what is to be done about it. God bless you my dearest Chats, give many loves to all, mine included & believe in the affections of your loving

Edwin

Tell my mother that I only opened the parcel containing my flannel waistcoats yesterday, & that they fit me very well I found her little epistle, the razor case &c all right. Adieu Edwin. Remember me to Bin when you write.

---

* It may have been mooted that the regiment would proceed a squadron at a time; however, it seems clear from the adjutant's diary that the regiment actually proceeded in just two divisions.

Deep into Spain

It is rather surprising that neither Edwin nor Frederick mention the problems the regiment encountered with the discipline of the men on first landing in Spain. The adjutant's diary clearly records that Privates Oakley and Jones were tried by regimental court martial for 'mutinous expressions' on the 15 November; the following day he records 'the men of the regt. Behaving very ill, much drunkenness, and great many confined' and the next 'Privates Wright and Foster were court martialled'; however, things seem to have calmed down after this.

On 20 November orders were received for the regiment to forage for two days and Captain Dalrymple* was sent forward with a Spanish officer to arrange the cantonments for the end of each days march. We resume Edwin's journal as the regiment set out from Corunna, his troop forming part of the second division commanded by Major Forrester,† which left the day after the first division.‡ It is clear that Edwin was shocked by his first views of Spain and betrays a strong dislike for the Spanish people.

Having visited all that was worth seeing in and about Corunna, I was not sorry at the preparations made for our departure from thence, which took place on the morning of the 22nd of November and on the night of which we halted at Betanzos, eighteen miles on the high road to Madrid. Betanzos is a wretched old town upon a little round hill at the foot of which runs a river navigable for boats down to Ferrol; the streets are narrow and some of them so steep & so ragged from the rains having guttered them that it is a service of danger riding through the town. I was billeted upon a barber who gave me a bed, such as it was, and having dined off a piece of English cold beef brought with me from Corunna which I eat by the light of a lamp by my bed side and drank some sour wine, I laid down not very much elated at the prospect which had that day dawned upon us. The next day's march was through a finer country than we had seen, it being in a tolerable state of cultivation & the great vineyards which extend quite to the tops of the hills from the bottoms of valleys gave me the idea that it might be in the proper season almost pretty.

About ten miles from Betanzos we passed over a hill which we were a full hour in ascending and from the top of which we were gratified by a very extensive prospect; bounded in our rear and on our left by the towns

---

* Captain Leighton Cathcart Dalrymple seems to have been a particularly good friend of Edwin. He rose to lieutenant colonel of the 15th in 1813 and as such commanded the regiment at Waterloo where he lost his left leg. He was the second son of Sir Hew Dalrymple and died at Delrow, near Watford, on 6 June 1820.

† Major Francis Forrester retired soon after the Corunna campaign in August 1809 by sale of his commission.

‡ Major Leitch commanded the first division of the regiment on the advance.

of Corunna & Ferrol with their harbours & shipping; by great black hills on the right, and by the tops of the snowy mountains of Asturias in our front at an immense distance. Four miles from this spot & half a mile out of the high road is situated the miserable village of Caballo Torto, where we were to pass the remainder of the day; nothing of any sort except a few apples & some sour wine was to be procured at this place, my English beef therefore rescued me from starvation a second time, and having with difficulty persuaded the people to let me have a little fresh straw I rolled myself up in it and slept as soundly as a parcel of old sows who were quarrelling all night in the adjoining *bed*, would admit of.

To give some idea of the extreme dirt & wretchedness these people live in, it is necessary to describe one of their farm houses. The whole consists of one large apartment, in which cows, mules, asses, sheep, pigs, poultry & children are all huddled together; a fire of wood is made in the middle of the floor; windows and chimneys being equally unknown the smoke finds its way out where it can; two large chests are placed on each side of the fire one containing chopped straw for the mules, the other meal for the hogs; the tops of these chests do duty as beds at night and which with a couple of benches constitutes the whole of the furniture. Even the simple contrivance of a lamp is not used in some houses, so when there is occasion to go for fuel or straw after dark a wisp of the latter is carried flaming in the hand at the imminent risk of setting fire to their whole property in order to save a farthing a week in a rush light. It was sitting round the fire at this place that I first learnt the art of making Spanish soup, or as they call it *sopa*, which is their principal food, and for which the following is a short recipe. To four quarts of hot water put half a pint of train oil, a handful of garlick, some red pepper and salt. This when boiled is poured into a little trough full of broken bread, out of which the whole family feed with wooden spoons; I have frequently been invited to partake of this feast and as regularly declined the honour.

After passing the night in the manner I have described, it is not to be supposed that I felt much reluctance on quitting the premises the following morning;* the country did not improve upon us this day's march; we halted that night at the village of Baamonde which although miserable enough, is something better than Caballo Torto. We put up at a *posada* which is the name for a Spanish inn & having come to the determination of drawing rations of provisions with the dragoons we contrived to make

---

* Edwin was actually much luckier than his men who had to encamp this night in tents. Adjutant Jones wrote '... an excessive cold night. The wolves were so plentiful here on this wild high ground that they attacked the men as they lay sleeping...'

some excellent beef soup which we eat by the light of a candle stuck into a potato; and our host who had been bribed into civility by the sight of a few dollars supplied us with clean straw in the recesses where we slept.

A posada is the most miserable apology for an inn that can be imagined; the ground floor is a stable, over this are two or three large rooms which would make indifferent hay lofts; each room has a table and two benches; a mattress and some straw lays in the corners and this is the whole of the furniture; the people of the house never come near you; you can get nothing to eat but what you bring with you or send out to buy in the neighbourhood and there is a plentiful scarcity of everything *except* vermin and dirt.

On Saturday the 26th of November we arrived at Lugo. This city is surrounded by a high wall with a gravel walk on the top of it from whence you have a fine view of the country which is tolerably level hereabouts; it contains many good houses & handsome churches & convents; the cathedral is extremely grand, and the inside of the choir particularly beautiful. The roof which is admirably painted is supported by a great many pillars of different coloured marble and the quantities of images in the most expensive dresses, the immense gold and silver candlesticks & lamps, the rich gildings, carvings & paintings of which the altar is formed, together with its massive & costly ornaments, give the whole an air of grandeur & magnificence that I never had seen in any church before. The streets are narrow & dirty, but there are several good shops where one may purchase almost every necessary of life; inns there are none with the exception of a miserable hovel where the muleteers put up, & which nothing but dire necessity could induce one to set foot into. This being the case I was very glad to find myself quartered at the house of an ecclesiastical who appeared to be a man of some consequence, though what his precise title was I never could learn, who very kindly insisted upon my living with him the two days we were to remain at Lugo. The lower story of this man's house like all the others is divided into stables & pigsty's, a wide stone staircase led to the first floor on which there was a *drawing room* not less than 40 feet long, with an excellent bedroom at the end of it; on one side were three windows which opened into a balcony, and on the other folding doors leading into another large room through which you pass to a third, forming altogether a handsome suite of apartments, well furnished. With such a house it is not a little surprising that the master should chuse to live in the kitchen among the servants, yet such was his taste. Our dinners each day consisted of beef, black puddings & large peas boiled up together; a dish of stewed pears, some cheese & wine; all tolerably good except the wine; the parson ate most enormously of the beef & marrowfats, & being troubled with a good deal of flatulency, he loudly set the fashion at defiance for a considerable time

after every meal. As soon as we had finished, his cook and two maids sat
down, & we retired to the chimney corner to smoke segars [*sic*] :– as we
were to march early the following morning I retired betimes on Sunday
night to a very comfortable bed, but which according to the custom of the
country was without curtains.

I remarked at Lugo as well as at Corunna that the shops are open, and
work goes on the same on Sunday as any other day; this is the more to be
wondered at when it is remembered that the Spaniards are an extremely
bigoted people, and naturally so very lazy & indolent that one would think
they'd be glad to have any pretence for remaining idle, at least one day out
of the seven.

At Lugo the troops foraged for four days' supplies in preparation for a further
advance but orders arrived at midnight to halt. The news of Spanish reversals*
and a consequent French advance which threatened Baird's forces induced the
infantry to retire from Astorga on Villafranca. Orders had been changed at 2
a.m., with the cavalry and artillery ordered on to Villafranca to support the
infantry. The 10th Hussars were despatched immediately but the first division of
the 15th remained, allowing the second division to catch up, which they did at 3
p.m. The regiment would still move by divisions, but provisions for a retreat
were still being made and Lieutenant Baron During† was sent to reconnoitre the
roads into Portugal. The adjutant's diary indicates that there were several arrests
for drunkenness and that Edwin was sent with dispatches from Lugo to
Corunna, but Edwin indicates that he remained with his troop. Gordon in his
journal states that it was Cornet Laroche‡ who proceeded to Corunna and this
seems more likely as this was hardly work for a captain. Edwin continues:

The next stage beyond Lugo is the village of Constantine; here we were
gratified by the sight of some green meadows & beautiful valleys; a rapid
river takes its course along the bottom receiving its supplies from several

---

* General Blake's Spanish army of the left was defeated at Espinosa de los Monteros on
  11 November 1808, losing all their equipment, and the armies of the Centre and Reserve
  under Generals Castanos and Palafox were smashed at Tudela on 23 November.
† Lieutenant Lewis Alexander During, a Hanoverian by birth, served with the 15th until
  1813, when he joined the staff corps as a captain. He served the latter years of the
  peninsular war as aide-de-camp to Sir Lowry Cole and fought at Vitoria, Nivelle, Nives,
  Orthes and Toulouse. He went on half pay in 1819, then became a captain in the 98th
  Foot in 1829 and major in the 89th Foot in 1833, but again went on half pay. He
  eventually rose to the rank of general in 1877 and died at Hornburg in Saxony in 1880.
‡ Cornet James Laroche became a Lieutenant in July 1809 but was superseded for absence
  without leave in early 1810.

rivulets which fall down from the rocks in numerous cascades on every side; the situation of Constantine is altogether romantic & beautiful; but smiling meadows & purling streams afford little consolation in the month of November without a good house to put ones head into, & never shall I think of the night I passed in this beautiful valley without horror. The wretchedness & the filth in which the family lived with whom I *pigged*, 'beggars all description'. Three or four women, or rather *she men*, with as many young children, 3 cows, one mule, 8 or 10 hogs, with a proportion of chickens ducks & geese, & by far the greatest beast of the whole family the old farmer himself, all tryed [*sic*] who could get closest to a wood fire that smoked in the middle of the hovel. The glimmering of the fire enabled me to contemplate, (though not without emotion) the savage group that surrounded me, but all I can attempt to say of them is, that three better witches for Macbeth, or a better Caliban for the Tempest, never were seen; it was with difficulty I could persuade myself that I was living among Christians, much less among a *race* of *Christians* who think & stile themselves the elect of heaven, and who affect to smile with equal pity and contempt upon every other nation under the sun.

As soon as the embers of the fire died away, the family stretched themselves upon their dirty rugs laid on the floor; I occupied the top of a chest with my cloak for a bed, and a sheaf of straw for a pillow; 'tired nature's sweet restorer', did *not* forsake the wretched that night, for in spite of the hardness of my bed, & in spite of the grandest concert of vocal & instrumental noses I ever was at, he gave me a refuge in his arms from all the wretchedness that surrounded *me*. This blessing was however of short duration; an envious cow who seemed to live upon short commons had observed the sheaf of clean straw placed for my pillow & no sooner was all quiet than she came to the diabolical resolution of eating it, from which resolution I found it quite impossible to dissuade her and in spite of my repeated efforts she kept snorting & grinding away the whole night close to my ear.

Although sleeping in one's cloaths is not reckoned in general so refreshing or comfortable as getting between sheets without them, it has at least this advantage, that you just get up & shake yourself and there you are, dressed for the day without any of the troubles of the toilet. The Spaniards seem so fully aware of this, that in all the nights I passed among them I don't recollect ever seeing any part of their dress taken off except the shoes. Having mentioned shoes I must remark that those worn by the common people are nothing more than a log of wood hollowed out & set upon three feet like a stool; a great sharp hook turns up from the toe & almost touches the instep, the inside is lined with hay or straw; they are altogether very clumsy & resemble a *boat*, a *stool*, or anything you please but shoes.

We quitted this abode of misery soon after daylight on Tuesday the

29th and after marching five or six hours through a hilly, bleak & barren country, we arrived at the filthy village of Nogales situated at the foot of a great mountain. I shall pass over the sourness of the wine, the grittiness of the bread, the impenetrable toughness of our beef and the incivility of the people at Nogales and wish I could have passed over the great mountain that lay in our next days march with equal facility; we commenced ascending this hill as soon as we were out of the village, it is seven miles long & very steep; we crossed a level on the top about a mile broad, and descended nine more which brought us to the village of Trabadelo. The road is a very dangerous one, being in many places no more than a shelf cut through the rocks with tremendous precipices & without the most trifling fence; the summit of the mountain is generally enveloped in clouds the consequence of which was that we all got drenched to the skin; it also separates the kingdoms of Leon & Galicia. The posada where we put up was miserable enough, but thanks to the accommodating disposition of our landlord he commanded to make ourselves tolerably comfortable. The honesty of this man's countenance & openness of manner would have been prepossessing in any country, how much more so then in one where meanness, deceit & suspicion form the distinguishing characteristics of the people.

Having received information on our arrival here that Sir David Baird who had been some days at Astorga was retreating, we of course expected not to have advanced any further in that direction; & happy had it been for the army, for the cause we had embarked in, & for the friends of the thousands who were lost, if this decision had never been altered. If we had then retreated upon Corunna, or Vigo, the whole army might have been re-embarked without the loss of a single individual; it might then have proceeded to some port in the south of Spain or of Portugal, on which Sir John Moore would have fallen back from Salamanca, & where not only the people but the climate would have been more congenial to our wants & our operations: at all events the armies might have formed a junction, have established magazines & probably have laid some plan of future operation which held out a prospect of success. In the north there was no such prospect; the country was thinly inhabited and barren of provisions; instead of the zeal, & enthusiasm which we were taught to believe animated every Spanish bosom, we found them indolent and phlegmatic: their *patriotic armies* were *invisible* and it was generally remarked that what few terrified peasants we did see with arms in their *hands*, had their *faces* invariably turned *from* the quarter of the enemy.

Orders arrived at 5 a.m. for the first division to march to Bembibre with two guns and the second division to move to Ponferrada to cover the retreat of the infantry. When Captain Gordon's division (he commanded the rear division of the brigade to pick up the stragglers) reached Villafranca, Frederick was ordered back to Lugo in command of 170 sick horses and 100 sick men who were unable to continue with the brigade. Edwin was surprised at the order to advance:

Not expecting as I said to advance further, we were rather taken by surprise on receiving an order early in the morning of Thursday the first of December to march on towards Astorga. Our route lay through Villafranca [del Bierzo] where we were directed to take two days provision & forage, to leave all our baggage & women, and such men & horses as were in any way unfit for action. Villafranca is situated on the banks of the River *Minho* [actually the Burbia], & in a sort of amphitheatre of mountains ; it is a place of great natural strength and may be properly termed the key to Galicia, as were it well defended, no numbers could force this pass.

We quitted Villafranca at sunset, & after marching four hours by moonlight along a flat gravely [*sic*] plain, where we met the First Division of Sir David Baird's retreating army, arrived between nine & ten at Ponferrada.

Not having had anything to eat since morning we were all pretty hungry by the time we got here, and as soon as I had seen my troop put up I repaired to my billet which was at the house of an apothecary who I had the good fortune to find just setting down to supper on an [*Olla Podrida?*] of fish and parsnips stewed in oil; bad as this may sound, I contrived to make a very hearty meal to which I was invited by the lady, the don looking ready to eat *her* for making, & *me* for accepting the invitation. The kindness and civility of this woman was greater than any I had met with in Spain; to the beauty of an English woman she united the frankness & affability of the French, which gave her many an opportunity of displaying an even & white set of teeth; the first I had seen in the country. With such an obliging creature I was happy to stay two days, although her husband did everything in his power to make it unpleasant, being stingy, ill tempered & jealous.

Ponferrada is built upon a rock at the bottom of which runs a large & rapid river; behind it is a range of immense mountains, whose craggy & lofty points are continually lost in the clouds; in front of it a beautiful & level country, tolerably well cultivated extends as far as the eye can carry; this direct contrast has a very pleasing effect, and I have little hesitation in setting down Ponferrada as the prettiest situated town in Spain. Its castle which was built by the moors is very large, and must have been a place of great strength. The adventures of Gil Blas and his gang of thieves did not escape my recollection at this place.*

---

* *The Adventures of Gil Blas of Santilanne* was a novel written by Alain-René Lesage in 1715 and translated into English by Tobias Smollett.

On 2 December Lord Paget sent an order to select the best 400 men and horses and to prepare to march over the mountains to join Sir John Moore who was expected to retreat from Salamanca into Portugal. The remaining troops were to march back to Corunna to embark and sail to Portugal by sea. Baird's infantry continued to retreat:

> On Friday the 2nd the Brigade of Guards under General Ward* marched in, and on Saturday morning we were ordered to proceed to Astorga from whence it was intended the cavalry should make their way either by force or stratagem to join Sir John Moore at Salamanca.
>
> We stopped that night at the villages of San Roman [de Bembibre] and Bembibre and on Sunday at [blank] within two leagues of Astorga. I put up at one of the best houses in the village, but the *best* accommodation they could give me was an arm full of straw in an apple room the roof of which was perforated in so many places that I contemplated all the stars of the heavens in station as they passed over me; a delightful birth for an astronomer, but a very miserable one for any other person in a frosty December night.
>
> As our last two or three days marches had been unusually long we never arrived at our halting place till sometime after dark, which circumstance encreased [*sic*] the difficulty of getting shelter for man and horse, and frequently have we sat for hours before the inhabitants could be prevailed upon to open their doors, although it was an invariable rule never to quarter more dragoons upon any individual than could conveniently be accommodated, & most scrupulously to pay for every article with which we were furnished. Such was the disposition, & hospitable reception of this people, in whose cause, & for whose sakes we were suffering every species of privation & fatigue!

Such trying marches in inclement weather caused the numbers of sick to increase rapidly and Lieutenant Buckley† and Assistant Surgeon Forbes‡ were ordered to take the sick and lame to Lugo, where they would join Frederick. Gordon was ordered to force march his detachments to catch up with the brigade, which he did on 6 December at La Baneza.

On Monday the 5th we marched into the plains of Astorga, where we took

---

* The 1st and 3rd battalions of 1st Guards under Major General Sir Henry Warde.
† Lieutenant James Ogden Buckley had been promoted from sergeant major in the 44th Foot to cornet in the 15th in 1804. He rose to captain, retired on half pay in 1817 and died in 1824.
‡ Assistant Surgeon James Forbes had joined the 15th Dragoons from the 30th Foot in 1804 and joined the 95th Foot as surgeon in 1809. He went on half pay in 1814.

leave of our infantry & and of the mountainous country. The hussar brigade consisting of the 7th: 10th: and 15th: Regiments and two troops of horse artillery* being formed under the walls of this ancient & handsome city, Lord Paget collected the officers & made a speech, the *substance* of which was, 'that in consequence of the French being in great force, & nearer than was expected, it had been deemed too hazardous for the infantry to attempt forming a junction with the army of Sir J Moore; that he had however come to the resolution of doing so with the cavalry; confessed his want of information with regard either to the position or numbers of the enemy; that if we did fall in with them our point was to be carried with a dash, and concluded by entreating that good order might not be lost by an over anxiety to come up with them'. We then proceeded to La Baneza, a town about three leagues from Astorga, in the direction of Salamanca, where I had the choice of three billets, and as I had long before this formed the greatest aversion to every thing Spanish, I took up my quarters at the house of a French *Medicin*. As it was customary for the officer who went forward to the different juntas for billets, to procure more than were wanted, it frequently happened that I had this sort of choice, on which occasions I used to show my billet & ask the first person I met, which was the way to it? But they almost invariably shook their heads & said '*No entendi*', 'I do not understand you', and of this you may be assured, that a Spaniard when you ask him a question will if it is possible say he does not understand you, merely to save himself the trouble of giving an answer; if however they were inclined to be communicative I used to say '*esta Buena casa senor*?', 'is this a *good house* sir?', if it was a bad one the answer used to be 'Bueno Senor', '*good* sir'; if of the better sort the answer was 'si senor *grande, muchio grande*', 'yes sir, grand very grand'; but on inspection these grand mansions were generally found to be of the usual stamp of wretchedness.

Uncertainty as to the position of the French determined Lord Paget that our *rest* should be taken by day; and consequently our marches by night; we therefore remained the whole of Tuesday at La Baneza, and assembled on the road leading to Benavente at eleven o'clock at night. Owing to the extreme caution that it is necessary to observe during an advance by night, we did not arrive at Benavente which is only two and twenty miles till between six & seven in the morning; when having made the necessary dispositions for our security,† the next thing to be thought of was some

---

* B & C Troops Royal Horse Artillery were attached to the hussar brigade.
† Not knowing where the French were, a picket of 100 men from each regiment was posted along the banks of the river.

breakfast, & then a dinner, the former we made on some excellent chocolate, of the latter every man was his own cook, our servants being employed in the care of the horses, & the Spaniards we could not trust as they spoilt everything with garlick and oil. Thus between cooking, eating & drinking, sleep, which was by far the most necessary article, it was quite impossible to procure; at half past ten at night we were again on horseback.

Of all the disagreeable sensations to which we are subject, there is none can be compared (I speak *feelingly*) to that of having an irresistible impulse to sleep without a possibility of gratifying it. To *such* a degree have I experienced this, that I declare I have often envied and would gladly have exchanged conditions with the very stones by the road side merely because they were at rest. This *doziness* was considerably augmented by the extreme cold; for though the sun in the daytime was sometimes unpleasantly hot we had sharp frosts at night accompanied with thick fogs which numbed our hands & feet, and stiffened our cloaks with ice. The breath too with the assistance of the fog formed large icicles to the men's mustachios, & though the different faces at daylight were all *greatly* expressive of misery, it was quite impossible to help laughing at some of them.

The town of Benavente has nothing remarkable in it, though from the circumstance of its being built upon a rising ground, situated in a level country, & surrounded by a high wall and old towers, its appearance from a distance is imposing and grand. The brigade being formed on the plain below the town began to move off at about twelve at night, and we soon afterwards passed the bridge across the River Esla since rendered famous by our victory over the Imperial Guards, and capture of General Lefebvre.

Just as our rearguard had passed this bridge a sudden & large blaze of fire appeared about ½ a mile upon our right flank; it did not last above a quarter of a minute, and was evidently intended as a signal, as we saw it answered by similar blazes for many miles in front. Whether it concerned us or not, we never learnt, but it had the effect of putting us more than usually upon our guard; the artillery marched with their matches burning, and we loaded our pistols.

We had learnt at Benavente that a corps consisting of 8,000 infantry, & 1,400 cavalry were at Toro, who would probably attempt to frustrate our intention of joining Sir John Moore; what grounds there were for *believing* this I know not, but from the directions given out, and the order in which we advanced, certain it is that Lord Paget expected to be attacked on that nights march.

The brigade was now close to Zamora and there was a nervous tension as all were keenly aware that the French were close at hand, but were quite ignorant of their actual position or strength; however Edwin was still guilty of falling asleep when in charge of the picket, perhaps a sign that these young 'gentlemen' were yet to appreciate fully their roles and responsibilities as cavalry officers.

Twilight at length glimmered in the east but no French appeared; the men and horses were sinking through fatigue, yet it was deemed unsafe to separate them, we were therefore drawn up near the roadside at about eight o'clock in the morning, dismounted, & ordered to make ourselves as *comfortable* as we could till eleven at night; and to encrease *mine* I was sent out with a picquet of thirty men to protect the front of our position. As soon as the videttes were placed I set all hands to work to make a fire but owing to the scarcity of wood, and what little there was being covered with hoarfrost, it was some time before we could persuade it to burn; as soon as it did I made myself some chocolate, a plentiful supply of which & a pot to boil it in, I always carried about with me, and extending myself upon the ground sunk into a profound sleep, but from this I was soon roused by one of the men who came galloping to say that as the fog cleared away he distinctly saw the French cavalry manoeuvring about two miles from us; information was instantly sent to Lord Paget, who with his staff & a party of dragoons set off to reconnoitre them, whilst we waited impatiently for the order to advance; he however soon returned laughing, the enemy being nothing more than a herd of wild horses who animated by some gleams of sunshine were 'fetching mad bounds & galloping to & fro' as fresh colts often do, begging me therefore to caution my men against receiving objects with such quixotic eyes for the future. He left us to enjoy the joke & to prepare something in the shape of dinner, which I made on some portable soup, & a piece of cold beef that had been several days in my haversack, & which was both in quantity & quality very different from what I could have wished it to be. As it may be supposed that we lived well as long as we had a piece of beef left, I shall here once [and] for all give a description of it. The oxen are invariably small and of one colour, a sort of yellowish dun; at two years old they are put into harness and being kept constantly at hard work & having nothing but chopped straw to eat very soon become a mere bundle of bones & sinews; of fat they do not possess a single spark, & what little lean they have is so indescribably tough, that it is perfectly impossible to eat it under six hours stewing at least, and as we hardly ever had above half of one to spare for cooking, it was of very little use excepting for the broth. At five o'clock the sun went down, & soon afterwards the cold fog came on; we encreased our fire, lighted our pipes, which on these occasions I found of the greatest comfort, & thus passed the time till near twelve, when we were called in to the main body & the whole resumed their former order of march. Nothing remarkable occurred this night except that it was as much as ever

we could do to prevent the men from tumbling off their horses during a
tedious march of between five & six Spanish leagues.*

But at daylight in the morning of Friday the 9th of December† we were
gladdened by the sight of the churches of Zamora just in our front. The
great cathedral, the lofty convents & other public edifices of this city give
an idea of grandeur & magnificence that but ill prepares one for the
reception you are to meet within its walls; but I must do the natives the
justice to say that they paid us every mark of attention in their power, and
which made the greater impression as it was the first time we had met with
any. The windows and balcony's even at that early hour were crowded with
ladies, and the shouts of '*Viva Los Ingleses*', '*Viva Jorge Tercero*', 'long live the
English', 'long live George the Third', resounded from all quarters. As
soon as we had formed in the great square an invitation was sent to the
officers from the junta requesting we would honor them with our
company at breakfast, an honor which we very readily conferred;
accordingly as soon as our troops were put up we repaired to a sort of
town hall, where we were received in form by the members of the junta,
and introduced by them to the bishop who was arrayed in his pontifficals
and seated upon a throne at the upper end of the room. The breakfast
consisted of chocolate, biscuits, fruit & liqueurs, all very good, but
forming rather a slight repast for a parcel of hungry hussars who had been
marching all night; the dons declared that we each eat enough to serve a
Spaniard for a week; rather an unseasonable remark I thought, but
however we cleared the tables, when another scene of bowing & scraping
ensued, and we each retired to our billets.

Not having had our cloaths off (except to change linen) or any comfortable rest since leaving Ponferrada, I was not a little rejoiced to hear that
we were to halt for twenty four hours at this place, & my joy was much
encreased by finding that myself with 3 other officers were billeted at the
bishop's palace, where we had a prospect at least of cleanliness & comfort.
This house is built in form of a square, & encloses a courtyard to which
you enter by folding gates; the apartments on the ground floor, for we got
no higher, are numerous and spacious, but with regard to comfort, suffice
it to say that the floors were of tile, the walls were base, there was no
fireplace, nor did either door or window shut by several inches. The bishop
sent to us to say that as he knew the English liked dining late he would not
pay us the compliment of asking us to dine with him, but begged we

---

* Note by Edwin: 'A Spanish league is about four & a half English miles.'
† The adjutant records that they arrived at Zamora on the 8th, but Edwin and Gordon
   both agree that they arrived on the 9th.

would give orders to have dinner at what hour we pleased, so having named five, we dressed ourselves, and sallied forth to take a survey of the place. Zamora is a very large and very ancient city; it stands upon the right bank of the River Duero, which is here very considerable, and over it is a handsome stone bridge of seventeen arches. It contains some magnificent churches & convents, & is surrounded by a high wall; the entrances to it are over draw-bridges, defended by towers and portcullis's; the streets are as usual narrow but have some good looking houses in them and a few tolerable shops, and the people altogether bore a more Christian like appearance than any we had seen.

Here, as well as at every other place that the opportunity offered, I paid a visit to the grates of a convent; *why* I do not exactly know, but there was something in the life, and I believe name of a *nun* which always prepossessed me in their favour and made me anxious for acquaintance among them; I pictured to myself beautiful and interesting young women who from some cross in love or rather disappointment in early life had sought for that peace of mind & happiness in the arms of religion of which the uncertainty of world affairs had bereft them. However right I might have been with regard to the *causes* of this seclusion, certain it is that I was very far from right in picturing the *objects* of it, as neither *youth* or *beauty* were visible within the walls of a convent, or at least never presented themselves at the grates; on the contrary I found them in general old and ugly, *with* beards, *without* teeth; they however covered a multitude of imperfections by their vivacity and affability, by their expressions of love and veneration for the English character, and particularly for English *officers* who they declared were the first of men.

Returning from our stroll at the appointed hour, dinner was served up to us in the following order; first a great stiff dish of vermicelli and bread, called by them sopa, and which would have been tolerably good but for the quantity of saffron which was mixed with it; next came the principal dish at every Spanish dinner which is a piece of beef, the fat of bacon, black puddings, hard pease [*sic*] & cabbages all boiled up together and turned out into a kind of turene [*sic*]; the garlick with which the black puddings were stuffed, gave the whole a most *vile twang,* but we had fortunately the best of sauces; next came two split boiled tough old cocks which they had vainly attempted to moisten with bad oil; then a great roasted fish of the haddock kind, and lastly a course of sweet things which was much the best part of the dinner, and indeed would have been commended on the table of an English bishop.

It being thought a mark of respect in Spain for all the family to attend during the dinner hour, the bishop sent the whole of his, which including chaplains, stewards, housekeepers, valets &c, amounted to about twenty persons, who formed in a double row round the table criticising on our manners, and the quantity we devoured; nothing could be more disagreeable; but as it is a ceremony never to be dispensed with, we were forced to *eat & abide*.

Being all tolerably well fagged, we retired early to our beds, which were very comfortable, and I do not hesitate to assert, that the great luxury of getting between clean sheets, and warm blankets, can only be fully felt by those who have experienced the deprivation of it for many successive nights.

While at Zamora intelligence was received which proved that all the previous alarms had been false rumour. The French armies had struck south to capture Madrid and had never been close to Zamora. Baird's retreat had been unnecessary as the junction with Moore's troops at Salamanca had been perfectly feasible. This information had already been received by Sir John Moore at Salamanca and it was at this point that he decided to advance into northern Spain to threaten the communications of Napoleon's army and to help the Spanish armies in the south by drawing off some of Napoleon's forces. Baird's forces were ordered to advance again and Moore set out to join him near Astorga, the cavalry were ordered to Tordesillas.

We had now got from eighty to ninety miles distant from Astorga, and within thirty of Salamanca, and not a symptom of an enemy had appeared; a plain proof that the intelligence given to our commanders was false, and that the people were not to be depended upon. The French had not been at Toro, nor had there ever been the smallest impediment to Sir David Baird's infantry forming a junction with Sir John Moore according to the original plan. It was probably about this time that Sir John determined to take a northern direction; Madrid had fallen, which destroying all hopes of joining the patriotic armies in the south of Spain, (if indeed there were any, which is extremely doubtful) the making a diversion in their favor in the north, by drawing the attention of the French in that direction was the most essential, and at the same time the most promising piece of service we could perform. Orders were therefore sent to Sir D. Baird to advance again immediately, & Lord Paget was directed to push forward with the cavalry brigade in the direction of Tordesillas.

In compliance with this resolution we were formed in the great square at nine in the morning on the 10th of December* and after being inspected by the Spanish general commanding the garrison of Zamora, where by

---

* The adjutant again records their arrival at Toro on the evening of the 9th, but Edwin and Gordon both agree that it was on the 10th.

the bye there was *not a single soldier*, we marched out on the road to Toro.

The 10th were left at Zamora and the 7th took outpost duties; it is clear, however, that the hussars had yet to perfect their role as pickets; the adjutant records 'the outposts were in general harassed by their own want of knowledge'.

Toro is only five leagues from Zamora, but owing to the badness of the road, which in some places was almost impassable for the artillery, we did not reach it till dark. Nothing could be more flattering than our reception at this place; the town was illuminated, which is not done in our way by sticking candles *in* the windows but by placing great flambeaux on the outside of them, to the balcony's, door posts &c. bonfires were made in the open parts, and the streets rang with '*Viva Los Ingleses*'.

But amidst all these appearances of rejoicing we had a fresh proof of the insincerity (to call it nothing worse) of this nation; the junta sent to Lord Paget with many apologies to say that 'the British troops having arrived rather unexpectedly they had not provided the billets which would otherwise have been done, that they were however happy *we* should not experience any inconvenience on that account as the inhabitants all *eager* to testify their *love* for us had voluntarily thrown open their doors for our reception.' Such was the substance of the message from the junta, and which was by order communicated to the troops, accompanied by many encomiums from his lordship on the generosity of the *brave Spaniards*, and with strong injunctions that no abuse whatever should be made of such unbounded confidence and hospitality. Each officer was then directed to take his troop off and put them up.

But where now had flown this extreme *love*, this *great generosity*, this *unexampled hospitality?* Suffice it to say that *I* was two hours, and other officers more in the streets, before our entreaties, persuasions, & latterly threats, could prevail upon these *eager* inhabitants, (who had barricaded the lower storys, & taken refuge themselves in the upper) to give our men & horses shelter for the night!

I got admittance to a priest's house, which were always the best, as however it went with the rest of the world these good people were sure to have plenty of provisions. As luck would have it, I found a friend supping with him who happened to be an Irishman. He was a Catholic priest & had quitted Ireland during the rebellion in that country, & having some friends in Toro settled himself among them. I found this man in common with his countrymen, friendly, communicative, and entertaining; I gave him the best account I was able of our proceedings both at home and abroad, and he in return imparted to me all the information I wished for on the country & place we were then in. Toro and its environs is reckoned famous for the fineness of the bread, the excellency [*sic*] and abundance of its wine, and for the extreme productiveness of its vineyards & fruit trees of every description; it is so famous as to be termed by most people the *Garden of Spain*. Here then was I in the garden of that country which is itself esteemed the garden of Europe.

'Bear me Pomona to thy citrus groves, to where the lemon, & the piercing lime, with the deep orange glowing thro' the green their lighter glories blend. Lay me reclined beneath the spreading tamarind, that shakes, fann'd by the breeze, its fever cooling fruits.'*

Full of these luxuriant ideas & all impatience to behold this terrestrial paradise, I was soon after daylight on the walls of the town; the morning was uncommonly fine, my station was very high, and I eagerly bent my eyes on the extensive prospect before me; at first I was rather disappointed for there were neither tawny citrons or orange *trees* to be seen much less *groves*. The River Duero however winding majestically along watered some fine meadows, & here and there a few dusky vineyards appeared; thinking I had made a mistake & that the great beauty of the country lay on the other side of the city, I hastily passed through the streets & ascended the opposite walls. But *here* a vast, flat, & sandy plain extending in every direction as far as the eye can carry, & unadorned by a single twig, might safely have disputed the praise of sterility with any desart [*sic*] in Africa. And *here* ends my description of the *Garden of Spain*.

Toro was too cramped for the brigade and the left squadron of the 15th which included Edwin's troop, was ordered forward to Morales de Toro.

Toro stands upon a hill, and is altogether a handsome place; it is a Bishop's See, with Zamora, the same as Bath & Wells are in this country. As we were rather crowded here, & a division of infantry was expected soon, the Fifteenth marched on the evening of the 11th to a large village about a league off, called Morales [de Toro]. Nothing can exceed the ugliness of the country hereabouts; there are a few small hills to be seen but all so exactly the same height and so very flat at the top that they look as if they had been mowed off with a scythe. With the exception of these you could fancy yourself at sea the moment you are out of a town, the country being so destitute of trees or any other symptom of vegetation, and so perfectly on a level that you may distinguish the steeples of churches for leagues in front of you.

Being now advanced a great way from the main body; we were directed

---

* This is a verse from James Thomson's *The Seasons* written in 1730.

to halt at Morales until the evening of the 14th.

It will be remembered that we left Frederick at Lugo with the sick men and horses. Cornet Jenkins and the twenty men released on parole, having been captured by a privateer and relieved of their arms, arrived at Lugo and Frederick happily handed over his command to Jenkins. He proceeded to join the regiment but Sir David Baird ordered him to halt at Villafranca to command thirty sick hussars who were lying there. Frederick wrote to his mother from here to update her with his movements; the letter was received at Bath on 31 December 1808. En route to Villafranca Frederick had been alarmed by the report of the enemy; it seems that it was not only Edwin's men who could see French cavalry where there were none!

Villafranca [del Bierzo], *December 13th 1808*

My dearest mother,

I am quite rejoiced to get a single halting day to let you know that I am quite well and in good spirits but I must begin with an account my peregrinations since I left Corunna. The first days march was to Betanzos which is about 18 miles, the country all the way to it is very fine and abounds in vineyards, but the town is a great deal worse than Corunna, indeed that is the best place I have seen yet, but to give you some idea of them all, I assure you that *Mold* is as good again as any of them. There is no such thing as an inn where you can get a dinner. The next place we came to is Caballo Torto, a miserable cottage village; about 14 miles further on, Edwin & I slept in the same cottage to which I assure you that [the one on the] other side of [Caer Estyn?] belonging to old Mary Reese is a *palace* to it. Three different families live in it, besides the cows, mules, pigs, fowls &c &c &c without any partition. We lay in our blankets & clokes in one corner of this wretched hut on a bundle of straw; but being now got used to this sort of rough work I do not mind it in the least. The next place was not quite so bad, but the poverty of the place is so great that we could not get anything but eggs and potatoes to eat. The next day's march was to Lugo which is a large town but is not half so good as Corunna. The streets are very narrow and dirty, and every thing very dear. We halted here a day to refresh our horses & I had the comfort of again sleeping between the sheets. The next day we set out for Nogales about a twelve mile stage where we were pretty well accommodated considering that it is only a small village; the two next places are likewise small villages not worth mentioning as they are almost all alike.

14th on getting up this morning I find that I am to remain here which gives me more time my dearest mother to continue this epistle but more of this hereafter.

On arriving at Villafranca I received an order being the junior cornet to return to Lugo with the command of the sick horses belonging to all the brigade which amounted to about 170 horses & 100 men, this I assure you was no sinecure as I had to pay the men regularly and draw forage and provisions for the horses & men in all the towns & villages that I stopped at and to take accounts of all, besides attending the men when I got in at night and see that they took proper care of the horses, being without Edwin or any officer at all to give me any assistance. However I got them all to Lugo but 4 men & horses which were unable to proceed. I found an officer of our regiment Mr Jenkins, at Lugo with about 20 men & horses who had been captured by a privateer and rifled of all their arms & appointments but had let them go on his giving his parole that neither himself nor the men would serve again during the present war, so there he is obliged to stay, much mortified he is not to be able to proceed to join the regiment. I stayed here two days without anything remarkable happening when another officer namely Lieut. During came in there from Santiago where he had been reconnoitring the country, & to my great joy he obtained leave from Genl Manningham* for me to return with him [During] with a detachment of about 50 men & horses which were fit for service to join the regiment and I had got again as far as Villafranca when I was ordered by Sir D. Baird to remain here with a detachment of about 30 men & horses; & here I am afraid I am likely to remain. 16th On enquiring to day I find that a post sets out for Corunna tomorrow morning so that I shall get this finished as quick as possible.

The state of affairs here look I am very sorry to say very unfavourably at present. The French are in the opinion of everybody in possession of Madrid; & Blake's army are all dispersed about the country; it is quite miserable to see the poor wretches laying about the streets basking in every gleam of sunshine they can meet with and begging their bread from every passenger! It is also a prevailing opinion that we shall all be in motion to retreat in less than a week but this is only report. I wish very much to get permission to join my regiment as it is very dull remaining here by myself. There is luckily for me another young officer of the 7th left here for the same purpose as I was, and he & I pass our time pretty well together as we have borrowed a couple of guns and he has got 2 dogs so that we have famous sport here shooting; there are a good number of partridges & hares and woodcocks and a few snipes, so that we do not want for game. By the bye I must not forget to tell you of a good joke which happened to me on my return with the sick horses. When I had got about 14 miles from

---

* General Sir Coote Manningham, 95th Foot.

Deep into Spain

Villafranca the corporal of the advanced guard came back with a very long face and told me that he thought there was a *detachment of the enemy* in our front on the side of a mountain. I halted the men and was really *half inclined* to believe it, as it *had* been reported that there had been some of the enemy near a bridge not far from it; I rode on and found that there was something very like what he represented so I had all the best men & horses to the front which amounted to about 60 & so proceeded on in due form. After we had marched about a quarter of a mile we found that the *detachment* of the *enemy* was nothing more than some new palings on the other side of a thick hedge which with the sun shining directly upon them looked exactly like a regiment of soldiers. What say you to that? Almost as brave as Don Quixote's encounter with the windmills. The living here is very cheap as we have our lodging for nothing and a pound of beef besides bread & wine allowed us daily, so that we have only little necessaries such as chocolate & milk to get ourselves. It is quite misery to write a letter here as I am sure to have five or six people all about me the whole time; some pulling my paper, some my pen and some asking me what one thing & the other that in English. I am getting on now pretty well in Spanish and can make myself understood tolerably well by signs and the little I know of it; the man I am billeted upon is very civil and tries to teach me as much as possible. I saw an officer a few days ago who had just come from the army and he tells me that when he saw Edwin he was looking very well and in good spirits. This is the last account I have heard of him as it is impossible for us to write to one another on account of their being no cross posts as in England. He desired me to be sure whenever I wrote to add a thousand loves for him to all at Rhual, Bath &c. He & I who to[o] often think of the namesake of this confounded place in the Bellan and wished ourselves there for a few hours but we both wish to see a little more of Spain before we leave it to the *mercy of Bonaparte.* I suppose you and the Morgans are comfortably settled in 28 St James's Square, or have you changed the house? I suppose Edward* will be off to join his regiment at Clonmel soon or has he got further leave of absence? I must now begin to conclude with my best love to my grandfather & grandmother, Uncle & Aunt Morgan, Louisa, Edward; tell the latter that I think he would not *relish* Spain so much as he thought he would. Pray give my best love to my sister Charlotte and tell her I often wish for her to see the ridiculous figures

---

* Lieutenant Edward Morgan 7th Foot rose to captain in the regiment but went on half pay from the 75th Foot in 1822 'from ill health'. His illness presumably led from his wounding at Albuera, for which he received a pension of £70 per annum. On retirement he married and lived in Italy.

that go about the streets. My paper grows very short so adieu! God bless you my dear mother & believe me your ever dutiful & affectionate

F C Philips

On 12 December the regiment moved up to Morales de Toro and the right squadron was sent forward to Pedrosa del Rey. Edwin was well aware that the French were now very near at hand and the regiment was constantly kept on the alert. There was time however, for a regimental court martial as the adjutant records that Privates Weir, Collins & Burton of Captain Broadhurst's* troop were tried and punished by the lash and sergeants Pugh and Milner of Captain Cochrane's† troop were reduced for 'irregular conduct'. Edwin resumes his journal with a description of Morales de Toro.

At such a place as this in England there certainly would not be fewer than twenty good shops at least; here on the contrary there was but one, and that for four articles only; viz, bread, butter, onions, & rice. Of butter there are two sorts, *Manteco de vaca*, cows butter, & *Manteco de porko*, which is hog's lard; it is sold in black pudding skins at so much an inch and does not look at all tempting; but of the Spanish butter I shall have said enough when I assure you that the worst hog's lard is preferable to it.

A dear *clean* little old woman made me very comfortable here, getting a dish of good eggs & bacon and a rice pudding each day for my dinner and making me a very tolerable bed, but as we were now getting into the neighbourhood of the French cavalry we were kept upon the alert all night and consequently had not much use for beds. What particularly charmed me in this old lady was, that I found all her kindness had proceeded from a wish to make me comfortable only, as at parting it was with the greatest difficulty I persuaded her to accept of anything in return for all the trouble I had given her, and all I had eat and drank at her expense. There is nothing in or about Morales worth describing; the inside of the church was extremely beautiful, and indeed all the churches in Spain are, and I attended Mass there several times. The outside of the windows and door frames were like most others surrounded with human skulls, the backs of which are stuck against the walls with mortar, some of them had beautiful teeth, which is more than any living Spaniard can boast, but they have altogether a most horrible grinning and ghastly appearance.

---

* Captain John Broadhurst had come from 27th Foot in 1803. He retired by the sale of his commission in 1809.

† Captain the Honourable William Erskine Cochrane became a major in 1813 and retired by the sale of his commission in 1819. He died in 1871.

Deep into Spain

A reconnaissance towards Tordesillas received reports that there was a French post there and the outpost picket being pushed forward, the French left the town to the British. The 15th were hurriedly sent forward to occupy Tordesillas.

> We quitted Morales on the afternoon of the 14th* and arrived at Tordesillas, four leagues and a half, about nine o'clock; the night was frosty and starlight [sic], our route lay most part of the way along the right bank of the Duero, and the quantity of swans, geese, herons and all sorts of wild fowl that we disturbed exceeded anything I ever beheld; they kept circling at a little distance over our heads, and on our firing a few ball cartridges at them almost deafened us with their screams. We were received at Tordesillas the same as at Toro with bonfires and illuminations, tho' our fare within doors was much as usual; the people were however rather more sincere in their rejoicings, as our approach had obliged *four & twenty* French hussars who had laid the town under contribution to retire; here then was a pretty specimen of Spanish heroism and intrepidity! Where the inhabitants of nearly as large a town as Shrewsbury had been dictated to for the space of a week by *twenty four* French hussars, had been obliged to contribute so many days provisions & forage for the use of the French army, & not only that, but had been forced to convey it to them at their own trouble & expense! And yet these are the heroes whom the English newspapers would fain persuade one are to restore the balance of power in Europe and make the Imperial dynasty of Buonaparte [sic] tremble on its thrones.

Moore had now joined forces with Baird but before advancing further he received news that Madrid had capitulated and he quickly realised that there was now extreme danger in remaining on the Spanish plains. However, Moore saw an opportunity to attack an isolated corps under Marshal Soult on the Carrion River numbering only 18,000 men before he would be forced to retreat. This movement initially required a short retrograde march which did not please the army.

Following the arrival of additional cavalry with Moore's force, the cavalry was now formed into two brigades: Brigadier General Slade commanded a brigade consisting of the 10th and 15th Hussars and Brigadier General Charles Stewart commanded the 7th, 18th and 3rd Hussars KGL.

> Early on the 15th we left Tordesillas, & made rather a retrograde movement to a small town called Mota [del Marques]. It is built in [the] form of a crescent round a sugar loaf hill on the top of which stands an

---

*   Again the adjutant's diary seems to be in error stating the 15th moved to Tordesillas on 13 December; whereas Edwin and Gordon both agree that this occurred on the 14th.

old Moorish castle (which like everything else in Spain is rather famous for what it has been than what it is) and at the bottom of it is a palace belonging to the Duke of Berwic[k] & Alva a descendant of our James II.

According to the adjutant, a trumpeter was placed on the top of a tower in this castle ready to raise the alarm.

> This being the greatest object of attraction we naturally went to look at it as soon as we were able; the duke was at Madrid but we were invited in by one of his relations and introduced to three of the most charming young women I almost ever saw; their feature & persons were really beautiful one of them perfectly so, and their manners were elegant and fascinating; they told us that the Duke was particularly partial to the English, and would be very angry if we did not send to his house for everything we wanted; they then shewed us all over it, but there was nothing worth seeing except indeed some paintings on a gallery wall which were of so indelicate a nature as to make *me blush* although they were particularly pointed out to us by these young virgins; such is the difference of ideas between different nations.
>
> We took leave of these Spanish beauties who were the first (and last) I had seen on Saturday the 17th: and got to Villabragima before dark; one league from [Medina de] Rioseco, famous for the great victory obtained there over the patriots* during the summer months and which was the last attempt at opposition made by them in these parts; Rioseco had been in possession of the French ever since, but was abandoned on our approach; they had not however retreated far, and as an attack was expected that night we lay on our arms till daylight. On Sunday the 18th we proceeded to Villalpando, where we joined Sir John Moore and the infantry. A council of war was held, and it was then I believe determined to make an attack upon Marshal Soult who with an army of sixteen or seventeen thousand men was posted along the River Carrion, three days march in front of us. With this determination the cavalry were detached to drive in his outposts and the infantry were to follow with all convenient speed.

When close to Medina de Rioseco, a picket was sent to within a mile to reconnoitre, as it was reported that some 700 French cavalry were in the town. However, on the approach of this patrol, the French abandoned the town and Captain Dalrymple was despatched to report the matter to Paget who ordered them on to Villalpando and on the following day to Mayorga.

---

* The battle of Medina de Rioseco was fought 14 July 1808, when a heavily outnumbered French force under Marshal Bessieres heavily defeated the armies of Castille and Galicia under Generals Cuesta and Blake.

Chapter 3

A GLORIOUS NIGHT

The regiment still formed the advance guard of the army as Moore sought to catch Soult's force before he could escape. Paget gained intelligence that General Debelle's French cavalry lay nearby at Sahagun, apparently oblivious of their approach; Paget struck immediately and with venom. The night of the 20th would become very special in the memories of the 15th.

> After a tedious march through a deep country and during a heavy fall of snow, we reached Mayorga on the night of the 19th starved with cold and hunger. A few damp and dismal convents was the only shelter we could procure for the night, and at daybreak we were again on horseback; about noon we arrived at the little village of Melgar de Abajo.
>
> The fifteenth were now the advance guard of the British army, both the seventh & tenth having halted short of this place. The French cavalry hearing of our approach had abandoned all the villages which they had been laying under contributions and rendezvoused at Sahagun. Lord Paget who was with *us* having received certain information of this, resolved to attack them on the following morning and accordingly issued orders* for the fifteenth to assemble at half past eleven o'clock that night on the outside of the village leaving all the men & horses behind who were the least sick or lame, and as we had by this time a good many of the latter the regiment did not muster altogether above five hundred men.†

---

* The briefing was held in Paget's rooms; Adjutant Jones states that only commanding officers and adjutants were in attendance, but most other witnesses state that the commanding officers and commanders of troops and squadrons were present.

† As the orders were given late, when the troops had been scattered in their billets and the regiment was ordered to muster in silence without bugle calls, apparently a number of men were not called. Lieutenant Buckley and a small detachment also arrived that evening and were ordered to remain as the baggage guard. The numbers therefore engaged are problematical, but a good estimate would be 450 to 500.

From Corunna to Waterloo

The regiment had a ride of approximately twelve miles, not an easy task in the dead of night on poor roads covered with sheet ice and all to be completed in total silence. It was arranged that the 15th, who led, would skirt Sahagun and arrive at the far side of Sahagun at exactly 6 a.m., precisely the moment when the 10th, following with a detachment of horse artillery, would drive into the town. Caught in a trap, it was hoped to capture the entire force, an ambitious plan.

> The night was dark as the grave, the ground covered with snow, and so slippery that we were obliged to lead our horses out of the village; under all these circumstances it was one o'clock before we were formed, told off, and ready to march.* At length a guide having been provided and orders given for the strictest silence to be observed, we moved off at a few minutes after one. Nothing could be more perplexing than the route our guide led us, sometimes in a track but oftener not, across ditches, and over bridges so narrow as to be dangerous even for foot passengers, and all these difficulties were of course encreased ten fold by the darkness of the night. We however proceeded without any *mishap* till five o'clock in the morning when our advanced guard fell in with a small picquet of the enemy's hussars a few of whom after a short scuffle unfortunately contrived to make their escape, leaving about half a dozen in our hands, and gave the alarm;† had this not happened we should have taken the place completely by surprize [*sic*] and every Frenchman in it.

There was no time for delay and the 15th were ordered to advance as quickly as the conditions allowed.

> One hour after daybreak on the morning‡ of the 21st of December the battlements of Sahagun appeared in view and at the same time an officer who had been advanced to reconnoitre came forward to inform Lord Paget that a large body of French cavalry was formed upon a rising ground near the town waiting our arrival.

The French cavalry, two regiments totalling some 700 men, had lain with both horse and men fully accoutred and once the alarm was given, formed up with

---

* Some sources indicate earlier times for their departure but Adjutant Jones agrees with Edwin that it was 1 a.m.
† A few sources state that only one escaped but this is at variance with most witness statements including Edwin's.
‡ It is often stated that the charge took place in the dark or half-light of dawn, whereas if as Edwin states Sahagun only came into sight an hour after dawn and the action occurred at least thirty minutes to an hour later, then visibility would have been pretty good.

admirable speed. Once formed it would seem that they intended to retire slowly along the Carrion road to join Soult's forces; however, Paget formed the regiment into column of divisions and sought, by riding parallel to them on the other side of the road, to gain the advance of the French and bar their retreat. Seeing that the 15th were rapidly outpacing them, and believing they were against Spanish cavalry, Debelle ordered his two regiments to halt and wheel into line three deep, with the 1st Provisional Chasseurs in front and the 8th Dragoons directly behind. As the two lines were formed with virtually no space between them, to the British cavalry it appeared to be a single line, six men deep. Paget timed the order for the 15th to wheel into line to perfection and without hesitation ordered the charge. The British being only two deep in line would have formed a longer line than the French; therefore, it is unclear whether the French left wing overhung the British right as Gordon says, but the left of the 15th which Gordon actually led certainly overhung the right of their line and had nobody immediately in their front. Despite the half-light and the numbing cold, the 15th charged without hesitation across the snow-covered fields; darting through the withered stumps of the olive trees that were dotted so regularly across the fields and negotiating with apparent ease the snow-filled ditch which the French had anticipated would have disordered them, they drove the charge home. William states that if there had been any troop allocated as a reserve for the regiment, it must have been caught up in the affair and joined the charge.

As soon as we came in sight of them we formed column of divisions and took an oblique direction at a gallop in order to gain their flank; they performed a similar manoeuvre, and after having gone a few hundred yards parallel to each other we both halted, & wheeled into line; they then gave three cheers and waved their swords in the air, which we answered in the same way, our trumpets then sounded a charge which Lord Paget led at the head of the right squadron, and in a moment we were in their ranks.

Trusting to their superiority of numbers, and to their advantageous position in a vineyard with deep ditches, blinded with snow in their front, they foolishly stood their ground, hoping as they afterwards told us that the vine boughs or ditches would have thrown down all our horses, and that they should then make easy work of us; they also gave us a volley from their carbines as we were coming up which killed and wounded a few of our horses, but finding that we surmounted all these impediments, and that victory was not for a moment doubtful they flew in all directions. Between twenty and thirty were laid dead on the spot, others were killed or wounded in the pursuit, and about three hundred were taken prisoners; among the latter were two Lt. Colonels and eleven officers of inferior rank.*

---

* French losses appear to be twenty killed, 167 prisoners including two lieutenant colonels

Once the 15th Hussars had hacked their way through all six ranks of Frenchmen, the French broke and fled; the fighting rapidly deteriorating into a confused mass, with fleeing Frenchmen being chased by individual soldiers of the 15th, dead and wounded horses and men scattered on the white blanket of snow now pocked with patches of dark scarlet. During this confusion the 10th appeared, having passed the town and found it abandoned. In the confusion it was feared that this was a further French regiment and there were frantic bugle calls for the 15th to reform. William states that a reserve squadron had been ordered but that the men had been swept up in the excitement and joined in the melee. Soon their true identity was discovered but too late to continue the pursuit of the fleeing French and the 15th were slowly reformed under the protective shield of the 10th. The brigade then took quarters in the town, the prisoners being housed in the castle and the wounded in the convent, in the courtyard of which the men auctioned off the loot they had taken. It was discovered that the majority of the captured men were actually of German origin. It was also noted that their head wounds were not as deep as those on the soldiers of the 15th. This was blamed on the poor construction of the 15th's headgear; theirs only being stiffened with paste board, while the French one was reinforced by iron hoops. Among the 15th's wounded, William records that trooper Hawkins received no less than twenty cuts and trooper Vokins received a frightful gash across the face.

It was certainly a stunning feat of arms by the 15th for which the regiment eventually gained a battle honour, one of only two occasions such an honour was granted to a single corps action during the wars and the only one to a cavalry regiment. Indeed Fortescue describes it as 'a brilliant little affair, and very creditable to Paget.' while Oman calls it 'perhaps the most brilliant exploit of the British cavalry during the whole six years of the war', no small praise.

> Their numbers amounted to between 7 and 800 men composed of the 8th Hussars and 2nd Dragoons,* commanded by General Debelle who was one of the first men that took of his heels; his horses, baggage and portfolio containing some important papers fell into our hands, and the booty taken by our men out of the French saddle bags was immense, consisting principally of solid gold and silver which they had robbed the churches, convents &c of, and melted down into small bars about one inch

---

(Dud'huit & Dungens), three captains, eleven lieutenants and 125 horses.
* Edwin wrongly identifies them as the 8th Hussars and 2nd Dragoons; most witnesses appear to be confused as to the identity of the French regiments but it is generally agreed that they were indeed the 1st Provisional Chasseurs and 8th Dragoons. It is probable that the provisional regiment consisted of detachments from a number of regiments and the different numbers on their buttons presumably caused misidentification.

square and six or eight long. As soon as the different parties who had gone in pursuit were returned, we dismounted under the walls and fed our horses, and in the afternoon we entered the town where we were received very cordially by the terrified inhabitants. We had two officers, and about thirty men wounded in this affair, some severely.*

There cannot be a better specimen of the Spanish character than these people gave us; far from resisting the entrance of the French to Sahagun, they were on the contrary eager to serve them; but they no sooner found that the monsieur's were not the *strongest* party, than they exercised every species of cruelty upon them.† One poor Frenchman too sick to turn out with his comrades was found murdered in his bed; and a party of ours who were sent out to collect the dead found that the Spaniards had already stripped them all to the skin, and for fear they should not be *quite dead,* had perforated their bodies with knives, &c, in twenty different places.

The following day the infantry caught up and the hussars marched on to Villalebrin still in search of Soult. On this day Lieutenant During, who it will be remembered had been sent to reconnoitre the roads into Portugal, returned, unfortunately just missing the action. Edwin was ordered out on patrol to locate Soult's forces, which he succeeded in doing, but before an attack could be organised, devastating news arrived.

On the 22nd of December we were detached to the villages in front of Sahagun which was soon after occupied by the infantry, and Sir John Moore established his Headquarters there on the same day.

On the morning of the 23rd Colonel Bathurst, Deputy Quarter Master General‡ arrived at Villalebrin where I was quartered with my troop and ordered us to accompany him on a reconnoitring party; we proceeded in the direction of Carrion [de los Condes] and Saldana, which we came in sight of at sunset; at the latter Marshal Soult was stationed. Having

* Losses of the 15th were four men and horses killed; two officers (Grant lightly and Adjutant Jones severely in the face), nineteen men and four horses wounded and ten horses missing. Edwin's troop lost Privates Lathey and Clarke wounded.
† It was not only the Spanish that showed extreme cruelty, Gordon recalls that a man of Edwin's troop rode up to a wounded dragoon who had raised himself from the ground while indicating that he surrendered, only to split his skull with a crashing blow. He heard afterwards that his excuse was that he did not like 'to let the day pass without cutting down a Frenchman, and could not suffer such a favourable opportunity to slip!
‡ Lieutenant Colonel James Bathurst Assistant Quarter Master General was a very experienced officer, having served in Surinam, Egypt, Hanover and Poland. Later he served under Wellington in the early campaigns.

ascertained the exact position of the French army, Colonel Bathurst returned full speed to Sir John Moore, who he told me at parting meant to make an attack upon it at daybreak. I was directed to remain till the rest of the cavalry came up. The ground was covered with snow, and the cold most intense; it was much as ever we could do to keep the men from falling asleep.

Twelve o'clock came and nothing appeared; at length a few minutes before one the sound of our advancing army was distinctly heard, but no part of it ever reached us: a halt was sounded and orders were soon after given for the *whole* to return to their respective quarters; thus instead of reaping fresh laurels on the plains of [the] Carrion, the dawn of the 24th beheld us more dead than alive re-entering our miserable villages.

The cause of this disappointment was soon made known to us. On the night of the 23rd after the troops had been put in motion, Sir John [Moore] received intelligence that Bonaparte at the head of seventy thousand men was advancing from Madrid with rapid strides to get in our rear, and cut off our communication with Corunna and Vigo; had he succeeded in this, not a man would ever have returned to England.

The move back to Sahagun was very trying, the cold was so intense, indeed General Slade records 'some of the men got frost-bitten, and one poor woman, a trumpeter's wife, died from the cold'. It was not to be a good Christmas. The hussar brigade was to form the rearguard and so they loitered near Sahagun for two days while the army marched away as rapidly as possible with all the baggage to avoid being intercepted by Napoleon's force of some 50,000. The left squadron formed the rear-most picket and was the last to leave Sahagun on the morning of the 26th on the road to Mayorga. Lieutenant Penrice was found to be dangerously ill of typhus and he had to be left in the care of a Spanish physician.* Paget gave him a letter for the commanding officer of any French troops that entered the town, offering, in the event of his recovery, to exchange any officer of his rank taken at Sahagun. He did eventually recover and returned home.

A rapid retreat was the only chance; had we even delayed it long enough to bring Soult to action the army would have been lost, for as it was we clashed with Bonaparte's advanced guard at the bridge of Benavente.

The greatest possible number that the British army could have brought

---

* Lieutenant John Penrice survived and transferred to the 5th Foot with whom he served with Wellington in the Peninsula where he was wounded at Badajoz before reverting to the 15th as a captain. Wylly states that he served at the battle of Waterloo, but he is not shown in Dalton nor named in the Waterloo Medal Roll. He retired by sale of his commission in 1821.

into the field at this time did not exceed 23,000 effective men. The infantry moved off first & as they were to be covered during the retreat by the cavalry and artillery it was not till the 26th that we quitted the town of Sahagun.

As the brigade was arriving at Mayorga, news was brought that the French cavalry had intercepted the baggage; the 10th Hussars were sent forward immediately. The two lead squadrons were sent against the French force which consisted of two squadrons of the 15th Chasseurs. In a short but sharp action, the French were overthrown, suffering twenty killed and also lost one hundred men captured;* while the 10th apparently did not suffer any casualties.

In passing through Mayorga two or three squadrons of French fell upon our baggage and attempted to cut it off; part of the 10th and 18th Dragoons however got up with them, charged, and took them all prisoners; they were fine hussars, and belonged to the *Fifteenth* Regiment.

We halted that night at a place called Valderas & marched out early on the 27th; a few hours after we had left it Bonaparte established his headquarters there as appeared by one of their bulletins. We passed the bridge over the Esla that night and halted at the village of San Cristobal [de Entrevinas] near Benavente. On the night of the 28th; I was placed with a picquet on the bank of the river opposite to Villafer where the enemy were quartered; the river was deep, but so narrow that we distinctly heard their conversation; they also challenged, and fired a few shots at us.

The left squadron had been ordered to break all the ferries along the river to slow the French advance, which they did, although it was made difficult by the lack of proper tools. However, at dawn on the 29th the 15th were ordered out as the French had crossed the river in force. The French cavalry commander Lefebvre-Desnouettes† had crossed at a ford with four squadrons of the Chasseurs of the Guard numbering some 550 men; they advanced rapidly, driving the pickets towards Benavente. The inlying pickets joined in the attempt to slow the French but were slowly driven back by sheer weight of numbers; however, the French were advancing into a trap. Paget had formed the 10th Hussars on the French left flank and managed to keep them out of sight until the perfect moment. He launched a devastating charge which completely overthrew the French, who turned and fled the two miles back to safety. However, slowed down by fording

---

* Wylly says forty-eight but all other sources seem to agree with the higher figure of 100, including Oman.
† Lefebvre was sent to England and was allowed to live at Cheltenham on parole. He broke it and escaped to France in 1811 where Napoleon restored him to his rank.

the river, many were captured, including their famed commander, all of which it was rumoured was witnessed by the Emperor Napoleon himself. The French casualties left on the field totalled fifty-five dead and wounded and seventy-three prisoners. Although the 15th were called out and marched almost immediately, Edwin's troop took some time to close up to the regiment from his distant station and before he could reach them he was ordered to halt and was soon met by the regiment marching quietly to Villaquejida. The fighting had finished before the 15th had arrived, indeed the only casualty from the regiment was Private Charles Green, who had been employed as an orderly.

> Soon after daybreak on the morning of the 29th General Lefebvre at the head of seven squadrons of the Imperial Horseguards forded the River Esla about a mile & [a] half below Benavente. Their first object was to take prisoners a picquet consisting of about 120 men and composed of the 7th; 10th; 15th & 18th that had been posted opposite *that* part of the river which was deemed fordable; this picquet behaved most gallantly and kept the whole French force in check until the arrival of reinforcements from Benavente, when all those who could not regain the stream were either killed or taken prisoners, among the latter was General Lefebvre and many other officers of rank. Both them and their men declared that the bravery of our troops was unparalleled and that *they* were so little *used* to resistance of *that sort*, & looked upon the capture of our picquet as *so certain*, that they could hardly persuade themselves they were our prisoners.
>
> The fighting on both sides was indeed uncommonly severe, and many men were most dreadfully lacerated. Some few could speak a little English and they frequently said what a pity it was that the troops of the two first nations in the world should cut one another to pieces for the sake of such a parcel brutes as the Spaniards. The great Emperor (as his soldiers call him) was observed soon after this affair reconnoitring with a party of Mameluke Guards on the height opposite to us, and little doubt can be entertained of his having been an eye witness to the defeat and capture of his chosen troops.

That night the brigade marched to La Baneza; the weather continued to be atrocious and the strain of night marches and constant alarms meant that sickness increased rapidly. Captain Broadhurst became so ill that he was sent forward to Villafranca. William recounts how the men would battle with extreme exhaustion all night as they rode along, of the tell-tale swaying in the saddle as they lurched into somnolence and then awoke abruptly and occasionally actually fell from the saddle.

Edwin was overjoyed to meet Frederick again. He had been stationed here with Captain Thackwell to look after the men and horses that had been taken ill on the advance. The retreat continued at a pace and always by night but by some error the bridge was not blown; the next morning they arrived at Astorga. Here, they met the rag-tag Spanish army of the Marquis de Romana which had arrived having been defeated by Soult at Mansilla. It was already settled in the town and had taken up most of the billets when the brigade arrived.

In the evening we continued our retreat and arrived early in the morning of the 30th at La Baneza, moved again at night and on the following morning reached Astorga, where for the first time we fell in with a *Spanish army,* and such a group of half starved, sickly, terrified ragged wretches were never I believe got together before. The Marquis of Romana who commanded it was the only person who did not look frightened out of his wits altho' he had the most cause to be so. We *saw* this band of *heroes* assembled & should judge they mustered at the outside *3,000 men,** and this was one of the armies of patriots which the English newspapers asserted *at that very time* amounted to *upwards of ten times* that number.

After literally starving a whole day at Astorga, (for although these patriots could not fight they could eat), we assembled soon after dark under the walls of the town and at eleven began to move. I have slept, eat, drank and danced the new year in, and according to my taste found them full as agreeable as marching it in; we were the whole night passing great mountains covered with snow, and in my life I never felt or suffered so much from severity of cold; a great many men lost the use of their limbs and were obliged to be lifted off their horses on our arrival in the morning at the village of *Matachana* near Bembibre.

Their condition was not improved by having to ford a rapidly running stream in order to reach Matachana. While here the French attempted to surprise the picket, forcing the regiment to turn out, where they then stood all day before marching at night for Cacabelos.

We halted at this place for a few hours, and marched again at night for Cacabelos.

Owing to the badness of the road and depth of the snow our infantry got on very slowly, the consequence of which was we were overtaken on the 2nd of January by seven or eight thousand cavalry, who although so much our superior in numbers were afraid of making an attack upon us but kept continually skirmishing with our rearguard the whole days march; at night we drew up, and never doubted but that they would either attempt

---

* Romana's army supposedly amounted to some 10,000 men.

to surround, or cut us off; but this was not their object, they halted and dismounted when we did and our fires were not above ¾ of a mile from each other all night.

Sir John Moore's letters that have been printed give so clear an insight to the proceedings of the army from this period that I will not trespass upon my reader by detailing all the particulars of a most dismal retreat, or the various scenes of distress and wretchedness that it gave rise to. The enemy close upon our rear in immense numbers, harassing & annoying us in every way in their power prevented our ever halting except in the fields. The Spaniards altho' not at *open* war were equally hostile; not contented with running away themselves they took all the cattle and provisions with them that they could, and depriving us of the very necessaries of life, left us only the alternative of starving or plundering. Of course there was no hesitation which of the two to chuse and I grieve to say that the British army for the last two hundred miles were guilty of excesses which heaven forbid they should ever be again driven to!

But there is a great deal to be said in extenuation of their offence; exasperated by the numerous instances of perfidy that the Spaniards daily exhibited, they rejoiced in any opportunity of revenge; they were sent to Spain as auxiliaries but on their arrival found themselves principals; the natives so far from receiving them as their deliverers, treated them with a jealousy and indifference that soon created disgust; the rations of bread, meat & wine for the troops for which they were regularly & scrupulously paid the full value, were furnished and delivered in an ungracious manner; and they practised every species of fraud & imposition on our men to a scandalous and infamous degree. Added to this we were suffering privations and hardships that may have been equalled but never exceeded in any campaign. Exposed to all the inclemency of a winters sky by night as well as by day, the ground covered with snow, worn out by excessive fatigue and fainting for want of nourishment; unable to procure the usual conveyance allowed to the sick, and seeing those sick abandoned by the people for whom they were dying; under all these circumstances, it is not I say to be wondered at, if a retreating army should exceed the bounds of moderation; and that they did so, is too well known.

At Cacabelos, the 15th were formally attached to the rearguard of the army also consisting of the 20th Foot, two companies of the 95th Rifles and two guns. Captain Cochrane's picket was driven in and he was publicly censured by Colonel Clinton who was Adjutant General* – the incident led to a court martial in

---

* Brigadier General Henry Clinton, Adjutant General to Moore's army. He later commanded the 6th Division under Wellington and commanded a division at Waterloo.

England.* There was constant skirmishing and the 15th was stood to its arms all night. On the 3rd the French cavalry made a serious attempt to take the narrow pass at Cacabelos but their attempts were thwarted by the 15th and 95th. It was here that Tom Plunket of the rifles became famous for killing General Colbert† and a man of the 15th reputedly decapitated a French chasseur with a single blow. The constant rearguard duty being done by the 15th was openly criticised by the officers of the regiment; they believed that Paget sought to save his precious 7th and the Prince of Wales' 10th from too severe an exertion. Certainly the sick list in the 15th grew rapidly and Captain Murray‡ was also given leave to retire to Villafranca through extreme illness. Leaving the town that evening was complicated by the number of men who had discovered the great wine stores and were so drunk that they were thoroughly unable to stand, let alone march. Lacking the facilities to carry them, these men were left to the mercies of the French, who simply butchered them as they rode after the rearguard. Corporal Smith of Gordon's troop was one of those lost here. On 4 January the 15th retired through Villafranca where they witnessed the burning of the great mass of supplies deposited there and rode on to Constantia. Having arrived in the mountainous regions where cavalry could not operate easily, the rearguard was handed over to the infantry and the 15th could gain some respite when not marching. On the 5th they arrived at Lugo which was already full and they were forced to remain in the streets. Cornet Laroche was sent ahead from here to Corunna with the sick men. On the 6th a further batch of sick was marched to Corunna led by Edwin and also containing Lieutenant Jones who presumably suffered from his wound and Frederick who was suffering very badly. Surgeon Lidderdale§ had also marched with them to tend the sick en route. Edwin's invalids rode into Corunna on 10 January and the regiment arrived the following day, taking up their billets at the St Lucia barracks.

We re-passed Villafranca on the 3rd, Lugo on the 6th, & reached Corunna

---

* Cochrane was charged with giving false intelligence and was placed under arrest. At the court martial in England he was honourably acquitted. However, evidence has since come to light that the cavalry he ran from were actually Spanish.

† Tom Plunket became a minor celebrity in England having shot General Auguste de Colbert, but the bottle eventually affected him and he got into serious trouble, including at one time threatening to kill his company captain. After Waterloo, this embarrassment to the army was pensioned off. He cashed in his pension to buy a plot in Canada but did not like frontier life and saw out his days in virtual penury.

‡ Captain Evan John Murray transferred as captain to the 52nd Foot in 1810, became major in the 8th Dragoons in 1811 and rose to major general in 1837. He died in Barbados in 1841.

§ Surgeon William Lidderdale joined the 15th in 1796 and became surgeon to the forces in July 1809.

on the 10th, where contrary to Sir John Moore's expectation there were no transports ready for our reception.

As the cavalry brought up the rear almost all the way, *we* had the best opportunity of beholding the effect produced, and the horrors attending on that country which is unfortunately made the seat of war, and never will it be effaced from my memory. We also passed hundreds of our brave countrymen who unable to proceed further were left to the mercy of their enemies; & our road was strewed with dead horses.

At Lugo, Lieutenant Knight* and a detachment of the 15th of forty men were organised as a guard for Sir John Moore. A large amount of money being left at Lugo, the cavalry were each given 500 dollars in a bag to carry to Corunna but at Guitiriz mules were found, and the 30,000 dollars transferred to them under charge of Sergeant Roberts. Roberts eventually deposited 27,000 dollars with the Paymaster General at Corunna. They marched to Betanzos that day and the next Corunna was finally reached.

The cavalry, apart from providing pickets, lay quietly in their barracks as the country was not conducive to their operations. This was fortunate as William of the 15th described the regiment as 'almost horseless, bootless, shoeless, ragged, dirty and something worse', though boots were soon forthcoming from the stores.

Despite all their recent privations, as soon as Sir John Moore ordered the army to prepare for battle outside Corunna everyone formed with gusto, they blamed the French for their hardships and wanted to wreak revenge. The French army under the command of Marshal Soult had arrived before the army could be embarked and they would now have to fight to gain the time to do so safely.

The state of the army when it arrived at Corunna was indeed truly deplorable; a sickness had spread throughout it, and the men and horses were worn down with fatigue, and perfectly bare foot. Notwithstanding all this they were in excellent spirits, and so eager to charge the French in the battle of the 16th that Sir John Moore did little else than gallop about to the officers of regiments entreating them to keep their men *back* as much as possible.

However, the army clearly had strong misgivings as to Moore's tactics in the campaign. Edwin's views were commonly expressed at the time.

---

* Lieutenant Edward Knight commanded Moore's escort of fifty men at Coruna and was near him when he was struck. He became a captain in 1810; he transferred to the Portuguese service and served as a brevet major commanding 11th Dragoons at Vitoria. He went on half pay in 1816 and died in Dublin in 1847.

A Glorious Night

This gallant but unfortunate commander's character is so well known that it is unnecessary to make any comments upon it further than what immediately concerns the retreat and the last fortnight of his existence, during which period he certainly forfeited to a very great degree the confidence of his army. The province of Galicia is perhaps the strongest by nature, and the easiest to be defended of any country on the face of the earth. Surrounded by mountains whose sides are almost inaccessible and height immense it would be hardly possible even for infantry to enter it except by the passes; and in these passes there are positions where (like Thermopylae) a handful of men might arrest the progress of millions; there were also bridges thrown over the chasms at the bottom of which run large and rapid rivers; had these been destroyed as soon as we had passed, it must have stopped the pursuit of the French cavalry for a certain time, and the artillery for many days. Unhappily these advantages were neglected, and trusting more to celerity of movement, than to the usual stratagems of war, Sir John subjected his army to the humiliating accusation of being actually driven into the sea by the French. The want of provisions too was a still more alarming grievance; but although the censure on these occasions always falls upon the head of the commander, I must do him the justice to say that I believe the neglect of both is to be imputed entirely to the ignorance of the people about him, and most particularly to the engineers & commissariat department, which latter was conducted in a most shameful manner.

During the whole of the retreat placed in the most arduous situation and harassed by continual reports of the most disagreeable nature, Sir John's presence of mind never forsook him and he gave his directions with a clearness and precision which evinced that he was fully equal to *his* share of the task, although unfortunately he did not meet with that assistance and support which he had a right to expect from others. In action his post was always the post of danger, and if the coolness for which he was remarkable on these occasions be a sign of courage, he was one of the bravest men that ever lived. Perhaps indeed he did commit some errors, but he has fully expiated them by the manner in which he terminated his career and he will ever remain a bright pattern for emulation to all those who like him, are desirous of leading a life of honor and dying a death of glory.

A more surprising view of Edwin's was his open criticism of Lord Paget, who is generally considered a very able cavalry commander and certainly saw some great successes during the campaign.

One of our greatest misfortunes was not having a man at the head of the cavalry who understood the nature of that service, for it is generally allowed that Lord Paget did not; his character for courage no one will dispute, but courage alone is a very vulgar quality unless regulated by wisdom & *judgement*. He in common with the rest of the Staff seemed to think that the cavalry never could do enough and we were constantly marching, counter marching, and harassed in every way to such a degree, that if the main object had been to kill all the horses as soon as possible they could not have taken a more effectual method for the purpose. The consequence of this was that the horses were knocked up before the retreat commenced; were reduced to half their numbers long before that retreat was accomplished, & what there was remaining were in such a dreadful unserviceable state that the French might doubtless have annihilated them if they had made an attack; and that they did not is solely to be attributed to their ignorance of our situation.

There was always time for some army discipline and the regiment held a court martial at St Lucia barracks to try all those accused of misdemeanours during the retreat. Assistant Sergeant Major Hickman was reduced to the ranks; Farriers Kelly and Wall were punished for neglect of duty, Wood and Smith for plundering and Ellestrow for losing his 500 dollars. The transports having arrived, the cavalry commenced embarking, but this led to horrible scenes on the beaches. Each regiment was restricted to loading only thirty horses, this in relation to the 15th, out of 682 horses landed in Spain the previous November; the rest were to be shot to prevent the French utilising them. Soon the beach was a charnel house and many could never erase those awful scenes from their memory; the regiment was completely embarked by 16 January. Following the victory at the battle of Corunna which took place as the cavalry completed their embarkation, the army was able to embark in relative ease despite the last-minute intervention on the 18th of a battery of guns that caused consternation amongst the transports. Baron During's transport was one of those that beached in the confusion but they were apparently saved by one of the warship's long boats and the fleet sailed safely for England.

> The Battle of Corunna, and the confusion attending the re-embarkation of the army are well known, I shall therefore merely say that our voyage home was as prosperous a one as could be expected at that time of year;

That evening on board his transport Edwin wrote a few final notes in his Corunna journal.

> The weather at that time was delightful; a light breeze from the NW just sufficient to fill the sails set us on at the rate of about four knots an hour;

the moon rose bright & clear, & the fleet collected as near as they could in the wake of the convoy formed altogether a beautiful & interesting scene. I sat upon deck enjoying it till nine o'clock at which hour I retired to my berth.

The ships passing through the Bay of Biscay were soon dispersed in bad weather, some running aground with many lives lost but thankfully none of the 15th Hussars; the ships landed at the first port after landfall, some arriving at Falmouth, others at Plymouth or Portsmouth, towards the end of January.

We sailed from Corunna on the 17th of January and arrived at Plymouth on the 23rd: the inhabitants of which place by their extreme kindness and humanity to every soul who put in there belonging to the army, and particularly to the sick and wounded who composed the largest part, made them ample amends for the variety of miseries they had been suffering for the last three months.

On landing Edwin hurriedly penned a letter to his sister to reassure her as to the health of Frederick.

Plymouth, January 24th 1809

I am happy to inform you, my dearest sister, that after numerous hardships misery & privations of every description your dear boy & myself arrived here safe yesterday afternoon after a fine passage of five days from Corunna but it has been far from a pleasant one as the lad has been very ill the whole way; he was attacked a few days before we sailed with a cold & fever, which had we been able to nurse on shore would have been trifling. Marshal Soult however decided that we should not & to sea we were forced to go; the dirt, stink & wretchedness of a transport, added to the tumbling about we got in the Bay of Biscay made him worse, & although he has never been alarmingly ill, he was sufficiently so to destroy my comfort. Lidderdale our surgeon, was on board with us so he had every assistance necessary, & I rejoice to say is recovering very fast; this day has been so wretched that it was impossible to leave the ship, but tomorrow I intend getting him into a comfortable lodging for a few day's rest, & then proceed on to Dawlish where I hope to find the Morgan's settled; in the mean time I hope to hear from you & know if you approve of my places.

Lidderdale says that he requires nothing now but rest and good ruming [*sic*], & that you may depend upon it he shall have as long as I have charge of him, & when we find Louisa he will be still better off. I have not time at present to say more – pray write by return of post, & direct to me Post Office Plymouth dock, as it is the best place for a sick person than

Plymouth itself. God bless you, Rico joins me in best love to yourself & Charlotte & believe me ever your most affectionate Edwin.

Orders awaited those able to march to make their way by easy stages to Romford where the two depot troops had been moved from Dorchester. Edwin completed his journal with a short diatribe on the Spanish people and culture; his views reflect the poor impression that northern Spain had made on most observers of this campaign.

I shall now wind up my journal with a few observations on the country of Spain, and its natives.

The country generally speaking is certainly the ugliest by many degrees that I ever saw, and which is to be accounted for in the first place by the nature of the climate, it being not uncommon for the sun to shine there for intense heat for six or seven months of the year without so much as a single cloud intervening during the whole period; the consequence of which is that every sort of vegetation is burnt up so completely that it never recovers the appearance of verdure, but gives the whole country a chocolate colour. In the second place the want of enclosures, and what few there are being made with stone walls has a very disagreeable effect; but as they fancy their sheep would not prosper and that they should not have the satisfaction of supplying the rest of Europe with coats if the country was enclosed there is not much chance of this being remedied. In the third place you hardly ever see a habitation out of the villages, and although I marched three hundred miles up the country I never saw anything the least like a gentleman's country seat, or *even an apology* for a wood of timber trees.

But one of the most serious misfortunes is the difficulty of communication between neighbouring places, for although there is a good hard road from Madrid to the principal towns such as Corunna, &c, there are no cross-roads, and the *tracks* are so easily lost that you are obliged to have a guide to go the shortest distance.

There is no sort of public conveyance except by mules, which is a very tedious one as they are twenty four days going from Corunna to Madrid; they form caravans of 30 or 40 mules & 8 or 20 muleteers; the dress of the latter is curious, their bodies are cased in stiff leather stays with a deep flounce round the bottom, immense plush breeches, & jack boots; and leather hats on their heads as large round as an umbrella; thus equipt [*sic*] they are proof against all weather, & with a long carbine and sword they set defiance to all robbers.

The stile of travelling is highly entertaining, I had the good fortune to meet two or three gentlemen's families on their *retreat* from the capital; the shape of their coaches is something like what were used in England some centuries ago; huge, heavy, & clumsy, with so many people both inside and out, so much provision (for as there are no inns they always carry enough for the journey) and so many packages, that it is as much as ever seven mules can do to drag them along at a slow walk, nor did I ever see a carriage go at any other pace.

Luxury has certainly not yet found its way into Iberia; contented with a base sufficiency of the necessaries of life there is no effort made at improvement in any thing; their manufactures, their implements of husbandry, in short their contrivances of every sort are clumsy and unfinished, and appear more to have been the invention of a rude and savage people than of Europeans. But what of all others appeared to me the greatest mark of indolence is their not having a regular intercourse between the different provinces; thus for instance the Galicians are as perfectly ignorant of what their neighbours the Asturians are about as the moors can be; and the arrival of a common courier in a Spanish town creates a greater sensation there than the arrival of an ambassador extraordinary would do in England.

I have so often commented on the Spanish *people* that I shall make but few more remarks upon them. There cannot I think altogether be a more disagreeable nation; deceitful, passionate, bombastic, imposing, inquisitive, vain and satirical.

These are the leading features of a Spaniard's character. But the female sex I must do them the justice to say are an exception to these rules; them we generally found sincere, obliging, hospitable and kind; on the advance we were almost always indebted to them for every little comfort we experienced, but on the retreat they often absolutely saved us from starving. The men forbidding and ungenerous cared not a farthing for your wants or distresses, while the women on the contrary did everything in their power to alleviate them. Often on these occasions have the beautiful lines on *woman* written by an officer occurred to me:

No proud delay, no *dark suspicion*
Stints the free bounty of their heart,
They turn not from the sad petition
But cheerful and at once impart.
Formed in benevolence of nature,
Obliging, modest, gay and mild,
Woman's the same endearing creature
In courtly town or *savage wild.*

They are however possessed of a most insatiable curiosity which was frequently very tormenting. The first thing they ask you on entering their houses, is, if you are a Christian? Then how many Gods there are? If you believe in the infallibility of the Pope? What your name is? If you are married? How many miles it is to England? Whether they have any grapes there? &c &c. then you have to tell them the price of every article of your dress and not contented with that, they make you say what you think *their* cloaths would have cost in England; in this sort of way I've been bothered for hours and gave any answers that came uppermost, always impressing them with the idea that I was accustomed to live in a most splendid manner in England, and that I had left a wife and children to mourn my absence; this latter circumstance always raised me in the[ir] esteem, and had its due effect on the fair part of my audience, particularly if I added that my wife was in a *family way* when I took leave of her.

Of all the miserable beings on the face of the earth a Spanish beggar appears the most so; I have heard somebody once remarked, that until they had visited Ireland they never knew what the English beggars did with their old cloaths; had this person extended his travels to Spain he might perhaps have accounted for the fate of the garments after they had been thrown aside by the beggars of Ireland.

But having extended my observations considerably beyond the limits I had originally intended, and further than I fear will be acceptable, I shall conclude with a quotation from the works of an eminent traveller & historian which will I hope serve to convince my readers that however prejudiced I may appear to be against the people of Spain and however harsh my remarks on their character may be, I have not formed an opinion hastily, nor am I *singular* in that opinion.

My author sums up a long dissertation on the Spanish character in the following words:-

'The Spaniards and Portuguese' says he 'appear to be a mixture of *Jews, Moors, Negroes,* and *French* – and to have reserved to themselves the worst part of each of these people. Like the Jews they are mean, tricking and avaricious. From the Moors they are jealous, cruel and revengeful; As the Negroes they are servile, indocile [*sic*] and deceitful; and they resemble the French in vanity, grimace and gasconade.'

Chapter 4

RIOTS & REVIEWS

By early February most detachments had arrived at Romford to reform and refit but many sick had been left behind, particularly at Haslar naval hospital in Plymouth, some eventually succumbing to their illness, others left too weak to rejoin for many months. Edwin delayed travelling to tend to poor Rico, but by early February he was writing home to his father advising him of the improvement in Rico's health whom he had left recuperating at Dawlish and adding a final description of their departure from Spain and the subsequent voyage home.

> *Blandford, February 8th 1809, to Thos. Griffith Esq. Rhual Chester*
> My dear Father
> Harriet & Louisa being so very much better correspondents than myself, to them I resigned the office of transmitting a regular bulletin of the state of Rico's health from the third day after our landing; but being cast abandoned on the worlds wide stage once more the functions of the pen must be resumed with increased activity. I am happy to say I left Frederick quite well on Monday, with the exception of a slight bowel complaint, which if you recollect tormented me at Southampton so long after I had got the better of everything else; his appetite partakes of the voracious, he sleeps well; and is in good spirits, a slight cough he had onboard ship has quite left him, in short nothing can be doing better; poor Morgan was also in a convalescent state, but looking deplorably I think. Louisa is not only looking well, but is in high beauty, & in her usual excellent spirits; she has made us laugh every night till our sides ached, and has hampered my delicate appetite with such immeasurable good things that I declare to you I should have been quite afraid of staying here any longer as Lidderdale cautioned us against over indulgence in that way so soon after the starvation system we have been going upon, & it was in vain attempting to refuse them from her. Harriet is also looking better [than] I had expected to see her after all her anxiety & the young ones are in a thriving condition

but I shall dismiss the Dawlish party for the present & take a introspective peep at my proceedings since the date of my letter on the 13th ult.

It is impossible to describe to you the misery I suffered till I got that dear boy (who grew so much worse as to become perfectly helpless) safe on board; the difficulty of getting a boat for the purpose was very great but the getting him into it still greater & the crowd & confusion at the point of embarkation, added to a high swelling tide rendered it a service of danger; twice were we fairly chucked on shore & left dry, and how we were not swamped is to me a wonder. The timely assistance of a man of war's boat at length extricated us from the perils that surrounded us, & we reached our ship in safety, where I had given directions for an arm chair to be in readiness, & Mr Cub [Rico] was run up to the yard arm & lowered again upon deck before he knew where he was. This transaction took place on the evening of the 16th & in the midst of the battle where Sir John was killed, the whole of which I was an eyewitness to. On the morning of the 17th the French batterys opened upon the harbour & produced scenes still more distressing than those we had just left on shore, on the 18th we lost sight of the coast of Spain. On the 19th & 20th we had a fine run going eight knots the whole time & made Ushant on the 21st met with a buffeting for 24 hours in the chops of the channel, & arrived at Plymouth as you have been informed already. Of my peregrinations from that period Louisa has no doubt given a detail, it only remains for me therefore to say that no transported convict, no dungeon'd captive ever hailed their restoration to liberty & to light with greater satisfaction or glee than I have experienced since I touched my native shore; not from any dislike to foreign service, but from my detestation of every thing Spanish when I think of their uncultivated country, their stone walls, their ill contrived houses, their filthy towns, their wretched food, & their disgusting manners, & compare them to our fields, our hedges, our woods, our clean wide streets, our comfortable houses, & the hospitality of the inhabitants; above all when I contrast the cleanliness, the bloom, & the beauty of our country women, to the sallowness & the dirting of the dames of Iberia, I can leap from the earth for joy, and in an ecstasy thank the gods that I was born an Englishman. I have lost my three horses, & some baggage, but the reflection that I was in some degree instrumental in bringing poor Rico off safe amply repays me; three other officers of ours who were exactly in the same state are now prisoners in the hands of the French, & in Spain!!!

Perhaps you are wondering what I do at Blandford all this time? You must know that I am on my road to Romford again; I left Exeter at four o'clock yesterday morning post coach, slept at our old quarters at the King's rooms Dorchester last night & came here to breakfast, in a return chaise this morning. I mean to wait here till I can get conveyance to

Salisbury where the division that marched from Plymouth is to be tomorrow, & proceed with them to the place we are destined to. I also mean to make application for leave till the 1st of April as soon as I have an opportunity but not with the slightest expectation of getting it, there will be so much for the officers to do, & particularly us captains; I don't believe there is above 8 or 10 horses per troop came home, the arms & appointments are deficient in proportion. Harriet tells me you never received a letter from me after I left Corunna which is very unfortunate as I wrote from Zamora and two about the 6th of December & from Sahagun on the 22nd the day after our engagement. I hope I shall find a letter from you on my arrival at Romford where I expect to be this day week till then adieu & with best love to all believe me most affectionately yours

EG

Salisbury Thursday, I have just arrived and found my division that I was in search of, we march to Andover on Saturday, a pretty mistake I've made.

There were joyful reunions at Romford as the scattered parties returned in early February. Edwin's troop was one of the last to rejoin. The men were inspected by the surgeon and generally found to be 'in a tolerable state of health & cleanliness'. Now the urgent requirement was for remounts and the official guidelines as to colour and gender were waived in the rush to re-horse. By late February, when Frederick rejoined, sufficient numbers of horses were available that regular drills commenced but it was 18 April before sufficient new uniforms and accoutrements had arrived so that their first full dress parade could be held. It would appear that it was at this time that the heavily criticised fur caps were relegated only to full dress and for other occasions a peakless shako was employed which offered much greater protection to the head. Edwin was involved in a small scandal at this time, when he joined Captain Gordon in refusing to assent to the presentation of plate to Lord Paget to commemorate the campaign. It would seem that this was due to their continued ill feeling towards Paget for what they perceived as his protection of the 7th and 10th from fatiguing outpost work during the rigours of the retreat at the expense of the 15th. This would be, however, in direct contrast with the view of Paget by the other ranks, as William says they 'would follow him to hell'.

In September 1809 the position of troop quartermaster was abolished and the rank of troop sergeant major introduced. A commissioned officer was to be given the role of regimental quartermaster; this post was first given to Cornet Jenkins. In October the regiment moved to Guildford and Godalming where the regiment celebrated the fiftieth anniversary of George III's reign. As part of the celebrations, the King announced a general amnesty and remission for all military offences, whereby the sole prisoner in the 15th, Farrier Girling, was set free. In

December the regiment celebrated the first anniversary of Sahagun; Colonel Grant was presented a sword for his bravery and the men received ten guineas per troop; this was paid for by a subscription from all field officers and captains in the regiment, and it seems that this time Edwin was happy to contribute.

In February 1810 they moved again to Hounslow and Hampton Court, where on 16 March they joined a huge parade consisting of 3,500 cavalry and six troops of artillery and were inspected by Sir David Dundas* and the Dukes of Cumberland and Cambridge. The Persian ambassador apparently stole the show with his two lady attendants gloriously accoutred in vividly coloured traditional Persian dress. There were problems being situated near the great city though, and William recounts that the number of desertions from the new recruits rose markedly.

Suddenly on 7 April the regiment was rushed into London, five troops being stationed at the Queen's palace, three at Knightsbridge barracks and two at the riding school in Gloucester Road. The reason for this emergency deployment in the city was the expected serious rioting following the committal to the Tower of London of the radical MP Sir Francis Burdett. Sir Francis had long been a thorn in the side of the government, championing parliamentary reform, Catholic emancipation, freedom of speech, prison reform and against high taxes. However, he seems to have overstepped the mark when he published a libellous article in Cobbett's weekly *Register*.† He was made the subject of a debate in Parliament on 6 April, and a warrant was issued by the Speaker of the house. It was obvious that the execution of the warrant was likely to lead to serious disorder as Burdett was the people's champion.

The Sergeant-at-Arms attempted to carry out the arrest on the morning of 7 April but failed, and there was serious unrest that night. A further attempt the following morning by an official from the commons ended in ignominy and a troop of Life Guards was positioned outside Burdett's house to drive the crowds away. The troops were hissed and the Riot Act read but, aside from a number of windows being broken, the mob remained generally peaceful. On 9 April the Sergeant-at-Arms finally succeeded in arresting Sir Francis who was placed in a coach for his journey to the Tower. Two troops of the 15th with two of the Life

---

* General Sir David Dundas was Commander in Chief at this time, the Duke of York having been forced to resign following a scandal over the sale of commissions. Originally an artillery officer, Dundas made his name by writing a number of drill books which, although heavily criticised for concentrating on the outdated Prussian system, did achieve a standardised drill throughout the British army.

† William Cobbett edited the weekly '*Political Register*' which he began publishing in 1802. Although often referred to as a radical, he actually struck a chord with the masses with his deeply conservative views, hankering for a return to an imaginary period of rural bliss which supposedly existed before the devilry of commerce and industry, which he blamed for the subversion of traditional liberties.

Guards headed the procession; the coach was surrounded by two troops of Lifeguards and a single troop of the 15th, immediately followed by two battalions of Foot Guards and at the rear of all another party of the 15th. By the time that this cortège had reached the vicinity of the Tower, a huge throng had massed in the streets and it was with great difficulty that they forced a passage to the gates of the Tower. At this point the rioters began stoning the 15th who retaliated by forcing them at sword-point into the Tower ditch, which was virtually dry at this state of the tide. Having safely deposited Burdett within the Tower, the troops retired, upon which the mob pelted them with mud and stones. During these disturbances a number of carbines and pistols were discharged killing three and wounding a number of others. Much of the animosity of the crowd was particularly vented upon the 15th; it is believed that the hussars with their drooping moustaches were mistaken for German troops by the mob, who did not take well to foreigners policing the capital. After this incident London remained calm, even when Burdett was released, as he retired by barge to his country seat at Putney leaving the expectant mob deflated. Edwin's next letter from Hounslow fails to mention this episode; presumably it was included in a previous letter that did not survive. The letter speaks of parades and the very healthy social life of the city. Rico, however, had been sent with a detachment to Richmond.

Hounslow barracks, April 22nd 1810 to Miss Griffith, Rhual.
I am afraid I shall have many a harsh expression from you my dearest Chats for never having written one line to you since we parted six weeks ago, & particularly as your younger sister has been honoured with a letter from me, but the fact I do assure you is that I was on the point of writing to you at the moment when her letter arrived & which seeming to require an immediate acknowledgement I altered my determination and having made thus my apology I shall proceed to give an account of myself from the date of the last letter to my mother on which day after taking our usual ride in the park, Rico and I at six o'clock, to a moment, entered our good uncle's house where we met the following generals; Sir Charles Greene, Sir Thomas Trigge, Craig, Balfour, Harris, Keppel, & Colonel Marlton,*

---

* These men may be identified almost certainly as:
Lieutenant General Sir Charles Green, who had served in America and Corsica and who captured Surinam in 1804; General Sir Thomas Trigge, who had been Governor of Gibraltar and who died in 1814; Lieutenant General Sir James Henry Craig, who had just returned from service in Canada; probably General Nisbett Balfour, who had served in America and the Flanders campaign; Lieutenant General George Harris, who made his reputation in India; Lieutenant General Sir William Keppel, who became equerry to the Prince Regent; and Lieutenant Colonel William Marlton, 60th Foot.

gentlemen of so much older standing than Rico and I, that it was not the pleasantest party I ever was at, and indeed if it had not been for Harris, I much fear I should have given them ocular demonstration of my sentiments, he was however, so full of fun, & humoured all Sir Alured's particularities in such a perfectly ridiculous manner that we were in fits for a part of the time, and in which the gravest of the company could not refrain from joining us.

Tell my father, Harris made many enquiries after him and said a great many civil things to me when he found I was his son. At half past ten the party broke up and I don't think we ceased laughing from Mansfield St to Pimlico. On the following day (Thursday) the whole of the fashionable world assembled in Hyde Park soon after breakfast where between 7 and 8 thousand infantry were reviewed by the Commander in Chief; the spectacle was very beautiful but not compared in grandeur to ours, which took place on the preceding Monday. As soon as the review was over I went to make some calls in town, among others the Dean, who with Miss George & Penelope I found at home & looking all, remarkably well. William's little boy was with them, and a nicer child I have seldom seen both in appearance & manner. By the bye I have taken a great fancy to Miss Shipley, I often ride with her in the park & think her particularly pleasant & good humoured. I dined that day with the Hunters again, where I met his mother, & a Miss Addison who came with her, Lord Yarmouth, Ld Tyrconnel, Mr Burges,* Mr Dalsey &c. Miss A is a devilish fine girl but a bit of a glist of which I had a good batch when we went up after dinner, neither of the peers standing the least chance against the brilliance, of my soldiered attire. Miss Daly played on the harp and sung and the evening passed away so delightfully that I was quite harping'd on going out of the house to hear 'past twelve o'clock'.

On Friday morning Frederick and I rode to call on the Wymes in Norfolk St when I delivered into his charge a little box which has been at my uncles many days & which I think he said was left at his house by somebody from Mr Williams the jeweller, but of this I will not be quite certain; it is directed to my mother. I dined that day at Sir Hew Dalrymple's;† apropos the youngest Miss D is to be married on Wednesday next to Capt Dacres of the navy, son of the late Admiral, he is a most

---

* Almost certainly Charles Montolieu Burges, eldest son of Sir James Bland Burges, the Knight-Marshal. The family name was changed to Lamb in 1821. I must thank Philip Haythornthwaite for this information.

† Lieutenant General Sir Hew Dalrymple, who had become infamous for signing the Convention of Cintra, by which the French forces in Portugal were repatriated in ships of the Royal Navy.

excellent little fellow* and they are all in high glee about it. Tell Cony that her music was the subject of general commendation after tea, Lady Dalrymple claims she never saw anything so beautifully written in her life, & that she should like of all things to [see] Cony at their house that she might give her daughters some lessons. I think she had better take this as an invitation and immediately set out, for they are a charming family.

On my return home that night I found a note from Orly Hunter begging me to dine with them the next day to meet Miss Fortescue & Lord Clermont, but alas! On the same table lay an order for the Regt to return to their quarters at nine in the morning and here ends my account of a fortnight in London that will ever be memorable to me, both from its inauspiscious commencement and particularly happy and pleasant conclusion. We took possession of our old apartment at noon yesterday and (to be very minute) I am at this period undergoing the discipline of a dose of salts for the purpose of destroying two or three little grog blossoms which the disciples of the metropolis have brought to life. I suppose you have seen that the numerous ills the D[uke] of C[umberlan]d has been heaping upon Foskett† of this regiment are at length brought before parliament. No good is likely to result from it to Foskett immediately I fear, but it is sure of being attended with salutary effects for the army in general, & he deserves the greatest praise for the spirit and firmness with which he has displayed to the world at large a system of the most unjust & infamous oppression. If you have not seen his petition verbatim, I will send it to you & will vouch for its accuracy in every particular. Frederick is gone to Richmond to remain, with which he seemed well pleased. Let me hear from you very soon & with a thousand loves to all believe me &c Chats and most affectionately yours Edwin.

---

* Captain James Richard Dacres was on half pay at this time. He was appointed to command the *Guerriere* (48) in 1812 which was famously captured by the *USS Constitution* later that year; however the loss of his ship did not hamper his career and he eventually rose to admiral. The 'youngest Miss D[alrymple]' mentioned in the text was named Arabella and married Dacres in May 1810.

† Captain Henry Foskett had joined the 15th in 1797 but retired by the sale of his commission in 1810. His central complaint was that although he had been the senior Lieutenant for over three years, he was ignored for promotion when both majors (Francis Forrester and Walter Leitch) left the regiment, both positions being filled by officers (John Waldegrave and Alexander Belcher) transferring in from other regiments. Soon after resigning he published his defence as '*The rights of the Army vindicated: in an appeal to the public on the case of Captain Foskett: to which is subjoined the whole of Captain Foskett's correspondence with the respective Commanders in Chief (His Royal Highness the Duke of York and Sir David Dundas) and also with the officers successively commanding the 15th Light dragoons*'. He died in London in 1853.

Life for the officers of 15th Hussars took on a monotonous regularity, only interspersed with occasional parades and ceremonies to liven things up; but the lively social life in nearby London helped to pass the time. The sudden death of Princess Amelia seems to have triggered the King's final bout of madness from which he never recovered and the Prince of Wales was formerly sworn in as Prince Regent. On 2 March 1811 the 15th were again employed in London where they formed part of the funeral procession for the Duke of Alburquerque, the Spanish ambassador, who was temporarily interred in Westminster Abbey. The colonel of the 15th, the Duke of Cumberland, was wounded on 13 June by his valet who then committed suicide – rumours abounded that Cumberland had murdered him. Four days later, a Grand Review was held on Hounslow Heath before the Prince Regent and the Dukes of York, Cambridge and Kent. Following an inspection of the troops, the whole force was taken through their paces in a long series of complicated manoeuvres which were performed in exemplary style. Afterwards the staff and regimental officers were treated to a sumptuous dinner at Richmond Castle consisting of turtle, fish, venison, followed by every exotic fruit and washed down with liberal quantities of champagne, hock, burgundy, claret, vin de France and [*Crozes*] Hermitage. Paget produced a very flattering order of the day.

Hounslow, 17th June 1811

Lord Paget has the honour to announce to the troops of the Royal Horse Artillery, the Prince of Wales' Own, the King's, and the 18th Regiment of Hussars, which he had the honour to command this morning, that he has received the Command of the Prince Regent to convey to them His Royal Highness' entire approbation of their appearance and performance.

His Royal Highness was pleased to express himself upon this occasion in terms that were singularly flattering to every individual concerned, and to order that these His Royal Highness's sentiments might be made known.

Edwin would have partaken fully of these festivities, presumably unaware of the near death of his father who finally succumbed on 18 June, a date that was to become very significant to the Griffith family. Edwin presumably returned home for the funeral, but there is no hint of this in the official reports. A week later the regiment was moved to their old quarters at Romford with one squadron at Colchester. Edwin commanded a detachment at Hornchurch but he clearly visited the nearby delights of London regularly.

1811 was a year of bad harvests and as always unrest in the country grew as bread prices soared. All was quiet in the south-east however and Edwin and Frederick looked forward to a spot of leave at Rhual.

London, Nov. 8th 1811 to Miss Griffith

My dearest Chats,

I sent you word through sister that I had a letter on the stocks which was to be dispatched from hence to day; but on my arrival here I discovered that I had very ingeniously left it in my desk at Hornchurch, but you will have no loss in it as I had not written above half a dozen lines, & those merely to thank you for your last long & entertaining letter franked by Mr Bankes, as I was afraid of your kicking the bucket while I was in your debt: a letter from Morgan received by Sir Olly while we were at breakfast says you are all going on well & which I suppose implies you are on the mending hand. I hope soon to hear my dear Chatling of your being perfectly restored, and indeed have little doubt of it if you can only be prevailed upon to take as much nourishment daily as would keep together the soul & body of an abstemious cock sparrow. I was very glad to hear from my mother that Morgan & Louisa are preparing to settle once more at dear old G[olden] G[rove] & have such cheering prospects of the teddy boy recovering the use of his leg again;* ask him (the latter) if he is not ashamed of himself to put the puff he did in the British press newspaper of yesterday? The heads of the poor people of LLanasa† must be suffering still if they swallowed all the cwrw, coorw (I don't know how to spell it) in his cause, which they have the credit of. I trust & hope we may all be once more assembled in that neighbourhood early in the ensuing year; at least both Frederick & I have applied for leave, & have every chance of obtaining it, I look upon it I am certain of it.

I had a tete a tete yesterday with my uncle, & today I am to dine with a party & go to see Kemble & Mrs Siddons in *Venice Preserved*,‡ how I do wish you & the Zwickle were going with me; it would be as great a treat to you, as to her, after that other Romeo business we saw there last year. Not having your letter here I may leave something unanswered but I don't recollect any queue besides desiring to know what sort of a man C. Blunt is? From the little I saw of him I should say his parts were not brilliant nor his appearance captivating at the same time he is quiet and gentlemanly & sufficiently good looking. Do you hear any thing of the happy couple at Vroniw?§ he is going to exchange out of the 15th & I believe try to get on

---

* His nephew, Lieutenant Edward Morgan 7th Fusiliers, was at home still recovering from a serious leg wound he had suffered at the battle of Albuera.

† Gyrn Castle at Llanasa had originally belonged to the Griffith's family and they obviously maintained their ties.

‡ Sarah Siddons, the sister of John Philip Kemble from south Wales, was a famous tragic actress who regularly performed for her late father's company now run by her brother who part-owned Covent Garden Theatre.

§ Almost certainly Vyrnwy in mid Wales where there is a river and large lake. This must

the pay. This will not benefit Rico I am sorry to say. Let me hear from you if you do not feel too lazy to write; I return to Hornchurch tomorrow. My best love to all; I hope Cony benefited by her life in the gutter & is well. Adieu for the present my dear Charlotte. Believe me ever most affectionately yours Edwin. And that's the way to polish a letter.

The general unrest began to manifest itself as mob violence in the autumn of 1811 and a number of outrages were committed including the murder of Mr William Horsfall, a Huddersfield manufacturer, and the burning of several mills. Within a week of this letter it had become obvious to the authorities that a military presence was required to quell these disturbances and the right squadron was rushed to Nottingham by forced marches. By early December eight troops including Edwin and Frederick had marched for the same destination, leaving the headquarters at Romford. In January the murderers of Horsfall were hanged and a number of rioters soon shared their fate. The riots did not cease, however, and the 15th were destined to remain in the Midlands throughout 1812. The rioters were known as 'Luddites', named after one Ned Ludd, a person of low intellect who was believed to have lived in Leicestershire in 1779. Irritated by a number of young boys, he was fabled to have broken two stocking frames in his rage; the term Luddite was used hence forward to describe all rioters who mistrusted the new industrial age and sought to destroy the mills and factories of the Midlands which they believed would prove a panacea for all their ills. Edwin clearly grew tired of this police work but he supported the policy of ruthlessly quelling the lawlessness.

Nottingham barracks, March 25th 1812

My dear Chats

I have nothing to say, but this is the last time I shall be able to get a frank as my dear peer takes leave of us for ever. I am quite melancholy about his loss to us in every way is irreparable both as a commanding officer & a friend, qualities for which the many excellencies of his head & heart eminently distinguish him.* I would give worlds to get out of Nottinghamshire, & never felt so dissatisfied with my situation since I have been in the army

---

refer to Captain the Honourable Esme Stuart Erskine who transferred to the 60th Foot in 1812 and afterwards served as Deputy Adjutant General at Waterloo. In 1816 he was appointed to a staff appointment in Ceylon but died on the passage. His move from the regiment did not help Frederick rise in the list of lieutenants as, for reasons that are unclear, the post was not immediately filled from the lieutenants within the regiment.

* Major the Earl of Waldegrave purchased a lieutenant colonelcy in 54th Foot in November 1812. As the senior major, he would have commanded the regiment at home, a posting in the Midlands not being to the liking of the colonels!

before; but however there is no help for it & I must do as well as I can.

I send you some lines written on the death of our lamented commander Sir John Moore which I think are pretty.* There is not perhaps much originality in them but they altogether perhaps merit & I hope if you have not already got them they will find a theme to your book.

I had a letter from Edward a few days ago dated G[olden] G[rove] & as he does not say how they go on there I conclude well. Our assizes are over, three frame breakers were transported for 14 years, but no hanging matches. Write me an account of yours and believe me always my dearest Chatty

your most affectionate Edwin.

Fred is here, well, & begs his compliments.

On 20 April, the rioting not having abated, the headquarters troops were ordered to Nottingham and the regiment started to move further into Yorkshire, where the worst rioting now seemed to be occurring. Frederick moved with his troop to Sheffield as an advance guard for this move where news of his gaining his captaincy was expected daily.

Nottingham, April 21st 1812

Having nothing better to do, (complimentary this) I will scribble to you my dear Chats to thank you for your letter, & verses which I had never seen. The severity on a certain great personage for which you conceive them, is, I am afraid & think, their greatest recommendation; he has betrayed so much weakness, and done such odd things since his accession to power that he heartily deserves all that is said, & certainly the opposition papers don't spare him. 'Tell me your company & I'll tell what you are', is a maxim which he seems to have disregarded when he nominates to situations in the household his chosen friends Lords Yarmouth, Hereford, and Petersham; three of the most worthless characters that can be found in the peerage.†

As every little helps to fill the scrapbook I shall write across an epitaph taken from a village churchyard near the place. The theme is a hacknied one, but as this is very short, the idea novel & the argument good, I have thought you might like to have it. Perhaps however, you are so proper in all

---

* The verses were not found with the letter.
† Edwin rails against the Prince Regent and his cronies; Yarmouth, known as 'Red Herrings', was Vice Chamberlain to the Household and Petersham, a noted dandy reputedly with a snuff-box for every day of the year, was Lord of the Bedchamber.

your ideas of things of this nature, you may think there is a little too much levity in it: if so give it to Cony. I hope you were not disappointed in your promised visit from the Pontriffithites. My sorrow can better be conceived than expressed at not being at home to give the princess the reception due to her rank, and to explore the charms of unsophisticated nature with her in the alcoves.

Frederick is gone to Sheffield, and the chances are that we shall all follow soon, as our headquarters division amounting to about 400 men is on the march to this place: so there's an end of our getting into pleasant quarters again this summer. For my part I expect we shall have a regular campaign of marching and counter marching till the harvest; for as long as there is a scarcity of grain riot they will, and unless my hopes are realised of Chester becoming the most outrageous of all the towns in this latitude God knows when I shall see you again. I have every reason to expect Frederick will appear in tonight's gazette in which case you will have it at Mold in an evening paper on Friday. A lucky young rascal he is : I hope Humberstone will exert himself in getting the whole of the purchase money into the agents hands soon, as our good uncle has become responsible for £800, which he says will distress him to lay out of long.*

In Bradford churchyard
Here lies old John Hildibrod
Have mercy upon him good God
As he would do if he was God
And thou wert old John Hildibrod.

Tell me if you have written to Lady Cony & received any answer; I really am quite grieved to hear she still suffers. I always longed you may have heard me say, to feed her with bread & milk, a flat stick but should enjoy it more than ever now she is an invalid. Five o'clock the papers just arrived by which I see they have commenced operations in Cheshire, at Macclesfield. I hope they'll soon be in the abbey square, much love to all

---

* Frederick was only eighth in seniority as a lieutenant when he purchased over the heads of all to become a captain on 16 April 1812. One suspects the hand of Sir Alured Clarke in securing this appointment, as he clearly provided an £800 bridging loan towards the £1,785 cost of a captaincy (after the proceeds of selling his lieutenancy); it is also virtually inconceivable that all seven senior Lieutenants would have declined the opportunity to purchase if they had been offered first as they should. Indeed Lieutenant Charles Carpenter, one of those senior to Frederick, was successful in purchasing a captaincy only three months later and therefore went from being Frederick's superior by date to his inferior as a captain.

believe me dear Chats most affectionately yours

EG

I am happy to hear the front glass of the coach is whole & hope it will long continue so. Love to old lanky.

Soon after this letter the regiment moved further north into Yorkshire, stationing three troops in Leeds, two in Wakefield, one in Barnsley and two (including Frederick and Edwin) in Sheffield, with detachments posted in Huddersfield, Halifax and Bradford, the headquarters remaining in Nottingham. Edwin had clearly received leave to visit London in the May and much of the letter recounts his social life in the great city. It would also seem that difficulties over movements of rank were again causing serious unrest within the officers; Fosket had clearly not stopped the sharp practices.

Sheffield, June 19th 1812

My dearest Chats, I lose no time in obeying your mandate as far as lays in my power with regard to my proceedings while in London, but most particularly to explain away viz, my ambiguous giving out, if some friends being more cordial than others are with you have naturally enough continued into my having met with a cold reception somewhere. This I assure you was not the case, but proceeded more I fear, from a small degree of churlishness added to the result of compassion, which have at all times something odious in them, there is a certain quality appertaining to every member of particular families which Lord Chesterfield terms (a je ne sais quoi) that makes you like them better than any other. The Cottons* I think all possessed this indescribable sort of fascination, the Paulet family† was the next I observed it in and at this moment I know of nothing like the Harvey's when I used to assist them at their sweet place near Chigwell in Essex‡ I never took leave of them without being fixed for a dinner, or some party for meeting again on an early day and in town found them the same as a specimen of which I was asked twice to dinner (but only went once), went without them to Covent garden, to a ball, and our morning ramble to see Lord Elgin's marbles &c and then Liverpool§

---

* The Cotton family, of which the most famous was Sir Stapleton Cotton, were based at Combermere Abbey.
† Paulet was the family name of the Earls of Winchester who were based at Stoke Park, Wiltshire.
‡ The Harvey's lived at Rolls Park, Chigwell.
§ The first of the sixty-five cases of the marbles arrived in London in 1806. Lord Elgin rented a house in Park Lane where he started exhibiting the sculptures to selected

museum during the short stay I made there. For a rich or a titled personage this sort of attention might not be particular; but to see who has not even the prospect of either, and whose friends & family were perfectly unknown to them till accident threw me in their way, you cannot but allow that it is extremely flattering.

I partook of a pleasant dinner with the Brooks, meeting the two Cunliffe's, P. Shipley, 3 or 4 of his sisters; T. Pennant,[*] T. Brooke, & several Cheshire young men whose names I forget. I stuck to Emma who is certainly a remarkably nice girl, & saw her a few days afterwards at Mr W. Wyans with whom I sat nearly an hour one morning. Charles was not at home, their eldest girl is a sweet child & has quite got the better of the antipathy they took to me at Acton. I forgot to say that I was obliged to refuse an invitation from Ld Sandwich the day Chumley & I dined With Sir P. which me lord was pleased to express his sorrow at in very gracious terms, made kind enquiries after you all & desired I would remember him to my mother & I also dined with an Essex family of the name of Tower,[†] with a parcel of people you knew nothing about, and with that Ravenscrofts where I met the Hunters,[‡] Colonel Sebright,[§] Mr Stanley (Sir J's brother) & on the other days I dined till late with my uncle having refused Sir Charles Rich & Madocks on two of them. My evening dispositions were confined to Mrs Bochna & a Mrs Leigh to whom I went with the Harveys, the former a ball in their usual style of splendour. The dancing was almost all waltzing & cotillion which I never yet exhibited in & was glad to have so good an excuse for standing still, in which I had plenty of friends to keep me in continuance some for the same reason. But

---

visitors in a large shed which he had built in the grounds. They remained there until he had to move from Park Lane in 1811. He was allowed by the Duke of Devonshire to place the marbles in the grounds of Burlington House, Piccadilly (now the home of the Royal Academy). This would appear to be the venue Edwin went to in 1811. They remained there until the latter part of 1816 when they were moved to the British Museum. The reference to Liverpool Museum is obscure but almost certainly refers to Mr Bullock's Museum which moved from Liverpool to a new home at the Egyptian Rooms at 22 Piccadilly in 1812. The museum housed a vast collection of arms and armour and artefacts from Cook's voyages to the South Seas.

* These were, respectively, probably the Brooks of Haughton Hall, Shropshire, the Cunliffes based at Acton Hall, Wrexham, the Shipleys based on Twyford Moor, Hampshire and Mr Thomas Pennant, head of the family at Downing in Flint. Edwin's sisters were frequent visitors to his house.

† The Tower family were based on Weal Hall in Essex.

‡ Probably the Hughes-Hunters of Plas Coch, Anglesey.

§ Lieutenant Colonel Edward Sebright 1st Foot Guards had been severely wounded at the battle of Barossa.

more from principle a certain set still keep up this system of hugging one another in publick but I am happy to find it does not increase. When you have an opportunity make a novel by Miss Byron called *The Englishman*; it is in six volumes but I did not find it a bit too long;* there is a good deal about waltzing in the 4th & 5th.

My mornings were employed in doing correspondence for myself, & others, and in paying visits to those friends I have mentioned and many that I have not: among the latter who you know the name of were Lady South, Burges, Mrs Graham several times & even Williams's &c &c, I was also much with Ld. Waldegrave who was then preparing for Portugal; the Pennants of course claimed my earliest claims & it gave me pleasure to find them (David included) looking particularly well. They could not return the compliment, as I was then looking rather interesting not from illness, but the effects of physic I had been taking and I am now quite stout again. It was my intention to have called upon them again the morning of the day I left town, but the expedition I spoke of to Lord Elgin's defeated my plans! My uncle promised to tell them this; but in case he should not, do you. These various little visitations, which are all I can at this moment recollect together with the days of rehearsal & installation composed the whole of my London visit. Trifling enough you'll say but, alas, what is one's whole life more than a succession of such trifles? You say you believe I am already a letter in your debt, that I deny: this is my second to your one therefore I answer it & we shall be square again.

I had no idea that Cony had been so very much of an invalid as you describe her to be. The poor girl has I fear undergone a great deal of misery & would have suffered much more; but for the kindness of the Rowlands. My main wish is to know how Williams obtains such extended leave? He sent in his resignation soon after they were named & requested he might be allowed to go on half pay to which the Duke granted;† but no half pay captain being particularly anxious to give a large sum of money to enter the 15th occasions a delay at the time. Since which the senior lieutenant remonstrated against the proceeding & the dispute is as far from being settled now as it was at first. Williams however will never join again as he posted with his clothes, horses & all his appointments before he quitted to Romford. It is thought to be a case of particular hardship upon

---

* Miss Medora Gordon Byron was a prolific writer of novels at this time. *The Englishman* was published in London in 1812.

† Captain Martin Williams transferred to the 10th Hussars on half pay on 28 July 1812. Edwin seems to indicate that he wished to go on half pay to avoid going abroad as the regiment was 'named' for Foreign Service. However it was December before the regiment was actually ordered abroad.

Lieut. Buckley as the troop is one without purchase, which he would succeed to did W go out in the usual way. The Duke has some dislike to Buckley & therefore the only method he has of doing him an injury is too valuable to be lost, and he, it is believed, desired Williams to apply for an exchange to ½ pay.* Our expedition to visit Frederick was prevented by General Grey† fixing upon the same day to inspect the troops here. But I fear we shall have plenty of time to make it before we leave Sheffield. I would give the world to pass the next two months among you but am doomed to a barrack society, smoke & bucolic dust for the summer. After this, & a few apt quotations such as 'La patience est amore, mais son fruit et doux' 'than never is, but always to be, blest &c &c' I shall conclude with best love to all, and assurance of my ever remaining your most affectionate

Edwin.

I breakfasted and made my uncle's house my home but slept at Ibbetson's hotel. He does not like an inmate I know & the early hours he keeps don't suit me in town, he was all kindness as usual and paid the whole expense of my journey.

By November the riots were finally quelled and the regiment moved to Manchester, furnishing small detachments to Preston, Bolton, Rochdale, Bury, Shrewsbury, Macclesfield, Chester and Pwllheli. Edwin received good news from Sir Alured Clarke, accompanied by instructions on how to conduct himself in his new role; he was to get his majority.

To Captain Griffith, 15th Regiment of Lt Dragoons, Manchester.
Mansfield Street, Nov 7th 1812

My dear Edwin,
The letter I sent yesterday was written at the *Cocoa-Tree club*,‡ about four o'clock; and about seven in the evening I received a note stating that Major Belcher's resignation had been received in the afternoon by His Royal

---

* Lieutenant James Ogden Buckley had been promoted into the 15th Hussars as a cornet, having previously been a sergeant major in the 44th Foot. He would presumably have been unable to pay the cost of purchasing a captaincy and would have felt aggrieved at not being given it, as according to Edwin it was supposed to be 'without purchase'. It is quite possible that the Duke of Cumberland felt that his lowly background did not fit with such a high position in his regiment. Whatever the reason, Buckley did not achieve his captaincy until 1813.
† Lieutenant General the Honourable Henry George Grey commanded the district.
‡ The 'Cocoa Tree Club', 64 St James Street, was a regular meeting place for gentlemen in London and is mentioned by Gibbon and Boswell.

Highness,* The Commander in Chief, accompanied by the Duke of Cumberland's recommendation of Captain Griffith to succeed to the Majority, so I trust it will not be many days before I greet you Major of the 15th Light Dragoons, or Hussars, as you please. *Take notice* this will be a new era in your military life; the duties of a field officer being so much more important than those you have hitherto filled. And let me, as having much experience in *military*, and *other worldly affairs*, recommend it to you to establish a reputation for the strictest attention, and decided obedience to your superiors; and the scrupulous exaction of the same from those under your orders; for I believe that no officer can ever be respected, as such, that does not properly maintain the authority that belongs to his station. From what I have said do not conceive that I mean you should act with harshness towards any; but, on the contrary, that you should shew every reasonable & kind attention that circumstances will admit of to those under your command. I have said this will be a new era; therefore I would also advise that you *endeavour, all in your power*, to recommend yourself, *anew*, to your Colonel, & Lt. Colonel Grant; and, if possible, make them friendly to you; as nothing is more entirely to contribute to your present ease, and comfort; and future prospects in the army.

> *I am, my dear Edwin, yours, most affectionately,*
>
> *Alured Clarke.*

Edwin's majority was confirmed and dated 5 November 1812; but he had little time to acclimatise to his new role, for orders arrived at the end of the month warning the 15th for field service. They were to be formed into a brigade with the 10th and 18th Hussars and proceed to join Lord Wellington's army.

---

* Major Alexander Hepburn Belcher retired from the army by the sale of his commission 14 November 1811.

Chapter 5

SPAIN AGAIN

The Duke of Wellington began the year 1813 knowing that he now had an excellent opportunity to drive the French out of Spain. Although on paper the French forces in Spain remained significantly larger than any force Wellington could assemble, the balance of power had shifted dramatically. Following the devastation of Napoleon's army in the snows of Russia, many veteran units, including many of his dragoon regiments, were transferred to the army in Germany. Those that were left were thinly spread, vainly seeking to hold down a belligerent population. For all his impressive troop numbers, King Joseph* struggled to maintain an army of moderate strength to resist the coming attack. The hussar brigade was now being sent to increase Wellington's cavalry force, but this deployment was not without its critics in the army. Cynics pointed out that the Prince Regent's 'dolls' had sat out the difficult years of hard fighting in 1810–12 in cosseted luxury, only to be sent to Spain to steal the laurels of victory. Despite their good showing in the Corunna campaign, the hussars had much to prove in Spain.

The outlying detachments were recalled and the regiment re-formed at Manchester ready to march. The regiment was to send only six troops each of ninety men and horses for service in Spain, the remaining four troops forming a depot were ordered to Brighton and Arundel. Major Dalrymple was to remain with the headquarters along with Captains Whiteford, Carpenter, and Frederick Philips.† Frederick must have been devastated to be chosen to remain behind; he could only hope that he could proceed later with any further detachments.

---

*   Joseph Bonaparte was made King of Spain by his younger brother Napoleon in 1808; he was unhappy in the role, given such a thankless task, and retired to France in 1813.
†   These were Captain John Whiteford, who served with the regiment until 1822 and was wounded at Waterloo; Captain Charles Carpenter, who sold his commission in 1823 and died in Milan in 1861; Wylly states that Captain Seelinger was also left behind, but records indicate that he transferred to the 96th Foot.

From Corunna to Waterloo

The six troops ordered for Portugal* marched directly for Portsmouth, two troops each consecutive day from 15 to 17 December 1812. At Chichester the regiment was formed and paraded before Major General Hammond† and then loaded on to fourteen transports on 15 and 16 January. Eventually a fleet of nintey-eight ships sailed for Lisbon on 19 January under convoy of the *Aboukir 74* and *Spitfire* sloop. Major Edwin Griffith and Lieutenant Barrett‡ were placed in the *Clifford* transport where Edwin decided to start writing a daily journal, which luckily has survived intact. On the inside cover he wrote:

> Should this book, my journal, fall into anybody else's hands, either by my death or other accident, they will confer an obligation by taking care of it until a convenient opportunity presents itself of committing it to my sisters, Charlotte & Caroline Griffith of Rhual in Flintshire. In the hope that the perusal of it will impart to them a little of the amusement that the writing it has afforded E Griffith.
> The Daily Journal of Edwin Griffith, Major in the 15th or King's Hussars from the day he embarked at Portsmouth to join the British army in Portugal January 16th 1813.
> 'One line on the spot is worth half a page of recollections.'

To which a note has been added, presumably by one of his sisters – 'January 15th 1813 – E was 27'.

The troops being embarked, the officers would find better fare and more comfortable accommodation ashore until the fleet was ready to sail; Edwin stayed at the Crown. There were dangers in staying ashore, however, for the fleet could sail with little warning and there was a real possibility of being left behind, particularly in bad weather. Edwin only narrowly avoided this embarrassment and was fleeced by his boatman; this inauspicious start forms the beginning of his journal:

16th January 1813

The two last troops of the Regt forming a squadron under my command embarked at the dockyard Portsmouth. Myself & Barrett onboard the *Clifford* transport, Wm. Field, Master. Dined & slept at the Crown Inn.

---

* The troops ordered to Portugal were A (Captain Wodehouse), C (Captain Booth, F (Captain Cochrane), G (Captain Dundas), H (Captain Hancox) and I (Captain Thackwell).
† Major General Francis Thomas Hammond.
‡ Lieutenant Edward Barrett eventually rose to captain in 1815, but went on half pay in 1816 and died in January 1820.

Spain Again

17th

Barrett & I tried to get onboard at night, but not finding our ship in Stokes Bay we returned to the point after sailing for several hours in a small boat with a raw wind against us all the way back.

18th

We again made an attempt to find our ship, & as it was by daylight with better success, she was at anchor at Spithead. The boatsman asked us a guinea for taking us to her, which I mention by way of memorandum never to get into a boat at Portsmouth without first making a bargain, or to buy anything at that place that can be procured elsewhere as they know that you *must* have them and impose most *shamefully on the strength of it.*

19th

The fleet weighed anchor soon after daylight & worked down to St Helens against the wind & a thick fall of sleet; it became easterly in the afternoon, & before the close of day we had shaped a channel course, having a fine view of all the south part of the Isle of Wight, the Needles &c.

20th

At nine in the morning I went upon deck & found we were off the Start Point in Devonshire, distant about four miles & running right before a brisk gale. We soon after passed the Eddystone lighthouse, & at four o'clock in the evening were off Falmouth, tho' not in sight of land, when the Commodore (Captain George Parker* of the *Aboukir* 74 guns) made signals for lying to, which we did the whole night, and until . . .

21st

he had been to Falmouth to fetch some ships from thence. When they had joined, the convoy consisted of upwards of ninety sail exclusive of the *Aboukir* & two [other] ships of war; and in the evening we proceeded on our course, losing sight of the Lizard a little before dark.

22nd

The wind continued fresh at South East, & we ran S.W. at the rate of six & seven knots the hour the whole day.

---

* Captain George Parker had become famous for the capture of the Danish *Prindts Christian Frederic 74* and with the *Aboukir* had taken part in the 'unfortunate' Walcheren expedition.

23rd

Continued the same course, but were ordered to bring to in the evening for several hours for the stern most ships to get up to the commodore. This is the worst of going with a fleet, as some ships sail much worse than others, & the motion when lying to, is particularly sickening. It was the more mortifying now as the wind was favourable and blowing very hard.

24th

The wind more moderate & the sky perfectly clear, we did not run above 5 or 6 knots any part of the day, & before night it had become perfectly calm.

25th

Was one of the most beautiful days I ever saw; there was not a cloud in the sky, or a breath of air stirring the whole of it. The water was glassy & the ships laid like logs upon it, their sails all hanging loose. It was also so hot that we laid upon deck in the shade, drinking lemonade the whole morning. A great many porpoises & other fish came to the top of the water close to the ships sides, but we had not the means of catching any of them. According to an observation taken at 12 o'clock we were about 45 miles to the West of Cape Finistere.

26th

There was just air enough to fill the sails in the early part of the day, & the fleet collected very close to the *Aboukir*. It however again dropped calm at noon & we had the same beautiful sky, & glassy water that we had had the day before.

27th

An easterly breeze had sprung up in the course of the night, and we held our course south west by west the whole of the day.

28th

Fine clear day; ran due south the whole of it with a fresh wind at east; tacked at night & stood in for land.

29th

Wind south east, continued tacking towards land all day; went up the shrouds in the evening, & saw the top of Cape Royana or the Rock of Lisbon, at an immense distance.

Spain Again

30th

The wind right off the land, which however we had got nearer [to] in the course of the night. Towards evening it freshened considerably, & before 12 o'clock blew a gale from the east by south.

31st

The sea ran very high; and the ship pitched in the course of the last night the bowsprit several times under water, by which she lost her sprit sail yard. Neared the land by tacking, towards evening I distinctly saw the palace of Mafra with the hills of Cintra in the background.

February 1st

Wind contrary but more moderate. Got a nearer view of the extensive, & to appearance extremely magnificent palace of Mafra. Having reached the lee of the Rock of Lisbon, a current set us up towards the mouth of the Tagus where we fell in with a fleet of fishing boats of most uncouth construction, we boarded one of them, bought an excellent dish of fish & took a pilot, whom altho' nobody onboard understood a word that he said, continued to work us up the river by short but numerous tacks plump against a strong wind; & a little after midnight we cast anchor between fort St Julien, & Belem, in smooth water; to the great comfort of all the fresh water sailors onboard.

2nd

At ten o'clock this morning the tide served, & a little before two we were safely moored off the dockyard of Lisbon, being the day fortnight on which we left Portsmouth. It is impossible to do justice to the beauties that open upon one every hundred yards of the passage up the Tagus, but the inequality of ground, & the numerous villages, forts, castles, villas, summerhouses, &c &c, scattered in an irregular and beautiful manner along both banks is such, that a traveller must be hard to please indeed who is not delighted with the scene. As for myself I was lost in admiration, so much so that I hardly perceived the deficiency of *one* of the greatest beauties of nature; but not a *tree* is to be seen excepting in the gardens.

The passage may seem straightforward in Edwin's diary, but he fails to mention that the *Canada* transport, with two officers, forty men and sixty horses of the 18th, was captured by an American ship just off Lisbon, the Americans having just declared war with Great Britain. Edwin echoes the views of virtually every visitor to the city of Lisbon who has left a description of it.

Lisbon itself appears to uncommon advantage from the water, it is built on the side of a steep hill, or rather hills, the houses are high, and in consequence of the abrupt ascent appears one upon another to a considerable distance; there are a great number of churches, convents & other publick buildings, which from the same course, and being lofty, handsome, and the *whole* of white stone, leads you to suppose that you are approaching one of the most magnificent cities in the world.

Five minutes on shore though is sufficient to convince you of your error. You then see that the buildings are unfinished, or clumsy; that the houses will still less bear a close inspection, that the streets are narrow, & filthy; that a different stench assails you in each of them, while idleness & poverty stare you in the face at every corner you turn.

3rd

Went on shore after breakfast & staid there till evening, returned & slept onboard my transport.

It seems that the 18th hussars were offloaded on 2 and 3 February; the 15th then landed over the next few days and both regiments were housed at Belem barracks.* During the disembarkation, trooper Catling of Captain Cochrane's troop apparently fell from the yardarm of the *Xanthe* transport and was killed.

4th

Disembarked my men & horses this day, & marched them to Belem. Took up my abode at Brasins Hotel, but got a billet afterwards on the Conde de Ribiera. Left my name at the Envoys Sir C Stuart.†

The regiment initially spent their days cleaning their barracks which they discovered in a squalid mess; then preparing for the campaign; ensuring that all their equipment was in perfect order and allowing the horses to regain their condition after such a trying voyage. The 15th and 18th were inspected at Inquisition Square on 13 February by Generals Leith and Peacocke‡ and on 15 February the regiment was pronounced 'ready for immediate service'. Over the next three days the forge wagons and their establishment of drivers from the Royal Wagon Train arrived, but the call did not come.

The 10th Hussars arrived in Lisbon in mid February and Colonel Grant was unofficially acting as brigade commander and Lieutenant Jones, adjutant of the

---

* Wylly states in error in his edition of Thackwell's correspondence that the 18th did not arrive until mid February.
† Sir Charles Stuart was British Ambassador to the court at Lisbon.
‡ Lieutenant General Sir James Leith commanded the 5th Division and Major General Marmeduke Warren Peacocke commanded Lisbon.

15th, became brigade major. William relates that together the tall dark-haired and moustachioed Grant and the short red-haired Jones soon gained the unfortunate sobriquet of 'The Black Giant and Red Dwarf'. This meant that Edwin was now the senior officer actually with the regiment and he was given command.

Thomas Dundas explains that the cavalry regiments were allowed to acclimatise in the Lisbon area before joining the army, followed by moderate marches, which ensured that they arrived at the front in perfect health.

On 21 February the brigade paraded for divine service at the riding school of the Prince Regent's palace. They paraded again on 25 February for General Peacocke and afterwards the 15th alone were put through their paces in a series of field-day manoeuvres, which they performed to his entire satisfaction. There is little doubt that the 15th were seen as the most organised and best-disciplined of the hussar regiments and it is telling that they do not seem to have suffered greatly with the problem of severe drunkenness caused by the ready availability of cheap wine, which the others, particularly the 18th, did. The full dress uniform for the 15th was altered slightly in 1812 with the unpopular hussar busby being replaced by a very distinctive shako of scarlet cloth; the officers received their new shakos at Lisbon on 17 February 1813, the men on 17 March. Once Edwin had procured mules to carry his baggage and completed fitting himself out there was plenty of time for him to explore the delights of the city:

> The employment of my time at Lisbon had so little variety in it, that I did not deem it worthwhile to keep a *daily journal*. Regimental duties, with preparations for the campaign & contrivances for the conveyance of my canteens, & baggage in the most convenient manner; with occasionally a ride into the country, were my chief occupation in the mornings; the evenings were spent with dinner or other parties, two or three balls at the Envoys, Sir Charles Stuart, and twice at the opera house.
>
> Any account of Lisbon, a place so well known, would be superfluous, as well as beyond the limits of a journal. Suffice it to say that I was there two months & two days, & that it is my humble opinion, that one half the time is more than sufficient to satisfy the most inquisitive traveller. The mosaic altar in the church of the St Roque,* & the noble aqueduct of Lisbon, or more properly speaking of Alcantara, are indisputably the greatest curiosity of this famed city. A person who has time should also visit the resort town of St Ubes, famous for its extensive salt trade; the royal palace of Queluz,† about a league* [Griffith's own note overleaf]

---

* The Igreja de Sao Roque is a very plain church, but its simplicity belies a succession of beautiful side chapels adorned with multicoloured marble and painted ceilings.
† Built by Dom Pedro III in 1777, its low pink washed wings and formal gardens make it the finest example of rococo architecture in Portugal.

from Belem, & the whimsical and beautiful little town of Cintra, 3 leagues beyond it.* The former place I did not go to, the two latter I did, & was highly gratified with the expedition.

* A Portuguese league varies in length from 4 to 5 English miles, which they distinguish by calling them long or short leagues. I have however found some of their short leagues less than 4 miles & the long ones nearly six in extent.

With the approach of spring and the forage beginning to ripen, Wellington now drew his army closer, ready for his great advance. The 15th were paraded on 9 March in full marching order to ensure that they could march at a moment's notice. However, it was not until 3 April that the 15th were ordered to form with three days' supplies and on the following morning, with a strength of twenty-one officers, thirty-one non-commissioned officers, six trumpeters, 503 rank-and-file and 576 horses, they commenced their march to join the army. Edwin resumed his journal as he marched with the right wing of three troops, the left wing following the next day with the 10th behind them.

Orders having arrived for the Hussar Brigade consisting of the 10th, 15th & 18th Regts to march from Lisbon & occupy Cartaxo, Azambuja & Vila Franca. It commenced its march on the 2nd of April with the latter Regt on Sunday the 4th; the three troops of the 15th; composing the right wing marched under my command for the village of Sacavem. The rain fell in torrents & every man was drenched to the skin before we got through Lisbon, but it soon afterwards became fair & we had a very pretty ride for twelve miles through olive groves & by several gentlemen's villas; just before we reached Sacavem a sweet view of the immense lake formed by the Tagus in this part broke suddenly upon our sight. The river is ten or 12 miles wide at this place; a small arm was up to Sacavem which is crossed by a bridge of boats. The town rises abruptly from the water and is a poor place with nothing worthy of remark in it. The country round is hilly & well wooded with olives. The people at my billet were very civil & made me a comfortable bed on the floor.

5th
At nine o'clock the following morning we marched for Vila Franca [de Xira], the road lies along the right bank of the Tagus of which we had

* Spelt Sintra by the Portuguese, this town has been the summer residence of the rulers of Portugal for many centuries. In British eyes, it was home to the infamous 'Convention of Cintra' which so nearly ruined Wellington along with his seniors.

several beautiful views; on the left is a strong country intersected with valleys, woods, & hills, on the most commanding of which are erected batterys & redoubts forming the right of [the] D [of] Wellington's celebrated lines where he kept the whole of Massena's army in check for 7 months & eventually compelled them to retire.* At Vila Franca we met the 4th Dragoon Guards (on their route to Lisbon for embarkation, having drafted their horses into other Regts)† which occasioned our being much crowded, the inhabitants were however extremely civil to us.

6th Tuesday

We pursued our march to Azambuja, about 3 leagues; the whole of this ride is delightful, the hills wooded, the plains well cultivated, & the gardens which are numerous full of fruit trees in the fullest bloom & breathing nothing but sweets. Azambuja is built upon the side of a little hill & commands an extensive view of meadow and arable land through the centre of which meanders the majestic Tagus. The plain which was situated between the contending armies, & alternately in possession of each, exhibits the marks of desolation & misery which are naturally the consequence of such a situation. Most of the homes were entirely gutted for fire wood & have nothing remaining besides the walls; the inhabitants quitted the place with such part of their property as was portable, & few have as yet returned to their homes. The civility of those that have is wonderful when it is considered how constantly troops are passing & re-passing this road, the whole of which are billeted upon them.

The regiment was to remain at Azambuja until 20 April and, apart from occasional field days, Edwin was free to explore the Portuguese countryside. He seems to have found that the country had rapidly recovered from the ravages of Massena's troops just a few years before and his eye for the fair ladies soon reappeared.

---

* The Lines of Torres Vedras were actually a series of three lines of redoubts, dammed rivers and scarped slopes right across the Portuguese peninsula from the sea to the Tagus. They were ordered by Wellington and built in secrecy by Colonel Fletcher of the Royal Engineers with Portuguese manpower. In all 108 redoubts were constructed and equipped with 447 cannon at a cost of some £100,000. Massena's army drove Wellington into the lines by shear weight of numbers in October 1810. The redoubts and forts were manned by Portuguese militia, with the army stationed immediately in their rear, ready to fall upon any force attempting to breach the lines. Massena declared the lines to be impossible to attack with any chance of success but he stubbornly sat down facing the lines until starvation forced him to retire in March 1811.

† The 4th (Royal Irish) Dragoon Guards were being sent home to refit.

7th

The left wing of the Regt marched in; two troops were detached, the town not affording stable room for the whole. The 9th Lt Dragoons* also came in for the night, on their way to England, dismounted. Seeing the church doors open this morning I went into it & found two young girls with their confessors. A wooden screen about the size of a door is set up with a board to kneel on one side of it, & a seat for the Father on the other; a few small holes are bored through, to which the padre puts his ear, & the Senhora whispers her (supposed) confession, for by the youthful appearance of both – the expression of the priests countenance, & their well known hypocrisy, I could not help suspecting that they were planning sins to come instead of reporting those that were past.

8th

I rode to the village of Aveiras [de Baixo] belonging to the Marquis of that name situated about two miles on the left of the road leading to Cartaxo. He has a good house there with a large garden, vineyards & shrubbery, standing in a beautiful little valley, surrounded with hills covered with cork, olive, fir, & other green trees. Pleasure & luxuries of all sorts was once the order of the day at this Quinta, the marks of which are still visible, in the ruins of summer houses, walks, alcoves, terraces &c &c. On the arrival of the French he retired to Lisbon, & was so disgusted with the outrages committed on his property, that he has ever since left the place in charge of an old steward, it still does duty as a barrack for troops when they are too numerous to be accommodated in Azambuja. I remained this day with my friends who were quartered there, I returned to it at night well delighted with my excursion.

9th Friday

Passed the morning at a quinta between Azambuja and Villa Nova [da Rainha] belonging to the Prince Regent where he used to go for a few days amusement in country sports & bullfights; the courts for the latter are still

---

* The 9th Light Dragoons were also returning home. It will be noted that the returning cavalry did not take their mounts with them. It had been found that many horses fresh from England, where they had been well provisioned and housed in warm stables, suffered from the poor quality, often green, forage available in the peninsula. Losses of mounts in newly arrived regiments tended to be very severe indeed and remounts were exceedingly difficult to procure and of much inferior quality and size to the British thoroughbreds. Therefore, all regiments returning home had to transfer their horses to those regiments remaining as they were now well inured to the climate and hardships of Spain and Portugal.

in preservation, & have every contrivance for the safety of the persons engaged, & to entrap the bull when they have sufficiently tormented him. In this situation he has the honor of being spear'd to death by the grandees & sometimes, if he has shewn good sport, by the hand of royalty itself.

10th

Took a solitary ride along the side of the beautiful meadows in front of Azambuja, to the little village of Villa Virtudes, in quest of prog.* Found nothing of any sort in the place excepting a few fowls which they had the impudence to ask 10 testoons a piece for (about six shillings 2d). Returned home through a large wood of cork & fir trees in which I saw some prodigious lizards from one to two feet in length, as thick as my wrist, & of a most brilliant green & yellow colour: these monsters are I am told are perfectly harmless & make a fine rich soup, little inferior to turtle.

11th Sunday

The regt assembled this day, not for divine service as usual, but in field day order for the purpose of punishing some men who had been guilty of drunkenness. Rode afterwards 6 or 7 miles up among the hills. The country away from the high road is in general very wild & foresty; the tracks are rugged & bad, even for a horse, two or three small vineyards, with here & there a miserable cottage just served to remind me that I was not in a *perfect desert*, although what few *natives* I saw appeared to be *very few degrees better than savages.*

12th

The priest at whose house I am billeted, & who is Prior of Azambuja, invited me to accompany him on a walk to his vineyard which I did. We found six men at work in it with a kind of large hoe loosening the earth about the roots of the vines. The soil in this part of the country is a mixture of whitish clay & sand, extremely hard & dry, but very productive when properly cultivated. There were a few patches of beans & onions, & garlicks scattered about, without any regard to order or regularity, as well as two or three line of olive, pear, apple, & other fruit trees. The whole contained about three acres, and was no little worthy of admiration as anything I ever saw in my life, although from the pride & satisfaction with which the old prior viewed & pointed out each vinestalk & onion to my notice, I found it incumbent upon me to express perfect rapture. I concluded the day by a ride up to the same wild hilly tho' less woody

---

* Army slang for provisions.

country that I explored yesterday, saw three peasants, several lizards, some nightingales, & a cuckoo, the first I had heard this year.

13th

The regt assembled for a field day on the plain to the east of Azambuja. The early part of the day was extremely sultry, but it clouded over at 12, and we had rain, & thunder the whole evening.

14th

Took a long ride this evening through a forest of pines that lies between the river, & the Santarem road, of considerable extent. The trees are of dwarfish dimensions, stunted in their growth by drought, & the heat of the sun, from which they afford no shelter. The burning sand on which they wither, is nearly destitute of every symptom of vegetation, but abounds in large grasshoppers, lizards & snakes.

15th & 16th

Passed the mornings in exploring the country & trying to procure something for dinner; the lean, tough, scanty allowance of ration beef being the only eatable to be got in Azambuja. In the neighbouring hamlets we sometimes found a few eggs, for which they asked a vintem & half a piece (about 2d) & now & then a rabbit.

17th Saturday

The 18th & us met for a field day about half way between Azambuja & Cartaxo, on very rough ground. Letters from England arrived this morning; the report of the day was that a large force was about to be sent to the north of Germany and that Genl Stewart, (Adjt Genl to the army in the Peninsula) had set out for that destination in an official capacity.*

---

* A force under Major General Sir Samuel Gibbs, consisting of the 1st, 25th, 33rd, 54th, 73rd and 91st Foot, 2nd & 3rd Hussars KGL and a rocket artillery troop, was sent to north Germany in August 1813. Landing at Stralsund this force joined the Hanoverian army of General Walmoden who beat Marshal Davout's force at the battle of Göhrde. Fortescue states that the British were not engaged at Göhrde, but the memoirs of Thomas Morris 73rd Foot clearly show that the KGL cavalry certainly were fully involved. Eventually this force sailed home only to be ordered to join a force going to Holland under General Graham. Lieutenant General Charles William Stewart, later Lord Londonderry, did not lead this force, but was sent to Germany as an envoy to the Prussian court.

Spain Again

18th

Was a showery day which confined us to the house nearly the whole of it. The order arrived for the brigade to continue its march upon Thomar &c.

19th

Packed up my things for the march, rode over to Aveiras de Baixo to dinner, returned at night, & for the first time fell in with a storm of fireflies. I caught one & brought it home with me, they are of the cockchafer breed, but not longer than a small kidney bean, the hinder part of their bodies is of a pale yellow by daylight; at night they are very brilliant, & resemble the sparks of a wood fire.

The march to join the army resumed and Edwin records the journey in great detail, while betraying his antipathy towards the dirty Portuguese villages and the controlling influence that the Catholic church had on the country.

20th Tuesday

We marched to Santarem, I parted from my friend the Prior of Azambuja with respect, he has been so very good humoured & civil to me the whole time I was in his house. His name is, he wrote it down for me, was a Padre Joze Joaquinada Motta. He confessed he was *rich* & had every comfort to which money can procure; he was also blessed with a most excellent temper & disposition & went by the name of the 'good prior' in the village; his two servants had lived with him from their infancy; his house was small, but was fairly clean, & commanded a charming view of the Tagus with the little towns of Salvaterra [de Magos], Benavente & Samora [Correia] on the opposite bank. His church duty was soon over, & *that* with an occasional walk in his vineyard was his whole employment: the rest of the day was passed in his *siesta*, in walking up & down the rooms muttering prayers to himself; or in yawning out loud & repeating in a melancholy tone Paciencia! Paciencia!

The road from Azambuja to Cartaxo is sandy & through [a] forest the whole way. Cartaxo is a pretty little town & was the Hd Qtrs of the army for a time when the French were at Santarem, which is about two leagues beyond it. We crossed a flat between two ranges of heights in which the armies continued in sight of each other until the retreat of the French, both positions bidding defiance to the attack of the adversary. Santarem is a straggling dirty town, much destroyed by the soldiery; it has many churches & convents, the chief of the latter used either as barracks or as General Hospitals to the English army. The people were less inclined to shew us civility here than any other place we had been at, they did however make me up a bed at my house, in which I scratched (for it was vain attempting to sleep) till five o'clock, & at six we proceeded on our march.

21st Wednesday

To Golega. Descending a long & steep hill we passed through what is called the old town of Santarem and entered upon a flat country highly cultivated with vines, which produce a most delicious wine called after the town. The view of Santarem from these meadows & vineyards is particularly favourable, though the weather was much against us, so it proved with rain for the first 7 or 8 miles. The road in many places is impassable for any carriage except the little ox cars of the country. Our route was generally on a level, & through olive woods, cornfields & vineyards from Golega, which is a straggling large village on a rising ground & overlooked the whole of it, & the view was bounded by the hill of Santarem. I had an excellent billet here in the house which the French General Loison* occupied for 3 months. It belongs to an elderly lady who I saw walking in the garden with her daughter in law, a very pretty girl. I introduced myself, & entered into conversation as well as I could in broken Portuguese, which they returned with civility, but not with much cordiality, & I bowed off with as much politesse as I was master of & retired to my room to write.

I had not been at my desk long, before a fat, sturdy, dirty cook maid with an immense bush of hair tied up & plaited with grease on the top of her head, march'd in with her arms akimbo & placing herself exactly before me said, 'God damn your eyes', which repeated three times with a ghastly grin, she quitted the room no doubt highly pleased with [the] specimen she had given me of her learning. A stiff, starch, old house-keeper made me an excellent bed, which had no living creatures but fleas in it & as I had got quite used to them made up for the worst of the last nights rest.

22nd

We marched for Tomar, 4 leagues from Golega, & 8 from Santarem. The road as usual is very bad in many parts, generally deep sand & through olive & pine woods, the scenery however varies, & the country is rich & picturesque. About half way we passed through the village of Atalaia, nearly in ruins now, but it apparently had been a very nice place. The approach to Tomar is beautiful; it stands in a rich valley. The chief part of the town is built on a flat, & encircling a steep & almost perpendicular hill

---

* General Louis Henri, Comte Loison, had been in Portugal with Junot's army. He returned to fight in Spain until May 1811 when he was transferred to Eastern Europe.

Spain Again

on which are the ruins of a castle, & the convent of Christ, a large gothic building, the greatest part of which is now used as a barrack; the horses standing in the cloisters, and within the walls of what was once a beautiful chapel, a very handsome carved wooden pulpit served as a rack, & the rows of seats as a manger for several of the horses. A sad perversion of its original sacred use! But such is the natural consequence of a country being the seat of war. The fences in this part, are composed of a mixture [of] evergreens; the commonest, particularly between Lisbon & Santarem, are made of the Hundred year Aloe, & the Sticky Pear; both nearly impassable to man or beast from their great size and the extreme hardness of their thorns which are as sharp as needles and nearly two inches long. The Gum Cistus is common everywhere, which, with Wild Lavender & a great variety of the flowers regales your nose with every breath of air that stirs, in some hedges I have also seen quantities of Geranium but to my recollection never met with any perfectly wild.

The weather at this season was very pleasant in the morning & evening. The heat in the middle of the day was quite as hot as it is in England in the month of July, and as we found it very relaxing, seldom staid out at that time when it could be avoided.

May 1st

We marched from Tomar after having staid there eight days, and as it is probable I may never return there I shall say a few words more about it & then take my leave. With few exceptions Tomar is one of the very prettiest towns I ever saw *any where in point of situation*. The rides about it are beautiful particularly those on the banks of the River Nábao (pronounced Naoon) which is a rapid stream exhibiting numerous cascades artificial as well as natural. The country is rich, & in parts picturesque in the extreme. The most striking object from all points is the extensive & magnificent convent of Christ (before mentioned) partly surrounded with the ruins of a Moorish castle, which almost overhang the town.* The streets are well paved & tolerably clean. The market place is a good square, one side of which is formed by the principal church,† & on market day (Saturday)

---

* The Convento de Cristo and Castelo dos Templarios still stand guard over this elegant town. The order of the Knights Templar had a post here and when the Pope banned the order in 1314, King Dimis of Portugal neatly sidestepped the papal suppression by simply renaming it the Order of Christ, and Tomar became its headquarters. Successive Grand Masters employed the best Romanesque and Renaissance architects to embellish the convent and it is pleasing to note that the convent survived its period of use as a barracks.
† On one side of the Praca da Republica stands the imposing seventeenth-century Sao Joao Baptista, with its octagonal belfry and elaborately carved doors.

remarkably well supplied with fruit, vegetables, poultry, fish salt & fresh, eggs, &c &c &c, at a very reasonable rate. The shops are well supplied with all the necessaries, & some of the luxurys of life, particularly one for glass of Portuguese manufacture. A few hundred yards from the bridge, up the river, is a cotton mill of considerable size, established by a Frenchman much on the principal of our own but I understood it was not in a very flourishing state. To conclude, the *display of beauty* was very fair. I got acquainted with two or three very pretty girls who were well brought up, spoke French, & play'd tolerably on an *English* pianoforte. Heaven defend me from such an event! But if ever my untoward fate should doom me to drag out my existence in the Lusitanian regions, Tomar would be the spot I should chuse.

After scrambling 4 leagues of the most infamous road ever passed by cavalry, sometimes upon shelves of sharp rock at the risk of breaking our horses legs, others sticking up to their knees in stiff clay, (for we had had several wet days while at Tomar) we arrived at 3 o'clock in the evening at the miserable village of Cabacos & its still more deplorable adjacents. A dirty room without a window, & furnished with Lord Wellington's allowance of two chairs & a table was allotted to me as a billet, & as the evening was too wet to walk out, I dispatched my cheerless meal early, & soon afterwards turned into my palliase of straw; where, with the exception of being two or three times disturbed by storms of rain upon the roof, I slept well & dreamt of comforts & friends that an ocean separated me from.

2nd Sunday

Soon after daylight we were on horseback; it poured with rain, & as the regt was scattered in obscene houses & hovels all about the country, it was eight o'clock before we had all assembled to proceed on our route for Espinhal; the distance was the same as yesterday's march, the road rather better, & through a romantic, hilly, & in parts beautiful country. Self sewn woods of pine flourish luxuriantly almost to the tops of the mountains hereabouts. Espinhal stands at the foot of the Estrela range of alps which stretch half across the kingdom of Portugal; it is a pretty little town, from it you over look a rich valley at the other side of which standing very high is the town and castle of Penela the latter now in ruins & forming a fine feature for the artist's pencil. The left squadron was detached to Penela, the officers & men of the other half were tolerably accommodated at Espinhal.

3rd Monday

Was again a wet morning, we marched at seven for Foz [de] Arouce; part of the regiment however only went there, Colonel Grant & I were put up at Lousa about 3 leagues from Espinhal. The road was hilly, but considering the torrents that had fallen & were falling while we were on the march, very tolerable. It lays along the bottom of the Estrela range under which Lousa is situated, in a most delightful spot. The variety of scenery in this days ride was perfectly beautiful. The valleys rich to a degree, hanging woods of pines & cork trees forming a fringe to the mountains as high as we could see, villages at their feet buried in vines & fruit trees in full bloom; torrents rushing over declivities of the rocks, & visible only where the openings in the woods admitted; the whole overtopped by the huge black mountains of the Estrela whose summits are continually enveloped in clouds & storms.

4th

After an excellent breakfast of goats milk & fresh eggs, Booth,* Barrett, & I set out on foot to climb the mountain behind the village which is very considerable & excessively steep; we were however amply repaid for our trouble by the view, which I think is the most beautiful I ever saw in my life. In front of us (when we had ascended & faced about) laid the fertile valley of the Mondego like a map at our feet; the course of that noble river might be traced to its mouth interrupted only by the magnificent city of Coimbra, every church & convent of which might be distinctly seen although at the distance of 20 miles. My view in this direction was bounded by a line of breakers of the Atlantic Ocean for a great many leagues. Behind us & to our rear left, mountain above mountain appeared as far as the eye can carry; the view on the right was closed by the great Estrela, capped with eternal snow.

Returning from this scene of richness & grandeur we passed some goatherd huts, which for security's sake are built in the form of villages, array the hollows of the mountains, & the contrast was a melancholy one. Nobody can have an idea of the misery, poverty, & almost savage severity of the peasantry in this country. I saw their situation, they are secure from all enemies excepting wolves, & these gentry in a formidable army of two or three hundred often attack their hamlets & carry off all the goats that happen to be within their reach, nor are armed men secure from them when hard pushed by hunger; a soldier of the 4th Dragoons patrolling on horseback during the night about two years ago was attacked by them, &

---

* Captain William Booth had served with the 95th Foot at Corunna before transferring into the 15th Hussars in December 1809. He became a major in 1823 and retired by sale of his commission in 1824.

he and his horse dreadfully torn before his commander could get to his assistance.

5th *Wednesday*

Marched for Sobreira. I was sent with the right squadron to the dismal village of S[ao] Martinho [da Cortiça], where four of us pigged together in the true Galician state of luxury. Our route laid through the romantic country on the left bank of the Mondego; & we passed bridges over the rivers Ceira at Foz de Arouce, and Alva at Ponte da Mucela, which [bridge] had been blown up by the French on their retreat, but since repaired. We had also a fine view of the heights on which was fought the battle of Busaco.* The road was tolerable but the weather bad, & on the top of the hills leading down to Ponte da Mucela we were caught in a shower which wet me to the skin.

6th

Continued our march to Galizes, but the Regt was scattered in many villages & hamlets surrounding the country. The distance is called 4 leagues but I thought it more, the road was most excellent, the scenery the same, & the weather being fine we saw more of the snow on the Estrela than we had hitherto done; the sun at the same time being very hot. I went first to [blank] but afterwards moved to Vila Pouca [da Beira] where we were very indifferently put up. Here is a convent of the Santisima Trinidad, in which are immured 25 nuns whose laws are so strict that they are not allowed to converse with their nearest relations nor do they ever shew their faces to any body. Their Father confessor who we conversed with for half an hour, told us that he had lived there many years but had never seen one of them, altho' he constantly heard their confessions thro' a door with small holes bored in it; they never touch meat of any kind; & *two* of them are forced to be on their knees before the Virgin Mary *constantly, day & night the year round.* The only exception to any of these rules was in favour of an Irish woman, who is allowed to talk sometimes but never to be seen. She sent to Colonel Grant to say she wished to speak to him, & on his arrival at the grate told him her name was Hussey, & that she begged he would spare a field of rye belonging to a friend of hers that had been ordered to be cut by the commissary for our horses. She also sent him some preserves, but they were potted in a little affair which in make & shape so strongly resembled a pot de chambre, that we could not relish the contents.

---

* The battle of Busaco was fought on 27 September 1810 between Wellington and Massena during the slow retreat of the British and Portuguese army to the Lines of Torres Vedras.

Spain Again

Edwin, although cushioned from the worst himself, was not unsympathetic to the great fatigues that his men were put to daily, in all weathers, and the misery that the requisitions of the troops caused to the local population.

Was a cold, & determined wet day. We marched at six o'clock for Maceira, and Seia, the latter of which I was billeted at. The road was pretty good excepting a few parts which had been cut off by the mountain torrents crossing it. Seia is about four leagues from Vila Pouca, & as it poured with rain the whole way, we all got drenched; the clouds flew too low for us to get a good view of the Estrela, but the occasional peeps that we had through them were grand. The moment our men had got under cover & changed their wet clothes most of them were ordered out again to cut forage for the horses, in the execution of which they got a second soaking. Foraging is the worst part of a cavalry soldier's duty. In addition to the fatigues of the march, loaded with their kits, arms, & appointments, & the cleaning of those articles themselves, & their horses after they had got in, they had frequently during this march to go two or three miles with reaping hooks and cords to bring home *28 pounds of rye or barley for each horse*; from the difficulty of access to some of the fields thus allotted & the scramble across the country with a great load on their backs afterwards, it was sometimes dusk before they returned, and as the trumpets sounded for stables at ½ past six, & the retreat at eight o'clock, it might be said that they had not one minute to themselves for the purpose of cooking their rations. A wet day of course doubled their labours, & miserys, many of them being put up in open lofts or stables, & those that had the good fortunes to get into inhabited houses were very little better off, as the wretched little fires of smoking, spitting, green wood, made on the floor, did not afford warmth sufficient to dry their clothes. But the accumulation of all these misfortunes to our men, was, many times, less distressing than the witnessing the grief, & almost distraction of the poor people, particularly the women, whose property was thus, in its unripened state, condemned to the sickle. For, although on their presenting receipts for the quantity taken, to the commissary, they get a bill upon England for the amount at its fair valuation, the money was seldom paid before the expiration of a year, at least, after date. It then came perhaps at a moment when they did not want it, or when twice the quantity of bread, (taken in green corn) could not be purchased for the same. One poor woman near S[ao] Martinho was absolutely tearing her hair out in agony while we were cutting her field of rye, which she had cultivated at much trouble & expense, & was daily watching the progress of her crop, which bid fair to be a very good one, with an almost maternal care and attention. She said that it was her sole dependence for herself & children for the coming winter, that *money* was of no use to her in that out of the way place, and that should we persist in taking her corn she had every prospect of starving. My heart bled for this poor soul, & many others in the same predicament, but what was to be done? Hay or straw was *not* to be had, & it was necessary our horses should be fed! The person acting as constable, or any civil authority in the village, was applied to, according to the orders for foraging, & whatever field he sentenced, we were obliged to take or starve.

This system of giving bills on the English Treasury was a source of great profit to some of the commissarys who had plenty of ready money in hand (& few more without), for after giving these bills to the poor people it was not unusual, nay I believe their constant practise, to offer them *cash* not exceeding two thirds, & I've been told, sometimes not more than half their amount, which rather than be at any trouble about, & in conformity to the old adage of 'a bird in the hand being worth two in the bush', these unhappy cottagers have jumped at. The commissary thus secured an immense profit without the slightest risk, as they well know the validity of a Treasury bill.

8th

We remained all this day at Seia; it is a pretty little place upon a hill above some fine meadow land, & at the feet of the mountains. The Bishop of Guarda had a palace here, which was set on fire by Gen'l Drouet's corps, & is now a magnificent ruin. The morning was so excessively wet, cold, & windy that I did not show out of the town; I don't recollect ever feeling a more uncomfortable day at this season of the year in England, & I found great comfort in sitting over a brassiere of charcoal, which the senhoritas at my billet sent me, & not only that, but hearing that I had a friend to dine with me, they made an excellent pudding of rice, eggs, milk, & nutmeg with their own fair hands, as the servant who brought it me said, & agreeably surprised us with it just as we had finished our sinewy allowance of a lean ox. The general desire of the different people we were quartered upon all the way is to be civil, & accommodate as far as laid in their power, often surprised me. I really don't think there is another nation upon earth who after having been harassed for five years by foreign troops, & a constant succession of strangers in their houses, would not only give you a good room, fire (if wanted), lights, a comfortable bed, clean sheets, towels, table cloth, &c &c, but also receive you with the utmost good humour, & at the same time in the most respectful manner.

9th

Marched at seven this morning, the Head quarters to Vila Cortês [da

Serra], & I with the right squadron to Nabais & adjacents. The day was showery, the road tolerable. Lord Dalhousie,* commanding the 7th Division came to view us on our march, we afterwards passed the village of São Paio, full of German troops, about 2 miles on the right, standing high, is the town of Gouveia. The village of Nabais is like most others in this part of Portugal, difficult of access for cavalry owing to the extreme badness of the lanes which are often nothing more than deep troughs formed by torrents from the mountains.

10th

At half past five we were on horseback & proceeded to Maçal do Chão, the Headquarters to Baraçal. About two leagues from Vila Cortêz we passed thro' Celorico [da Beira], the town & castle† of which stand upon a high rocky hill above the River Mondego which we crossed about a mile on this side of it over a bridge that had been partly destroyed by the French but repaired by our troops. The Mondego is not very deep hereabouts, but from the rapidity of its current & the ruggedness of its bed it would not be easy to ford it. The country for miles around Celorico, indeed as far as we could see, is nothing but a continuation of rough & barren rocks, devoid of any striking or particular feature is extremely ugly. As we were now living near the frontier, the misery & poverty of the villages became more apparent. They presented nothing but an accumulation of the most abject wretchedness. Our accommodation was proportionately comfortless; at Nabais I slept in an old lumber loft over my stable with a very scanty allowance of roof remaining; at Maçal de Chão I was happy to take possession of an old poultry house, on the floor of which you might have set potatoes; but we were now familiarised with filth, & slept as soundly on our uneasy pallets, as in the perfumed chambers of the great.

11th

We marched at six this morning for Freixedas along three leagues of winding rough road between rocks & huge round stones in which this part of the country abounds, some of these are of vast dimensions & balanced so singularly on the tops of others that I should think the soil in which they grew must have been washed away from them in the flood, or that

---

* Major General George the Earl of Dalhousie served for much of the peninsular war. He later became Governor of Canada.

† The castle of Celorico, built to withstand incursions from Spain, is now in a very dilapidated state; indeed those brave enough to climb its tower take their life in their hands.

they fell in a shower from heaven. About half a league short of Freixedas we passed through the pretty little town of Alverca [da Beira], very much superior in every thing to our quarters which were very indifferent. Freixedas stands on very high ground without appearing to do so; as a proof of which from a sloping field about a mile off we saw, in our front Almeida, distant four leagues; beyond it Spanish mountains far across the frontier, covered with snow. On our right, Guarda, reckoned I'm told, the second highest city in Europe, behind us Trancoso and on our left Pinhel, & curiously situated on the top of a sugarloaf hill, the town of Castelo Rodrigo. Our old acquaintance the Serra de Estrela still formed a prominent feature in the view, which was bounded in almost every direction by mountains as far as the eye could carry.

Having now closed up with the army, the regiment settled into their billets at Freixedas and sought to refresh their mounts after the long journey before the army moved again. The weather, however, was unseasonably bad.

12th

Being now only 5 leagues from Freineda, Lord Wellington's Headquarters, Colonel Grant rode over there this morning to report the arrival of the brigade, and to ascertain whether he was to remain in the command of it. I mounted my horses for the purpose of exploring a little of the country, but finding no hills near enough to ascend, & seeing nothing but enclosures between stone walls all round me, fruitful only in worked pebble stones, I soon returned to my stately mansion, where I wrote letters & shivered the remainder of the day.

13th

A squadron of the 18th marched in. The day was wretchedly cold & wet. Colonel Grant returned from Freineda without having gained the information that formed the ostensible object of his visit; but Lord W.[ellington] told him he meant to see the brigade in a few days, after which we were to be advanced in front of the whole army.

14th

Another wet day, & so cold that I did little the whole of it except endeavour to keep myself well fortified by great coat and cloak against the effects of it; my large rooms not being glazed, I was forced to sit with the shutters open, or in darkness. Should if ever I get home again how I shall enjoy myself!

Spain Again

15th

Buried again this morning, the weather was however rather warmer. Colonel Grant & I rode a little way on the Freineda road, but the sky & the prospect were both so cheerless that we soon returned to our quarters.

16th Sunday

Was a fine clear day, I mounted my horse with the intention of riding to Pinhel, about two leagues from hence; the road is over & through rock almost all the way, & so excessively rugged & rough that I took compassion upon my poor nag before I had got half way there, and returned to Freixedas.

17th

Rode to Gouveias to visit Major Hughes* who was quartered there with a squadron of the 18th. An order arrived for the brigade to assemble on the Almeida road at nine in the morning.

Wellington was on the verge of issuing the long-anticipated orders for the army to advance into Spain and he ordered an inspection of the newly arrived hussar brigade in full marching order. Wellington was particularly pleased with the bearing of the 15th; indeed William believed that the strong discipline instilled by Lieutenant Colonel Robert Ballard Long when based at Radipole barracks accounted for their excellent showing. By contrast, it would seem that Colonel Grant, who had now been officially appointed in command of the hussar brigade, was far from happy with the appearance of the 18th on their arrival from Lisbon and reprimanded Colonel Murray and his officers. Lieutenant Jones, now confirmed as brigade major confirms this declaring that they were 'for the present unserviceable'. In his absence Sergeant-Major Eggleton was appointed to act as adjutant of 15th Hussars.

While the French watched Hill's army stationed near Almeida, (Wellington remained with this wing to make the French believe that this would be the main attack), General Graham drove his army through supposedly impenetrable country to the north; the French finding all their river defences turned by this movement were forced to relinquish their hold of Leon without a fight.

18th

Lord Wellington inspected the Hussar Brigade in marching order on a plain about six miles from Freixedas on the road to Almeida; and expressed himself highly pleased with their appearance in every respect.

---

* Major James Hughes, 18th Hussars, of Kinmel Park, Denbigh, was a fellow Welshman and a great friend to Edwin.

We had 496 horses mounted on the field; the 10th [Hussars] 494, & the 18th [Hussars] 456. The route arrived for the brigade to march on the 19th for Miranda [do Douro]. The weather was very hot yesterday & today appeared to be settled fine.

19th

This morning at six o'clock the brigade marched; the 15th to Coriscada, the 10th & 18th to Cótimos, & Ervedosa. The weather was extremely sultry particularly towards evening.

20th

The Tenth marched to Muxagata, the Eighteenth to Servado Chao & we to Freixo de Numão, a nice little place where we were well put up & got excellent forage for our cattle.

21st

The regt marched this morning at four o'clock in two divisions to pass the Douro at the ferry called 'Barca de Pocinho'. Two large boats sailed together with boards laid across them, conveyed us 18 at a time, to the other side of the river, where we bivouacked at the foot of a hill. I took possession of a small chapel where I made myself a bed of broom &c, and slept in very good company having the Virgin Mary as large as life on one side of me, & half a dozen saints on the other. It was intended the whole regt should have passed the Douro this day, but in consequence of the other boats being employed in getting the pontoon bridge over, the right squadron was forced to bivouack on the left bank. The road for about a mile from the ferry is in a zig zag direction up the side of a mountain; the pontoon carriages with 14 bullocks to each appeared one above another all the way up, the channel of the river is deep on either side, detachments of infantry, artificers, &c were encamped in an irregular manner. The muleteers, & ferrymen in their native costume assisting in working the boats across, the winding course of the stream, & the amphitheatre of rocky mountains which bounded the view, formed altogether one of the most busy & picturesque scenes I ever beheld, & would have been a most beautiful subject for a painting.

22nd

The right squadron crossed the river soon after daylight, when we broke up our encampment, & proceeded to the town of Torre de Moncorvo. We had now entered the province of Tras os Montes; and the view, which was very extensive, presented nothing but rocks & barren mountains, the tops of which are inhabited by wolves & eagles only. The Serra de Estrela was again within this days march at an immense distance in our rear.

23rd Sunday

The whole brigade arrived here last evening, & as there was not stable room for all a squadron of each regt bivouacked in an olive grove near the town. We remained this day at Torre de Moncorvo, but the sun was so hot that I was not tempted to look about me much. It is rather a handsome town, situated in a valley along the [River] Sabor, a mile or two before its junction with the Douro. Behind the town a hill rises very steep, but cultivated & planted [a] great part of the way up it; among the trees are several extremely pretty cottages belonging to gentlemen, and the Convent of San Francisca a handsome building.

Four divisions of the army having passed through the day before us,* we could not get many comforts; there is however a good market place and in general well supplied, and several tolerable shops. I was billeted at the house of a fidalgo which had just been quitted by Lord Dalhousie; everything was very clean & handsome, & I had the luxury of sleeping in an English four post bed with *curtains*, the first I had seen since I left Lisbon. My patraõ who is a brigadier in the Portuguese army, overwhelmed me with civility & begged I would consider everything in his house my own as long as I remained.

As the army now neared the French advance posts, pickets were set and orders were promulgated that bugles were to be used only for field duties and 'turn out'.

24th

The regt's were on horseback at half after four o'clock this morning and proceeded on their march *in brigade*. The rising sun upon the castle and town of Torre de Moncorvo, the groves & fruit trees dripping with dew, the white mists hanging over the rivers Sabor, & Douro, and stealing up the sides of the mountains where clear tops presented a surrounding barrier of rugged grey stones *had* altogether a most beautiful effect from a hill a mile on this side the town. Next to Tomar, Torre de Moncorvo is the most desirable place herein that I have yet seen in Portugal, and in its intercourse with Oporto by means of the Douro, even superior to the

---

* The infantry force passing the Douro at Pocino actually consisted of three infantry divisions (4th, 6th and 8th) with the pontoon train and the reserve siege train. These would meet up with the 1st, 3rd and 5th Divisions, two Portuguese brigades (Pack's and Bradford's) and four cavalry brigades (Anson's, Bock's, Ponsonby's and D'Urban's Portuguese) at Braganza.

former. After marching five leagues through an ugly country under a burning sun & enveloped the whole way in a cloud of dust, we arrived at the village of Fornos which held part of the 15th & 18th, the remainder encamped near the town, and the 10th occupied another village about a mile on our right. The *vanity* of a soldier's life on service is not the least common part of it. Last night I had two splendid apartments to myself, with matted floors, silken hung walls, glazed windows, and a carved ceiling beautifully painted with devices of war, music & husbandry, from the centre of which was suspended a cut glass chandelier with gilt ornaments wax candles. Today two of us were squeezed into a loft, dignified by the appellation of *houses*, with our servants & baggage, the roof barely kept out the sunbeams, the floor was an inch thick with dirt, the ragged walls hung with cobwebs & filthy garments; the light came in, & the smoke went out at the door, no there was neither window or chimney, the *bed in* which the family slept was separated from ours by a low partition, & we all turned in with our clothes on by the dim & cheerless ray of a stinking oil lamp, which had no sooner burned out, than a whole host of rats, attracted by the savoury smell of our canteens invaded the apartment, & continued squeaking & racing, round & over us the night through.

The inhabitants of this village having given Colonel Grant information of the French cavalry being within a league & half of us on the opposite side of the Douro, (but which has since proved to be utterly void of truth) a picquet was ordered out at sunset; the first since our arrival in the peninsula.

25th
The brigade continued its march at five o'clock for Vilar de Rei where a part of the 15th & 18th were put up; the remainder, with the whole of the Tenth, bivouacked under some trees adjoining the village. A report reached us last night that Sir Rowland Hill's corps had received a check on the Tormes & [had] been compelled to fall back.*

26th
Marched this morning to the village of Sendim where some of us were well put up, & the remainder slept under the canopy of the heavens. The 10th went on about a mile & ¼ to a place called Picote.

---

* This report was false; Hill's force consisting of two British divisions (Light and 2nd), Morillo's and Espana's Spaniards and Silviera's Portuguese with the cavalry of Sanchez, Long, Alten, Fane and Hill (his brother), steadily advanced towards Salamanca without meeting any serious resistance.

Spain Again

27th

It was intended we should have marched to Miranda today, but a route arrived last night for us to go to Brandilanes, & Castro [de Alañices], 6 leagues from Sendim. We turned out at ½ past two o'clock, & between seven & eight passed through Malhadas & here we saw several divisions of the army encamped on a hill; and about one league further on, entered Spain, the kingdoms have no natural boundary on this frontier. The country the whole of the last few days marches grew very flat & ugly & did not offer any striking feature. The villages intended for our reception not possessing any stabling, the brigade encamped under some oaks between the two, along the bank of a rivulet.

The hussar brigade was now to take the advance and to form the eyes and ears of the army; but Edwin had a bad start.

28th

This morning was ushered in by a most calamitous event to me, no less than the death of my *best* although not favourite horse, Emperor; of inflammation in his bowel. This would have been a most serious loss to me at any time, but to happen the very day we were put in front of the whole army, & within a few leagues of the enemy, when I was certain of having full employment for all my stud, was a misfortune that required an exertion of all the philosophy I was possessed of to bear with common fortitude & resignation. The 4th & 7th Divisions arrived in our rear this evening, and encamped near enough to enable Edward to come & dine with me.

29th

At three this morning we struck our tents & marched part of the way in company with the infantry whom we left just before we arrived upon the River Aliste, passed it at the ford of Muga [de Alba], went on through Carbajales [de Alba], the Hd. Qtrs of Sir T. Graham,* & encamped between that place & the ford on the River Esla. A picquet of ours which had been sent on to this ford the night before observed a picquet of the enemy on the opposite side, the first we had seen.

---

* General Sir Thomas Graham, Baron Lynedoch had joined the army late in life to gain retribution after the callous treatment by the French revolutionary authorities of his wife's body when she had died of natural causes in France. He served in the army in an unpaid capacity until through the influence of Sir John Moore, he had gained a full military appointment. He served at Corunna, Walcheren and won the battle of Barossa. Wellington clearly saw him as a safe pair of hands even when in independent command and entrusted him with the very important command of this turning force.

30th Sunday

Remained the whole day in our bivouack expecting orders to cross the Esla, Lord Wellington having arrived at Carbajales. At eight o'clock in the evening directions were received for the Hussar Brigade, the 51st Foot, The Duke of Brunswick infantry, & Captain Webber Smith's troop of horse artillery to form in column on the road leading to the ford at one o'clock in the morning.

The crossing of the Esla was vital to Wellington's whole plan and he arrived in time to oversee the tricky operation. The 15th were to lead a small force across the river to form a bridgehead, which would protect the pontoon bridge while being laid. This was not a simple task, the river; about as broad as the Thames at London, flowing rapidly and with depths of water up to four feet over the uneven ford would not be at all easy for the horses and particularly for the infantry weighed down with their equipment. Thomas Dundas goes as far as to claim that the crossing was not reconnoitred properly and that Captain Clements of 18th Hussars led the columns over without any prior knowledge of the ford. The soldiers were ordered to hold onto the stirrups, the troopers preserving their muskets from the waters.

31st

Soon after one o'clock this morning, the troops having formed according to last nights orders, began to move off left in front, the right squadron of the 15th; in advance. We arrived at the ford of Almendra a little after daybreak where we were overtaken by Lord Wellington who directed the cavalry to pass by threes, the infantry to hold by our stirrups. The Esla is fordable in this part by the river separating into four branches or streams with gravely islands between, & after gaining the opposite shore the road runs parallel to the river and at the foot of a precipice for two hundred yards, & there winds up to the top by a steep ascent forming a very strong pass, which pass was covered by Capt. W. Smith's troop of artillery,* formed on a hill facing to it.

Unfortunately by means of melted snow or some other cause, the river had risen considerably in the course of the last twelve hours, & as it was deep, & very rapid the infantry could not keep pace with us against it, many of our horses also finding themselves carried off their legs took

---

* Edwin states that the horse artillery troop engaged was that of Captain James Webber Smith, whereas Ian Fletcher identifies it as Gardiner's. Thomas Dundas agrees with Edwin, as he states that Webber Smith's battery of 9-pounders was with the regiment until 2 June and then was replaced by Gardiner's 6-pounder battery, as it could move more freely with cavalry.

fright, and plunging violently overwhelmed both their riders, and the men at their stirrups in the water, at one time I counted seven horses, & I should think twenty men hurried along by the current & struggling for life. Before these recovered the shore, they were in a similar horrid situation, everyone forced to press on, although they saw the inevitable consequence of attempting it. Never did I behold so distressing a scene, never shall I forget the agonising looks & cries of the poor infantry, who, loaded with their arms & accoutrements struggled as long as they were able, & then yielded themselves to their fate. Nine & twenty of these poor wretches sank, never to rise again,* and nearly double the number who had been set by a friendly undercurrent into their depth again were so exhausted as to require medical aid to bring them round. One horse of the 15th drowned, was the only casualty in our brigade. Soon after advancing a small patrole [sic] up the hill, some French videttes were discovered; the right squadron was pushed on, & at the top got sight of a picquet of 30 men, 17 of which they took prisoners after a chase of some miles;† with the officer commanding it. The brigade then proceeded to two small villages in the neighbourhood of Zamora. A squadron of the 18th & the horse artillery went with us to La Hiniesta, and encamped near the village.

The complete failure of Didgeon's force consisting of two dragoon regiments, a half battery of horse artillery and four companies of voltiguers, to discover and contest what was inevitably a tricky crossing, is impossible to explain away. However, Wellington was never slow to take an opportunity and having laid the pontoon bridge he rapidly moved an overwhelming force across the river to secure his advantage. The cavalry continued to spearhead the rapid advance despite some appalling weather.

June 1st Tuesday
We marched to Fresno [de la Ribera] where we encamped, the 10th and

---

* There has been some confusion over the losses incurred at the crossing of the Esla; Oman states the losses vaguely as ten of the 51st Foot and more of the Brunswick troops; Wylly quotes Thackwell, who states twenty to thirty of the 51st Foot and Chasseur Britanniques, and Lieutenant Jones, who states seventeen Brunswick Oels; Mollo (1997) simply restates the figure of seventeen drowned. Most authorities agree that the troops that accompanied the 51st Foot were the Brunswick Oels rather than the Chasseurs Britanniques, a French émigré unit. As to numbers, Edwin's figure of twenty-nine has the ring of authenticity as it was written down on the spot and it agrees with Thackwell.
† Oman states that the picket of the 16th Dragoons was captured entire; however Edwin's statement that one officer and seventeen men were captured from a detachment of thirty-odd has more of the ring of truth.

most of the 18th went into quarters in the village. We left Zamora about a mile on our right, where we got into the road leading from thence to Toro, which I marched along in the winter of 1808 on our way to join Sir John Moore. We had several thunderstorms in the course of the day; the night was very cold & wet, & did our horses much harm after the heat of the sun which they had been exposed equally to without shelter. At 12 o'clock orders were read to march at daybreak to Morales [de Toro].

As Grant's Brigade neared Morales they discovered the rear of Didgeon's force with the two regiments of French dragoons drawn up in line in a defensive position covered by a bog in front. Grant attacked without hesitation, charging furiously with the 10th Hussars and with the 18th supporting on their flank. The 10th broke the front regiment whereupon the entire French force broke and fled, the hussars in hot pursuit. After a chase of two miles, the hussars were confronted by more cavalry, infantry and artillery formed on rising ground. Grant sensibly reined in the pursuit, as to attack unbroken infantry with artillery support would have only led to failure with heavy losses and on this occasion the British cavalry seem to have heeded the recall. The 15th being the rear-most regiment formed the reserve and Edwin who commanded merely ordered the regiment to canter after the others collecting the prisoners and wounded.

2nd

Mounted our horses at ½ past three & proceeded to within a league of Toro where we were met and [were] informed by an officer who had been sent forward to reconnoitre, that the French cavalry were formed on the plain behind Toro awaiting our arrival. As the brigade happened to be marching right in front this morning, Col Grant pushed on with the 10th & 18th and directed me to follow with the 15th at a walk, which I continued until we had ascended the hill and arrived on the other side of the town when I rec'd orders to trot, & support the attack about to be made by the other regts. Just at this time we discovered the monsieurs formed in column of 4 or 5 squadrons across the road leading from Toro to Morales. Capt Webber Smith's troop of artillery, having been last night changed for Major Gardiners, that officer gave them a gun or two, when the leading squadron of the 10th charged the others following in support. The French at first made some disposition of resistance, taking us, as they afterwards told us, for Don Julian Sanchez's Brigade of Spanish cavalry; when however they found what we were, they commenced retreating round the village of Morales, which soon increased in rapidity, & ended in downright running for their lives. They crossed a ravine by means of a defile & went up a hill on the top of which was formed 13 squadrons of cavalry, a column of infantry, & eight pieces of artillery which played upon us as we advanced but fortunately did not do *us* any harm although a shell fell actually among the horses feet of our right squadron, another burst close to Col Grant,* and one man of the 10th & another of the 18th had their legs carried off by balls. Col. Grant prudently not chusing to push his victory up the hill in face of so superior a force ordered a halt, & soon afterwards we retired into Morales to feed & rest ourselves after the exertions of the day. The result of this brilliant affair was the capture of near two hundred horse, & two hundred & fifty six men; mostly belonging to the 16th Dragoons reckoned the best regt in the peninsula & one which had frequently disputed the palm of victory with our own cavalry.† Our loss was very trifling, Lieut. Cotton of the 10th was killed & Capt. Lloyd‡of the same regt wounded & taken but afterwards left, on his passing his word of honor that an officer of theirs (we took three) of equal rank should be given in exchange for him. Capt. Lloyd informed us when we saw him next day that the French surgeon who attended him, had dressed between 60 & 70 of their own men all badly wounded. Those I saw in the hospital at Morales were dreadfully so, many of them being completely disfigured by cuts about the head with severed noses, ears, eyebrows, cheeks, &c.

To give the finishing stroke to the business Don Julian fell in with 50 of the same corps retiring in confusion into an adjacent village, & killed or took them all. Thus this celebrated French regt of Dragoons may be fairly said to be annihilated on the opening of the campaign.§

---

* Colonel Grant was returned as slightly wounded at Morales.

† Oman states that two officers and 208 men were captured, all of which came from the 16th Dragoons, whereas Edwin says 256 men *mostly* of the 16th Dragoons. If one assumes that the additional forty-eight men in Edwin's count were from the 21st Dragoons, these figures are not incompatible. It does seem very unlikely that Oman is correct in intimating that no men from the 21st Dragoons were lost in such a scramble.

‡ The official return says that the 10th Hussars lost twenty-one men killed, wounded or missing. The obituary of Lieutenant John Cotton, 10th Hussars, states that he was wounded by a sabre over the forehead then almost immediately shot through the right breast, killing him immediately. Thomas Dundas confirms that he was shot by a pistol. Captain James Richard Lewis Lloyd was severely wounded and made a prisoner but given his parole. He transferred to 18th Hussars with which he served at Waterloo and quit the service in 1818.

§ Oman says that the 16th Dragoons' morning-state indicates that they numbered slightly less than 400. They appear to have lost one officer and seventeen men at the crossing of the Esla, two officers and 208 men captured at Morales, one officer and up to seventy men wounded but not captured, and Sanchez is believed to have killed or captured fifty more. This makes a total loss of 349 from less than 400; clear evidence that the 16th Dragoons virtually ceased to exist.

The march resumed but there were signs that King Joseph was concentrating his forces for battle.

3rd

Marched at daylight to Pedrosa del Rey, one league & half from Morales, where a squadron of ours had been left as a picquet during the night, they did not however think proper to show their faces more & we passed a day of rest in tolerable quarters although the place was almost quite deserted.

4th

At one o'clock this morning, the picquet having had some cause for alarm, & the country around being a plain, nearly level, & perfectly open, the brigade was turned out, & we stood shivering in front of the village till daylight when the advanced guard of the 7th Division arriving in our rear, we proceeded for the town of Torrelobatón where we were well put up & got plenty of bread & wine, but nothing else. The information we gained from the inhabitants was that the French were assembling in great force in the neighbourhood of Palencia, & that King Joseph had lately arrived from Madrid with 5000 cavalry & 28 pieces of artillery. We were cheered & welcomed into all the towns & villages we passed, but not with the same enthusiasm with which we were received when advancing through the same country in the winter of 1808 & 9. Lord Wellington had his Hd. Qtrs this day at La Mota,* the place where we saw & so much admired the sisters of the young Duke of Berwick & Aloa.

5th

Turned out of our quarters as usual before daylight, & halted a few miles from the town until Lord Dalhousie's division appearing in sight we proceeded toward Peñaflor [de Hornija], a miserable place situated on the edge of one of the steepest hills I ever marched up into a town. One squadron of each regt were put under cover here, the remainder bivouacked in the fields.

The 6th & 7th Divisions encamped close to us, & the Staff gentlemen took care to secure all the best houses & stables to themselves. The approach of these two divisions, Genl Alten's Brigade of cavalry, besides artillery, & followers innumerable, along the roads in the valley leading to Peñaflor, was one of the grandest military spectacles that can be imagined; & crossing the end of the valley on the road leading to Torrelobatón, at the distance of eight or ten miles we saw the dust raised by the army under Sir

---

* La Mota is near Medina del Campo; the right wing was now covered by Hill's force which had joined from Salamanca.

Rowland Hill, which nobody, with us, knew had crossed the Douro; such is the secrecy & dispatch with which all Ld W's orders are given & executed.

6th Sunday

The brigade turned out at three o'clock & marched four leagues to a bivouack at a place called Casa de Monte Torre.* Two miles short of the place in passing through some high brushwood one of our advanced guard came galloping back to say there was a French picquet before us; it however turned to be an officer of the (I think Chambrian†) hussars with a flag of truce & a letter for Ld. Wellington. He was accompanied by half his troop, which led our advanced guard to suppose it was a regiment. The letter was forwarded by an officer of the 15th to Ld. W. at Ampudia & a receipt given to the flag who set off on his return at a gallop. He bore the rank of captain was very much laced, & wore a huge fur cap on his head; his horse was English & he *said* he had *bought* it of Sir Edward Paget.‡ He was very gentlemanly in his appearance & manner, told us the general commanding the French was stationed at Dueñas about a league and half in our front, and was particularly inquisitive to know where Sir Rowland Hill was, which we as particularly avoided telling him. The officer who went to Lord W returned soon & said the letter referred to exchange of prisoners only; he bore his lordship's answer back to the French general at Dueñas, but was not admitted beyond the outposts which were formed of cavalry & infantry. The certainty of our friends being such near neighbours kept us pretty much on the alert all night, which was cold & wet; and as I was unhappily Field Officer of the Day I had to visit all our outposts in the dark, scattered over a flat & barren heath.

7th

At daylight we proceeded to Paradilla§ where we formed in column with

---

* I suspect that Edwin refers to the castle, now termed Los Viveros near Fuensaldana, which is sited on the edge of the Montes de Torozos.

† 2nd Regiment of Hussars, originally raised as the Hussars Chamborant. This regiment was in northern Spain at this time and did see action at Vitoria. The use of the pre-revolutionary title, presumably by the French officer, is interesting, indicating a dislike of the Napoleonic number system.

‡ Major General the Honourable Edward Paget, brother of Lieutenant General Henry Paget, Colonel of 18th Hussars, had lost an arm at Oporto and had been captured during the retreat from Burgos the previous year. He was to see out the remaining years of the war in France.

§ Possibly Paredes de Monte.

Genl Ponsonby's Brigade of Heavy Dragoons* & waited the arrival of Lord Wellington. As soon as he came we filed on towards Palencia, passed through it & got partly into the village one league beyond it called Villalobón. Palencia stands on the River Carrion, over which there is a good bridge of several arches, and in the middle of a large fertile valley full of corn & vineyards. It is in appearance a very handsome city with a fine cathedral & many other churches.† There is also a large canal with locks upon it, which we crossed, short of the town, much resembling an English one.‡ The shops appeared good & the streets handsome, but we had not much time for observation in marching through particularly as crowds had assembled, & the windows were full of ladies all waving flags, some in the shape of *counterpanes, sheets, towels,* pocket handkerchiefs, &c &c, & deafening us with shouts of 'Viva los Inglese, Viva Hispania!' Half of each regt was put up at Villalobón, the remainder were in a field close by. I was glad enough to get into a tolerable house here, not having had my clothes off for two days & nights.

8th

Turned out at 5 o'clock, but remained waiting for orders until half past ten when we proceeded through Fuentes [de Valdepero], & Monzón [de Campos], to Támara [de Campos], where we did not arrive till six o'clock & there found almost all the town occupied by the Staff of the 4th Division. To add to our comfort we were nearly wet through, & the night turned out a cold & soaking one. The 6th & 7th Divisions passed through [Villa]lobón before we left it; & at Monzón we passed the Household Brigade of cavalry & the 3rd Division, thus coming in contact with two thirds of the army in one day's march.

Nothing can be more hideous than the country all the way, from the Douro to this place it is mostly a barren, rocky, or chocolate coloured heath for leagues in every direction, uninterrupted by a single house or thing of any description, you now & then see a flat table sort of a hill, or a grey church tower at a distance which just serves to destroy the fancy you might otherwise indulge of being at sea, or in a perfect flat & interminable desert; but as to a gentleman's house or a tree, you might as well look for them among the sands of Africa. The villages are obscure & miserable; the inhabitants, by nature the most wretched upon earth, rendered ten times

---

*   Major General Sir William Ponsonby's brigade consisted of the 5th Dragoon Guards and the 3rd and 4th Dragoons.

†   Palencia has numerous plazas, mostly dominated by Romanesque churches of gaunt white stone, but has nothing of real note.

‡   The Castile canal.

more so by the length of time their country has been the seat of war, & the heavy contributions continually exacted from them by the iron hand of power. One article composing the *few necessary's* of life was to be had in the highest perfection, & in my life I never met with any bread to be compared, either in quality or excellence, to that which is common in the provinces of Valladolid & Palencia. When you have said *that* you have said all. Not a morsel of any kind of vegetable, not a drop of milk, an egg, butter, & numerous other little comforts (whose value are seldom sufficiently estimated till you experience their want) could be procured for love or money. Our rations were our sole subsistence.

9th

Marched at six o'clock from Támara to Frómista one league. It had rained all night & continued until three o'clock this day accompanied by a cold wind. The 4th Division were marching off to our left at the same time we moved; and before we entered Frómista we saw the 1st Division for the first time about a mile from us, on their march. It appeared to us all by the clashing of so many columns which had been marching direct upon Burgos & which were now all going right shoulders forward at easy stages, that Lord Wellington no longer meditated attacking that fortress, but rather turning the position by a flank movement. Colonel Elley, Adjt. Genl. to the cavalry,* who I saw today, was also of the same opinion. The three regts were well put up at Frómista which is a large, straggling, but poor place. Our quarters very tolerable, & for the first time since I commenced this march I was invited by the *lady* of the house to partake of their *family* dinner! I had however peeped into the kitchen before hand, & not relishing appearances I declined the feast in favour of my *clean* bit of tough ox. The evening cleared up, but was cold, and I much longed for a good fire to pass it before.

10th

Marched at five o'clock for Villasandino, the rain of yesterday had made the roads very heavy & hard for the whole army. Three leagues from Frómista after passing through some of the most extensive vineyards I had yet seen we crossed the River Pisuerga at the village of [blank]† & entered Old Castille. At the end of at least two leagues further we arrived at Villasandino, where we found numbers of the neighbouring villagers assembled to get out of the way of the French, who were they said at that

---

* Lieutenant Colonel Sir John Elley served as assistant adjutant general to the cavalry throughout the Corunna campaign, Wellington's campaigns and at Waterloo.

† The regiment probably crossed the Pisuegra at Lantadilla.

moment plundering their house. Patroles from each regt were immediately sent out but returned before night without having been able to get near any of the marauders or do anything more than ascertain the truth of the peasant's reports.

11th

At seven o'clock the brigade proceeded, the 10th to Castellanos [de Castro] & the 18th with us to Olmillos [de Sasamon], where Hughes & I were comfortably accommodated at the casa's of the two curates. We were agreeably surprised at this place by the arrival of three mules laden with eggs going from Santander to Burgos, no doubt for the French altho' the muleteer denied it of course. At all events we eased him of his burthen considerably & lessened their supply. Eggs were the greatest luxury that *could be* procured in this country; they not only formed a pleasing variety in various shapes at dinner, but also made an excellent substitute for cream with our tea, well beat up in a basin. It was fully expected that we should have halted here all the next day, and we accordingly went comfortably to bed under that idea.

Near the village of Hormaza, they came up against a force in excess of 30,000 men commanded by General Reille. The position was a bad one, the cavalry being able to turn and surround it at ease, but because of a lack of sufficient infantry support they were able to extricate themselves with some loss.

12th

At one o'clock in the morning orders arrived for the brigade to assemble at four half way between Olmillos and Castellanos, we then marched on in the direction of Burgos. Soon after we had ascended the hill from our valley we met with Lord Worcester,* who had been stationed on the top of it with a regiment & who informed us that all the peasants told him the French were at Isar, the place we were going to. We proceeded about ½ a league further on a level barren heath when some of the terrified inhabitants came running to tell us that a considerable force, both cavalry & infantry were drawn up to dispute our passage into the village. Colonel Grant at the same time received orders to halt until Brig General Ponsonby's Brigade of Heavy Dragoons, the Light Brigade, composed of the 43rd, 52nd & 95th under Major Genl. C. Alten,† and Major Ross's

---

* Henry Marquess of Worcester was then a Lieutenant in the 10th Hussars but acting as an aide-de-camp to Wellington.

† Major General Count Charles Alten, a very experienced Hanoverian officer, commanded the Light Infantry Division.

troop of Horse artillery came up with us. We then advanced driving their videttes before us into the valley along the bottom of which four columns had previously retired & taking up a position on the high ground facing us. We then got ordered to halt & wait for Lord Wellington, who on his arrival immediately put us in motion again. The cavalry & artillery of the right column attacked & carried the hill in front of their position, the Hussar Brigade & Major Gardiner's artillery turned their left & drove them into a village on the road leading to Burgos where they were too strongly supported by columns of infantry to attempt following them. The cannonade on the right was briskly kept up but without doing much execution. A storm of thunder & rain half drowned us during the latter part of this business & we returned to the miserable village of Isar for the night, where I got possession of & slept most soundly in a broad trough.

Edwin makes no mention of the huge explosion that night by which the French destroyed the castle of Burgos and retreated. This allowed Wellington to continue onward, outflanking the French positions on the Ebro by again turning them to the north. He drove towards Vitoria where it was believed that King Joseph was concentrating his forces.

13th Sunday
Marched late in the day & encamped about 3 leagues off near the village of [blank]* where the 4th Division were stationed. I paid a visit to Edward in the evening.

14th
We were turned out this morning suddenly at ½ past two o'clock, & had a tedious march of 5 leagues, the Heavy Brigade, & Genl Alten's following us, to the village of Cernégula, low filthy houses, & most miserable people contained the Head quarters of half of the cavalry & three Genl officers. We were however most agreeably surprised by some country people bringing in the course of the evening more fresh butter & ripe cherrys than they could dispose of. An order arrived whilst we were sitting after dinner at Colonel Grant's for the army to pass the River Ebro the following day.

15th
Soon after daylight we moved forward, General Alten's Brigade in front & the heavys in the rear, to Puente-Arenas, over which, without seeing a

---

* Tale states that they halted at Huermeces, which would be likely.

symptom of a *foe*, we passed the Ebro & established our quarters at Horna, near Villarcayo. A few miles north of Cernégula the scene, which for many days had presented little besides barren heaths, sandy ill cultivated fields, or vineyards, changed suddenly as we descended into the valley of the Ebro, into one of the greatest richness. Corn, fruit, & cattle were everywhere in abundance; the houses had an appearance of cleanliness & comfort which was novel, & there were a few quintas in which much taste was displayed. Such a spot in any other country but Spain would be crowded with villas, & inhabitants as nothing can exceed its temptations & luxurys for persons who would be contented to live retired from the world. The difficulty of access to it for any other animal than a mule is its only misfortune, & to which I conclude is to be attributed the ignorance we had all lived in of its unique, its indescribable beauty. The descent into the valley was down two miles of road cut through solid rock & steeper than any I had ever attempted to lead a horse down before; the way out was also cut through rock but at the bottom of it, & close along the bank of the river, which for miles is overhung with the most exalted & terrific looking crags I should think in the world, & what added much to their beauty was their being clothed with box myrtle, & other evergreens almost to their summits, the base & sides thickly wooded with magnificent oak & chestnuts. The valley is about two miles wide where we crossed, & as it takes a winding direction I am ignorant of its extent, but I am unable to give any adequate idea of the beauty and sublimity of this pass. The exclamations of wonder and admiration that it drew from the least observing of the soldiers as they passed through it, and which are so seldom excited by scenes of natural beauty, will perhaps say more in its favour than the most eloquent writer could. The Ebro in this part is rapid & narrow, and by no means a large river, although from its depth of channel & rugged sides difficult to cross excepting by the bridge.

16th

Marched to Medina [de Pomar] where we were desired to wait for orders. When they arrived it was only for us to go a mile & half further & encamp near the village of Torme, the whole of the inhabitants of which had fled to the mountains on hearing of our approach. We this day crossed the River Nela at Trueva, on the latter of which is situated Medina, rather a handsome town, but destitute of any of the necessarys of life which the people *said* had all been carried off by the French commissarys. They had also carried away two priests as hostages for receiving correct information of our movements, a capital plan this, as the priests are the only people who have any intelligence, any authority, or who have any thing to lose; to say nothing of their well known plan being worked upon by a repayment exhibition of a latter, or some such little persuasive argument against their giving false intelligence.

17th

The Heavy Brigade & ours proceeded 4 leagues & encamped near [San] Llorente at the skirt of a beautiful wood which extends for miles along the sides of a hill crowned with bare crags. I walked up there in the afternoon & saw many eagles, one of which came within shot of me.

18th

Marched in the same order to another bivouack in some cornfields where there was neither shelter of any kind for man or beast. I took possession of a loft in the adjoining village of Berberana, the ground being too wet from the quantity of rain falling before we arrived at it to have any comfort in a tent. From this ground we saw the Light & Fourth Divisions engaged with the advanced posts of the enemy which ended in the latter being driven into the pass of Subijana [de Morillos].

19th

Proceeded to, & encamped near Subijana, where Lord Wellington soon afterwards established his Hd Qtrs. The same divisions of infantry again engaged & drove the French towards Vitoria, near which we were informed they had taken up a position. The pass of Subijana through which runs the River Zadorra is one of the most picturesque, next to that of Puente-Arenas, I ever saw.

20th

Yesterday & today were cold, wet & uncomfortable. I was employed most of the morning in writing letters & in regimental duties. I dined early, & the evening clearing up I took a solitary ramble among the rocks & cascades of this whimsical spot. Ld. Wellington reconnoitred the French position, & it was whispered in the evening that he meant to attack them in the morning. Went to my downy couch betimes, that I might be fresh for the expected fight.

The rumours were correct. Joseph had decided to stand near Vitoria to gain time for the reinforcements under General Clausel* to arrive and to give time for his enormous train of treasure to gain French soil. Joseph was taking a calculated risk as his army only numbered 57,000 against Wellington's 75,000. Wellington

---

* General Bertrand, Comte de Clausel.

believed that the French position was fundamentally flawed and noted that several of the bridges over the River Zadorra were not defended. With Hill pushing back the French left, followed by a major assault on their centre, Wellington planned to pin down the whole French force while Graham led another wide flanking movement designed to descend on their right flank and rear, cutting off all escape. The undulating ground would make it difficult for cavalry and they were generally held in reserve. The hussar brigade was split, the 10th and 18th forming in rear of the 4th Division at Nanclares while Edwin with the 15th were attached to the Light Division originally near the village and bridge of Villodas but were moved with Kempt's brigade to the vicinity of Tres Puentes where the bridge was reportedly unguarded. The 15th were largely spectators to the battle, even when they crossed the bridge in single file with Kempt's brigade and formed on the French bank. It was a hard-fought infantry and artillery duel, with both sides contesting for every inch until Graham's force began to cut their lines of communication and the French realised that they were close to being trapped. The French army began to retire rapidly and with a little more pressure Wellington could turn a defeat into a rout; it was the perfect moment for the cavalry.

21st

In the dead of the night orders were issued to the different divisions of infantry & brigades of cavalry to march from their respective camps so as to arrive in front of the enemy's army soon after daylight. The Hussar Brigade, Heavy Brigade, 4th & Light Divisions, & two troops of horse artillery proceeded along the road to Vitoria; Genl Hill's column took a road a few miles on our right; and Sir Thos Graham was detached with the remainder of the army on our left to turn the enemy's right flank. When we had arrived within about two miles of the French lines Ld. Wellington passed by & halted us until Genl. Hill had gained a height on our right, where the action soon afterwards commenced by the skirmishers of the infantry driving those of the French out of a wood & along the top of the hill. The engagement became general towards two o'clock, & before five, Sir Thos. Graham having turned the enemy's right, they abandoned all their positions one after the other, & fled in confusion through & round the town of Vitoria. The 15th having followed them across the meadows intersected with ditches round the left of the town, came up with, & charged large bodies of both cavalry & infantry, killing & taking about a thousand prisoners, the remainder of the brigade having unfortunately been directed to go through Vitoria did not arrive in time to support the 15th who were consequently under the necessity of contenting themselves with victory & abandoning many of the prisoners taken. Part of the 10th & 18th soon afterwards coming up we continued the pursuit and captured the whole of the baggage publick & private; the military chest, & most of King Joseph's treasures. After following them up about a league on the road leading to Pamplona night came on and we got into a wood near a village happy enough to lay down & sleep off the fatigues of the day. We had been full sixteen hours on horseback with little enough to eat or drink the whole time; the day had been extremely hot, the night became cold & wet, & yet none of us suffered from either.

Here a large gap is left in Edwin's journal; presumably he planned to add further information to his initial entry at a later date, but never did so. Oman is silent as to the movements of the 15th at this period of the battle, merely mentioning the 10th and part of the 18th charging through the town; this is probably because he does not appear to have seen William's or Edwin's journals while writing his great history. Edwin's description is limited, but actually added to William's, gives quite a lot of information about the regiment's role at this period. The 18th and 10th, it will be remembered, were attached to the 4th Division and when ordered to charge and rout the enemy, their commanders took the strange decision to advance through the city of Vitoria instead of passing round it to the north, as an attack upon Didgeon's already depleted and demoralised cavalry would have greatly eased the pressure on Graham's force. The streets of Vitoria were congested with innumerable wagons and fleeing troops and it is not surprising that these regiments only emerged slowly and in straggling groups, with many, particularly of the 18th, failing to appear at all having taken to looting. Those that did emerge found themselves facing formed squadrons of French cavalry which threw them back; however, with this force of cavalry eventually retiring, some of the 10th and 18th did launch an attack upon the mass of vehicles of the artillery park and baggage which was striving vainly to flee from the battle and nearly captured King Joseph; but it seems that the regiments proceeded no further, the lure of plunder being too great.*

In stark comparison, the 15th emerged with honour intact. Edwin led the regiment forward at about the same time, but led his regiment to the north of the city from which position he could launch his attack against the fleeing throng. This movement was made tricky by the numerous deep ditches and embankments dividing up this plain and the regiment did lose some cohesion. However, nearing the fleeing mass, Edwin immediately launched the regiment against some formed units of infantry which they completely overran. Not all of these infantry were harmed, however, and many rose to fire on the 15th from the

---

* For unequivocal evidence as to the failure of the 18th particularly to maintain their regiment in any form of order, I refer the reader to the telling comments of several officers of the regiment quoted on pages 103–8 of Eric Hunt's *Charging against Napoleon*.

rear, requiring a few men to return to dispatch these niggling pests. Formed cavalry now made its appearance and the 15th hurriedly reformed to face this new threat, but were forced back due to a lack of any support. This impasse remained until these troops retired, the regiment then proceeded forward again at speed (William describes it as '*a la cossaque*') cutting off much of the baggage and many prisoners with the aid of the remnants of the 10th and 18th, but Edwin placed guards over the baggage and the 15th continued onward without stopping for plunder until some four miles from the battlefield, when darkness forced them to cease the chase just beyond Argomaiz and to encamp for the night. In his journal the brigade major recorded that 'The 18th Regt behaved ill, did not charge home & remained to plunder.' Reports were soon circulating in England regarding the failure of the 18th and it is indeed telling that although many cavalry regiments were awarded Vitoria as a battle honour, some of whom took very little part in the battle at all, the 18th were made conspicuous by their not being awarded the honour.

The regimental records of the 15th state that a general officer was wounded and captured by Private Mesham of I troop, and a colonel, several officers and 130 men and a standard were also captured. As Edwin says, lack of supporting troops meant that many of the prisoners initially captured were able to escape in the confusion; indeed both Thackwell and William agree that, with support, literally thousands of prisoners could have been secured.

The losses of the 15th were fifteen rank-and-file killed,* Captains Hancox and Thackwell, Lieutenant Finch,† one sergeant and forty-three men wounded, with twenty-four horses killed or lost and twenty wounded.‡ Colonel Colquhoun Grant as commander of the brigade and Major Edwin Griffith as commander of the 15th duly received a gold medal for this action.

22nd
I went this morning into the adjoining village§ to see General Anson¶

---

* Some of those killed were Corporal Ward, Privates Scott, Newman, Stanley, Ford, Rose, Mitchener, Cox, Leahey, Gillies, Lawrence, Johnson, Chapman and Loncely; who the others were is not clear.

† Captain Thackwell received a very severe contusion from a blow with a sword-hilt but was not named as wounded on the return. Lieutenant the Honourable John Finch became a captain in the 37th Foot in 1814. He eventually rose to lieutenant general and died at Dover in 1861. There are no details of Captain Skinner Hancox's wound.

‡ As is often the case, the regimental figures are at variance with the official return quoted by Wellington; this quotes ten rank-and-file and eight horses killed, one captain, one lieutenant, one sergeant, forty-six rank-and-file and sixteen horses wounded.

§ The village of Argomaiz.

¶ Major General George Anson commanded a cavalry brigade consisting of the 11th, 12th and 16th Light Dragoons.

which was the first opportunity I had of so doing. At ten o'clock, the brigade, under Sir Robert Hill,* marched to Salvatierra [o Agurain] near which the whole bivouacked in a miserable situation, no wood or water nearer than the town, & no shelter from the torments of rain that continued falling the whole day.† The province of Biscay, which we had entered on our march to Berberana on the 18th, is picturesque, but like other mountainous countrys, poor, & subject to bad weather & the boasted face of fine Biscayans I should pronounce to be, both in appearance & manners, as uncouth a gentry as any in the world, particularly the women who seem to try to make themselves ridiculous by the immense quantity of thick yellow worsted petticoats they tie on tight round their hips & reaching very little below the knee, tawdry coloured stockings with very high healed wooden shoes. Some other kind of coloured stays; mens shirts; & the whole of their hair, which is *never cut*, plaited back, & in some, reaching down almost to the ground in one huge greasy tail.

The unseasonable weather began to take a severe toll, particularly upon the cavalry. However, it was clear from the debris that they left in their trail that it was also affecting the French badly.

23rd

Continued our march after the French as soon as it was light. The rain had made the roads very bad, as there was a division of infantry, with its baggage before us we got on very little more than a mile an hour. At Ziordia we passed the river Arakil by a ford, the enemy having blown up the bridge, & entered the province of Navarre. A little before dark we arrived at & got into the village of Bakaiku, drenched to the skin, & covered with mud. This day's march did us much more harm than the Battle of Vitoria; many men & horses sunk under the fatigues & miserys of the roads & weather.

24th

We remained the whole of this day in our quarters, & a most seasonable

---

* Lieutenant Colonel Sir Robert Chambre Hill commanded a cavalry brigade consisting of two squadrons each of the 1st and 2nd Life Guards and the Horse Guards.

† Wellington has been criticised for not completing his victory by chasing the French hard. Although one has to allow for the very poor weather; this short march, which was clearly completed at a leisurely pace, and the following days of rest, or crawling along behind the infantry, clearly shows that the French were allowed to escape too easily. The cavalry had generally seen little or no action the previous day and no one can claim exhaustion as an excuse for such a lacklustre pursuit.

halt it was for us, as altho' thunder storms prevailed the whole day, the occasional gleams of sunshine dried our cloaks & blankets & renovated our appearance altogether.

Edwin does not mention the fact, but while at Bakaiku the 18th were forced to deliver up all of their plunder. Major Hughes states that he collected about £2,600 in coinage, not including the jewels and fine clothes from the regiment.

25th

Marched at daylight, passed Sir Thos Picton's Division at Irurtzun & halted at night at a little village Odieta, about a league from Pamplona of which we had a fine view, & saw French picquets posted round the town. Joseph Bonaparte and his army had all left it with the exception of a garrison to defend the town against our entrance, & taken the road, as we understood, for France. A priest in our village told us that he had a relation in Pamplona from whom *His Majesty* had *borrowed* some linen, & other articles, having lost the *whole* of his baggage at the Battle of Vitoria. Our pursuit of the French ended here, having followed them rather more than 12 leagues, great part of which was strewed [*sic*] with carcases of men & beasts, and all kinds of arms & accoutrements.

On this day Wellington summoned Grant to his quarters to express in the strongest terms his opinion of the 18th at Vitoria and 'desired' him to 'state his opinion of their conduct to the officers in the plainest manner' and that they could have captured Joseph 'at the time the 15th charged so gallantly on the left of the town'.* Just as it seemed that the regiment would now get some rest, as the Pyrenees mountains were no place for cavalry, they were ordered to proceed by forced marches in an attempt to destroy Clausel's force which had arrived near to Vitoria unaware of the battle that had occurred and was now retreating as fast as possible. The 15th led the pursuit.

26th

It having been ascertained that the French army had fled in small divisions towards the Pyrenees, where it was in vain following them, we had flattered ourselves with the hopes of being allowed a little repose before Pamplona, for the purpose of recruiting our strength, shoeing up our horses, and renovating the worn out boots and overalls of our men who had never had them off but for the purpose of cleaning since the affair before Burgos. Great therefore was our rage at being ordered suddenly this morning to

---

* Mollo (1997), page 132.

march in the direction of Tudela, Ld. Wellington having received information of a corps of 12 or 14,000 men being in the neighbourhood of that place on its retreat, after having attempted to form a junction with Joseph's army at Vitoria. The Heavy Brigade, 4th & Light Divisions are ordered to follow us. We marched almost the whole day, and as the 15th was the leading regt I was sent to the front and got well put up at the village of Barásoain for the night.

The brigade major recorded in his journal that Captain Booth and Lieutenants Mansfield,* Finch and Barrett 'had disgraced themselves by participating in the plunder which had been taken on the day of Vitoria & were ordered to give it up forthwith'.

27th Sunday

As soon as the other part of the brigade came up we continued our march to Tafalla one league & half where in consequence of the infantry being a good way in our rear we halted, and were just making ourselves comfortable in the best quarters we had occupied since our entrance to Spain, when orders arrived for us to turn out immediately as Ld Wellington intended establishing his Hd Quarters there. We accordingly got under weigh as quick as we could & marched to Olite, a very nice little town, though not so good as Tafalla, where we again all got under cover. The difference of climate in Navarre to that of Biscay was very striking, particularly in this part, where we found the people in the midst of their corn harvest, and plenty of ripe fruit; apricots, plums, & cherrys in quantities.

The welcome at Tafalla was particularly warm and the locals plied the troops with drink, in fact it is recorded that 'three fourths' of the 10th were 'rolling on their horses, quite drunk'. Twelve of the worst were instantly selected and punished as an example.

28th

Marched at six along the beautiful road leading from Pamplona to Tudela. On our arrival at the bridge of Caparroso upon the River Aragon we were halted until the return of some staff officers who had been sent to reconnoitre Tudela. They returned about four o'clock; with the information of the French having quitted it that morning at ten o'clock, & taken the road to Zaragoza. We then crossed the Aragon & Genl

---

* Lieutenant Ralph Mansfield was aide-de-camp to Colonel Grant. He became a captain in 1817 and retired by the sale of his commission in 1818. He died in 1854.

Ponsonby having assumed the command of both brigades, halted us about 3 leagues further in a wood, near the village of Carcastillo, which was occupied by the 15th, we being the leading regt. The divisions of infantry ordered with us, halted at Cáseda where Hd Qtrs were also established.

It was now clear that Clausel had managed to escape; pursuit was of no further use.

29th

Was a day of repose to us all; much wanted on account of the horses being shod and the appointments put a little to rights. We also finished our muster this morning.

30th

Orders arrived for the cavalry to return the road we had come; the Heavy Brigade to occupy Tafalla, & the hussars Olite. This was rather expected by us, Genl Clausel having executed his junction with Suchet,* & retired towards Catalonia where it would have been impolitic to follow them until something was decided about Pamplona. We accordingly marched at six o'clock, recrossed the Aragon, & before two, had again taken possession of my comfortable quarters at Olite.

Wellington was now faced with the problem of holding the line of the Pyrenees while taking care of the last two great bastions of French control in Spain. He decided to blockade Pamplona with his Spanish troops while he invested the fortress of San Sebastian on the coast. The cavalry were of little use in these proceedings and were sent into cantonments to rest and recuperate around Olite where they could cover Pamplona.

July 1st

Employed myself almost the whole day in writing letters, and refitting my kit which was getting the worse for wear.

2nd

Sat as president of a Brigade Court Martial, & rode afterwards.

3rd

Finished the proceedings of the court martial.† Rode afterwards to Tafalla

---

* Marshal Louis-Gabriel Suchet, Duc d'Albufera, commanded the French army in eastern Spain where he had enjoyed a great deal of success.

† Private Russell was charged with striking Captain James Hughes, 18th Hussars, when he attempted to prevent Russell from assaulting a woman.

Spain Again

& called upon Sir Stapleton Cotton* who had just arrived at that place from Hd. Qtrs.

With the return of Sir Stapleton Cotton, everyone had to step down one position. This meant that temporarily the most junior colonel had to lose his brigade; this was Colquhoun Grant who had to lose it in place of Lord Edward Somerset† and he duly sailed for home. Grant did not have to wait long before returning, however, being appointed to Long's Brigade on 6 September. In the orders of 2 July the 18th Hussars were to join the brigade of Victor Alten but it seems that the 18th did not transfer until 14 September. Edwin had the pleasure of dining that evening with his new commanders.

4th Sunday
Wrote letters in the morning, dined with General Cotton, met Lord E Somerset & Charles Manners,‡ Colonel Elley &c &c.

5th
Lord Edward Somerset took the command of the brigade, & saw us in watering order.

6th
Colonel Grant took his departure for England.

The regiment was now settled for a reasonable period and Edwin made time to make some observations. He wrote his thoughts on the evening soirees put on by his fellow officers, he betrayed his farming background with minute descriptions of the local agricultural techniques and ruminated on whether the war in Spain was really worth it; for, as he readily admitted, given a couple of years in charge, the French would soon have sorted Spain's problems out!

7th
Sir Stapleton inspected the 18th in service order, which I attended, & spent the remainder of the day in writing letters, &c. Lord Worcester gave a hop in the evening, being his second. The company upon these occasions was not very select, and the variety of figures which presented themselves,

---

* Lieutenant General Sir Stapleton Cotton had returned to England to recuperate after being wounded at Salamanca in 1812. He now returned to the army and resumed command of all the cavalry.

† Major General Lord R. Edward H. Somerset had already served much of the Peninsular War as a very successful cavalry officer.

‡ Lieutenant Colonel Lord Charles S. Manners commanding the 3rd Dragoons.

together with the little gallantrys that passed between the sexes were highly amusing. The natives of this place & Tafalla, and indeed the whole of Navarre that we had seen, are an enlightened & active race. The men are tall, athletick & comely; the women are brunettes, generally pretty, cleanly in their persons & have remarkably fine hair of a dark colour, which is all combed back, & worn in a thick plait reaching half way to the ground & finished with a knot of ribbon. The neatness of the women of Navarre reconciled me to this fashion of wearing the hair, which I had disliked so much in the Biscayans. We seldom or ever saw anything of the description of a gentleman or man of fortunes, but on the other hand, instances of extreme poverty were alike uncommon. Most of the land is cultivated with corn or vines, & the produce is sufficient to make everybody comfortable. They were at this time in the midst of their corn harvest, and it surprised me to see how very few implements they used besides the scraping hook. A spot of ground about the size of a bowling green is flattened, wetted & baked by the sun till it is as hard as a barn floor; on this the corn is carried in sheaves & scattered about, knee deep. Three or four mules, with heavy flat boards full of iron studs, tied to them, are then introduced, a man stands in the centre with a string in one hand and a long whip in the other, with which he keeps them in a jog trot until the grain is all beat or trod out, & the straw broken into short pieces, this is all chucked away by a forky branch of a tree & the grain is passed from one cloth to another for the wind to rid it of so much dust & dirt as it can, & it is then carried in bags to the granarys. The straw is collected as forage for the mules in the winter, & as the whole is got in as I have described, stacks are never seen. Hay they don't understand in most parts of Spain; & where they do make it, it is of a very inferior quality. The people apprised me that before the invasion of the French the cheapness of provisions in Navarre was beyond belief, but that now they were as ill off as their neighbours; this was the usual outcry; whenever the want of anything was felt, the misfortune was always laid to the account of the *French*, in which notion it was *politick* to give the most decided connivance and encouragement. *My* private opinion however is, that the French having possession of the country for a few years would make it one of the finest upon earth. They would establish a wise government, enforce salutary laws, suppress convents & inquisition, and receive a people, by nature high minded & enlightened, from the miserable effects of a religious despotism with which they have long been borne down. A Spaniard has such reverence for his ancient customs, that it would be next to impossible to convince them that change of any sort could be for their improvement in happiness, but at the same time every candid & impartial man must allow that England is at this moment, & has been for years wasting her blood & treasure for the avowed purpose of securing to them the same government & laws under whose authority they have already sunk, below the standard of every other European nation, & consequently inflicting the greatest curse that we well could, under the profession of unalterable friendship.

There is no entry for the 8 July except the word 'Rien', which is of course French for 'nothing'. However the next day the regiment was inspected by Sir Stapleton and Edwin was pleased to record that everything went well.

9th

Sir Stapleton Cotton inspected the Tenth & Fifteenth in service order, & expressed himself highly satisfied with the appearance of both in every respect. I dined with our new-brigadier, Ld. Edward Somerset.

There is a long break in the journal which is strange as it soon became evident that Olite was a dangerous town. The local Spanish men seem to have taken great exception to the amorous hussars and even a smile for a beautiful young lady was sufficient to cause great offence. The problems started on the night of 9 July, when the body of Private Wilks of the 15th was discovered near the south gate; he had been murdered, his brains knocked out and his mouth stuffed full of rags. Two days later an artilleryman of Gardiner's troop and Bansdman McNorton of the 18th Hussars were found dead, the latter buried in a wood. On 12 July brigade orders stated that no man was to leave his quarters without his side arms. The attacks continued, however.

During this period Edwin often dined with his fellow Welshman, Major Hughes of the 18th Hussars and he did write a letter to his old friend Major Edward Hodge of the 7th Hussars who was stationed in England,* particularly airing his grievances over the actions of the 18th at Vitoria.

Olite in Navarre July 21st 1813

Dear Hodge

I am quite ashamed at myself for never having answered your letter of the 28th April before now, but really from the time I rec'd it to the first of this month, a few lines occasionally to my old mother was all I could find opportunity to write. The newspapers will have given you so much better an account of our proceedings here than I can, that I shall confine myself merely to the enquiries contained in your letter, which is spread open before me. In the first place the great Colquhoun will answer his part in person, if you should feel inclined to visit the corner of Duke St,

---

* This letter was kindly brought to my attention by Eric Hunt.

Grosvenor Sq. He left us most decidedly in the — though I am sure secretly pleased at having so good an excuse to return to his Marcia again.* It was however a very awkward moment to supersede him in the command of the brigade which he'd had ever since we landed. Lord Edward Somerset, our new Brigadier, is a perfect gentleman, and it is wonderful how completely reconciled I am to the change. The 18th I am happy to say no longer form part of our Hussar Brigade, but are removed to Alfaro; they are a very loose lot, to say the least of them. Had they behaved as they ought at Vitoria we should have all shone in the Gazette upon that occasion but by their stopping by dozens to plunder in the town instead of pushing through to support the 15th, we were placed in a most critical situation surrounded by five times our numbers, and that we were not annihilated I attribute solely to the good countenance the regt put on upon the occasion. Ld. Wellington has threatened to dismount them and send them home the next time he has any fault to find with them. I don't think Grant was quite justifiable in ordering us to charge till he had a support at hand; but however the thing is over & there is no use in talking. If you should come out to this cursed country again,† which heaven avert the necessity for, I should recommend you bringing horses in preference to mares; a good canteen; a light tent, and a bed called a stretcher. A couple of small kegs full of brandy to throw across a mule are a great comfort, your kit should be small but good and don't spare expense in getting every thing of the best; it is in the end most economical. Above all bring out a good lot of cash, or letters of credit, as you pay for every article now. We are in a very good town; Tafalla, Sir Stapleton's Hd Qtrs is four miles from us, & I suppose we shall remain in our present state of inactivity until the French attempt to relieve Pamplona,‡ or Suchet makes a run for France. He has I believe 30,000 men at, & near Tortosa. Our nags have picked up their [croups?] famously within the last fortnight, ripe oats in the ear, & grains our forage and it agrees with them. We have never been in want of anything except bread for two or three days just before the Battle of Vitoria. If we are to winter in Spain I hope it will be on the line, or north of the Ebro. The country, towns, & natives are very superior to any other parts of the peninsula that I have seen. I however hope that affairs in the north will enable Ld. W. to expel the French this year, put the passes of

---

* Marcia was the wife of Sir Colquhoun Grant.
† The advice would have been of use as 7th Hussars were to land in Spain in September 1813.
‡ Edwin was quite correct, within the week he would be rushing to help stop Soult's advance close to Pamplona.

the Pyrenees into the hands of the patriots, & then bid them a tender and eternal farewell. Everybody is sick of the war here, & certainly if we do not get out of it this year with éclat, when in the name of God shall we? I hear you made a brilliant review the other day; so did we before Sir S. Cotton: is it not odd that the 10th, 15th & 18th should so long have been, & continue to be commanded by the junior Majors of each. Col. Murray's horse fell with him* in fording the Esla & bruised his knee so badly that we have seen nothing of him since, & Col Quentin† has not yet made his appearance. Our large sad chacos [sic] have been in wear ever since we left Lisbon: they are heavy, hideous, unbecoming, unserviceable, villainous affairs altogether. The tenth have not got theirs yet, but the regt looks very well in the old worn out black ones. We still muster between 50 & 60 file a squadron which is rather stronger than most other brigades. The portable [furnaces?] are good contrivances. You do not mention Mrs Hodge; I hope she is well, and that I shall not be presuming too far if I said to be remembered to her. My paper is full so adieu; whenever you have time & inclination, a letter full of home news will be a treat & pray tell me what our august Colonel is supposed to be about? Yours ever very sincerely

Edwin Griffith

Genl. Cotton for tells me you are moved from London but does not know where to, so I must direct this to the care of the agents.

The men now became tired of their enforced rest period and the 'nest of assassins', but all was due to change. On 1 July Napoleon removed Joseph and placed Marshal Soult in charge of the 'Army of Spain'. Soult did not waste any time; he was present with the army by the 12 July and having rapidly supplied the troops with equipment and rations, he launched a massive attack on the Pyrenees passes, with the ultimate aim of relieving Pamplona and forcing Wellington's forces well beyond the Ebro. The British were forced out of the passes of Maya and Roncesvalles by vastly superior forces and they were forced slowly back over the next few days. Wellington was not aware of the attack until late on 25 July and although initially planning to halt the French at Zubiri, events overtook things and a concentration at Huarte was ordered. The order for the hussar

---

* Lieutenant Colonel the Honourable Henry Murray commanded the 18th Hussars in Spain; in his absence the regiment was commanded by Major James Hughes.
† Lieutenant Colonel George Quentin commanded the 10th Hussars in Spain, but in his absence sick in Hanover, the regiment was commanded by Major the Honourable Frederick Howard.

brigade to join was very much a surprise; arriving in the evening of 26 July and after hurried preparations the hussars marched at daylight. Having arrived near Pamplona the confusion was evident, nobody initially knowing what to do with the hussars, then conflicting orders arriving. Somerset rightly decided that Wellington's orders were paramount and moved his brigade into position in the rear of Picton's Division* but with darkness coming on they sought shelter. That night of violent thunderstorms and torrential rain was perversely greeted with great satisfaction by Wellington's men as a good omen; Wellington's great victories were often presaged by a violent storm.

27th

An order arrived yesterday evening for the brigade to march at daybreak towards Pamplona, & we accordingly set out from Olite at ½ past three o'clock. We had been stationary at that place exactly four weeks, leading monotonous lives, & I was not sorry to leave it; particularly as the inhabitants were growing gradually less civil, & made continual complaints against the commissary's not dealing fair with them in regard to the rations of corn & straw they were compelled to furnish to the troops. The people whose house I was billeted at were always very accommodating, but they had got rather too familiar, particularly their fat, loud talking daughter Fermina, who to say the teeth had become damned troublesome . . .

On our arriving within a league of Pamplona we observed some skirmishing upon a hill to the right of the town, & Lord Edward halted us near the aqueduct to wait for orders. The heat of the weather was intense & we laid the whole day in a broiling sun without a twig or anything to protect us from it. While in this situation many peasants passed us with their bundles making off for the mountains, the French being near they said, in great force. At length Sir S Cotton directed us to take possession of some villages near & put up as well as we could: but while we were going to them, counter orders overtook us from Ld Wellington, (who had just taken the command) for the brigade to advance and post itself on the road leading from Pamplona to Roncesvalles. We did so, & were placed in support of Sir Thos Picton's Division behind a rising ground which he occupied & kept the enemy in check who we observed in force upon the hills to the right & left of the Roncesvalles road; our artillery opened upon them but they were too far to do much execution. It was now getting dusk, & night came on suddenly in a most tremendous thunder storm which terminated the operations on both sides. We got into a miserable little village† but were

---

* General Sir Thomas Picton commanded the 3rd Division.
† Wylly states that the 15th found shelter in the village of Olaz, which Oman's map shows

happy enough to have some sort of shelter from the pelting of the pitiless storm, to the whole of which our poor infantry were necessarily exposed. The cause of our sudden move from Olite, which had been matters of surprise & speculation to us the whole day, was now accounted for.

Soult, who had assumed the command of the French army soon after its retreat from Vitoria, 'Congratulated them on their heroic behaviour on that memorable day; exerted himself to re-equip them with arms & ammunition, promised to lead them to fresh glories, & pointed to the fields of Pamplona as the ones in which they might insure it'. Inspired with confidence by the presence of their favourite general, & burning with desire to wipe off the stain their arms had received at Vitoria, five & forty thousand of them rushed with true exultation & impetuosity of their symbolical eagle down the pass of Roncesvalles, driving before them the small but gallant division under Sir Lowry Cole* unequal to the task of stemming so vast a torrent. Already had their multitudes passed the Pyrenees; already had their advanced guard gained the mouth of that defile where they were to debouch their strength, already had their leaders pledge been more than half realized, & the gilded vanes of Pamplona already glittered in their view. That goal where their toils were to cease, their labours to be rewarded, & their glory consummated, was within a short hour's march of their leading column, and they already grasped it as their own. Fools to miscalculate the genius of your opponent! To underrate the influence of that star where brilliancy has so often confounded & put to flight your long boasted invincible eagles! You vainly thought that our Wellington, engaged in the attack on San Sebastian, would never hear of your operations in time to thwart them. You plumed yourselves in the hopes that your success would be the first intimation he had of your designs, and under that important idea seemed to forget, that 'Achilles absent was Achilles still'. But he comes; our Wellington has arrived in your front, & your career is instantly checked!

The following day the hard-fought battle of Sorauren began and continued on and off for three days. Soult initially had gained local superiority of numbers and launched his attacks against Wellington's left and centre but failed to break through after very severe fighting. The hussars were stationed on the right wing with Picton's division, the 15th in the front line between two infantry regiments

---

to be situated one mile south of Huarte however this is unlikely as the regiment moved here on 30 July and from Edwin's statement, this would appear to be their first night there.

* General Sir Lowry Cole commanded the 4th Division.

and the 10th and 18th on the extreme right of the line. It was feared that an assault would be launched against this wing by Foy's troops* but it never materialised; Edwin was forced simply to sit astride his horse broiling in the intense heat for three long days and watching events unfold before him.

28th

We took up a position on a rising ground to the right of the whole army & watched the motions of the enemy all day. Their cavalry, unable to procure forage in the mountains filed down, in numbers about two thousand, & bivouacked on the other side of a rivulet opposite to us just out of cannon shot, a column of infantry accompanied them. The action on the hills above the Roncesvalles road opposite the left of our position was very lively. The French fought hard for the heights but were repulsed everywhere. I saw several of these contests with my glass, & even my naked eye plainly; particularly a volley, and short charge made by the 40th regt posted on the top of a hill, which instantly put to flight a large column of French who they had allowed to ascend till within a few yards before they shewed themselves. The echo of musketry & a few pieces of artillery among the mountains, with the occasional cheers of our brave infantry as they rushed to the charge, was interesting to a degree *not to be described*, but it thrilled to our very hearts. When night closed in, part of us retired to the little village & the remainder stayed on the ground. By the result of this days work it became apparent that the enemy would never attempt an attack upon *our* position in *front*, but our right flank was deemed not invulnerable & on that, the picquets & patrols were directed to be most on the alert.

29th

We were kept frying in the same position all this day again. The operations of the active posts of both armies were nearly the same as yesterday. Our arms were ever successful in defence or attack, but sufficient support had not yet collected to drive the French from their almost inaccessible mountains. A small column of infantry and some cavalry having been passed to their left this afternoon confirmed a great many of us in the idea that our right flank would certainly be attacked the following morning. I was detached with the 15th to a little village among the hills on our right† where we found all the inhabitants, who had not fled, in the greatest

---

* General de Division Maximilien Sebastien Foy, comte, had served in Spain with great distinction and had recently won the action at the pass of Maya.

† Almost certainly the village of Gorraiz.

dismay, the French being then they said in the act of surrounding the hill. I confess I did not feel very happy in this situation as it was one where infantry would have had a dreadful advantage over us had they come on. The arrival of Sir Stapleton Cotton however soon put me quite at ease again as he said they were going back, & that I might remain were [*sic*] I was until an hour before daybreak when the regt was again to take up the position we had just quitted.

30th

At two o'clock this morning we were on horseback, & a little before three had arrived on our old ground where a squadron of the 18th had been all night on picquet. The fires in the enemy's encampment were almost all extinguished, and most of their videttes had been withdrawn, a proof that they were either retiring, or concentrating their forces for attack. The latter was the prevailing opinion among our officers, & it was curious to hear the different assertions they made respecting the enemy's movements, which they said, they *plainly saw, & heard*. Every tree, & bush on the side of the valley opposite to us was in motion, the vineyards were columns of infantry, & the hedges squadrons of cavalry. In the midst of these *alarms* Sir Stapleton arrived on the ground, his ears were instantly assailed with the different reports: the guns had been unlimbered & the matches lighted. He only desired they might not fire till they could plainly see what they were about, & directing me to send an intelligent officer & file of men to patrole the front till they came in contact with the enemy, he galloped off to another part of the line. In the meantime day dawned apace, Capt Wodehouse,* who I had dispatched in the direction pointed out, returned in about half an hour, & reported that he had crossed the rivulet & pushed on as far as the nearest village, occupied by the French yesterday, but that he had neither heard or seen anything of them, & stated his belief that they were all off. The reddening east as it enabled us to distinguish objects strengthened this opinion; at length, sol shone forth in all his glory & confirmed the fact. I will not be hypocrite enough to say that I lamented this retreat of theirs, although I entertain not the slightest doubt that any attempt to turn our right would have ended only in their complete discomfiture & disgrace, and added a fresh lustre to the fame of the British cavalry. At the same time to have had any chance of success, the attack must have been made with a spirit & desperation that we'd have cost the lives of hundreds

---

* Captain Philip Wodehouse had joined 15th on 31 December 1811; he eventually became a major in 1st Life Guards and retired by sale of his commission in 1837. He died near Bewdley in 1846.

of brave fellows on both sides. At seven o'clock we were ordered into the village of Olaz, on the Pamplona road leading up the pass, & saw a short but smart skirmish on the hills to the left of it between the allies and the rear of an immense column of French infantry. About 12 o'clock they disappeared & we saw no more of them. Our baggage which had been sent to the rear came up to us this evening, & for the first time since we left Olite we got a clean comfortable meal, & went regularly to bed.

Eventually, on the third day, Soult was forced to abandon his position and return to France; the cavalry remained in the vicinity as this mountainous country was not suitable for them. Edwin was clearly appalled by the devastation left by the starving French troops, who had destroyed everything in their search for hidden food and treasure. Major Hughes, 18th Hussars, records that he visited Edwin on this day.

31st

The regt moved this morning into the village of Elcano (close to the spot where the French had encamped) and which they had made their usual example of; the houses were all gutted, the chests, cupboards, &c broken open & sifted of all their contents, even the flag stones were taken up, & parts of the walls pulled down in all the kitchens & cellars, in search of hidden treasure: the table drawers, & furniture were strewed in fragments all over the apartments: the bedsteads were broken, & the mattresses ripped up, their stuffing (the husks of Indian wheat) scattered upstairs & down, added not a little to the scene of havoc, confusion, & filth which a village lately abandoned by the French presents to view. A few of the wretched inhabitants crawled back to their homes in the course of this evening from their hiding places in the mountains, where they always seek refuge when the French approach their houses, choosing rather to abandon everything to their ruffian grasp than run the hazard of suffering personal violence for *withholding that* which they *have not to give*. The man whose house I am now writing in was caught before he had time to make off, & an immediate demand for money and provisions to a great amount was made upon him; he declared his inability to answer it, on which they threw him down, knelt upon him, took up the skin of his throat & cut it slightly with their knives, while another passed the point of one against his breast threatening him with instant death if he did not produce all he was worth, but their barbarity was not confined to the men alone, a beautiful girl of sixteen was robbed of all the few trinkets she possessed in the world, even to the rings which she had in her case & which they were so eager to get that they could hardly wait for her to take them out . When I saw her she had tied two little bits of black silk in her ears to prevent the holes growing up. Ruffians! Is such conduct characteristic of bravery? Is this a specimen of the boasted gallantry of the French nation?

Edwin rode to the battlefield and was horrified by the carnage, which caused him to wax lyrical on the cost to humanity of Napoleon's unbridled ambition. Like many others, he was clearly tiring of the senseless loss of life and longed for peace.

August 1st Sunday

Barrett & I dined early & rode up the hills where we had observed the fighting for the last two or three days. The spectacle was horrible, some English were employed in collecting the wounded & carrying them off but it was impossible to find them all in time to save their lives. Their limbs wounded & their nature exhausted, they laid for eight & forty hours, & some of them more, exposed to the cold damps of night, & the broiling heat of the sun by day, without a morcel [sic] of food to support their sinking frames, or a drop of water to moisten their feverish lips! Many had been released from their sufferings; the placidity of some of whose countenances evinced that they had welcomed death as their kindest friend, while others appeared to have struggled against him with the keenest anguish. The offensive effluvia with which the air was loaded, emitted from hundreds of carcases in every state of putrefaction, & which laid all round the wounded adding tenfold horrors to the miserys [sic] of their situation, was not the least disgusting part of the scene. One only consolation I received amid this scene of death & that was the circumstance of there being ten Frenchmen to one English or Portuguese. Not that I exulted in their deaths, forbid it humanity! Poor fellows! They were torn from their homes by the tyrant who governs them to fight the battles of ambition that he may have dominion over Spain whilst thousands bleed! 'What millions die that Caesar may be great'. Tyrant of France! The inscrutable decrees of providence have granted thee strength & power almost absolute over the nations of oppressed Europe; but beware the severe account you'll one day be called upon to render up. Repent in time the enormity you have been guilty of, think that the daily prayers, the hourly supplications of childless parents, helpless widows, & friendless orphans for heaven to avenge their wrongs, to curse the author of them, may yet arouse its vengeance! May suddenly hurl thee from thy exalted station in this world to the lowest in that which is to come, where the tears, the groans, the miserys, the want, torture, & despair, that you have caused, & beheld with indifference *here*, may *there* be accumulated & settled eternally upon thy devoted, thy detested head!

2nd

I rode this morning up the pass of Roncesvalles through the villages of Larrasoaina & Auritz, the ride is romantic & pretty being between hills & along the right bank of the River Arga; any pleasure that I should have had in exploring it was however defeated by the desolation which reigned in the valley, & by the stench of the dead bodies which laid in numbers by the road side & on the shoals in the river. Few peasants had as yet returned, & as the ground was hard & the bodies very offensive they had made no attempt at burying them but had covered them with straw & boughs & then set fire to the pile, and by half roasting them only, rendered them still more frightful and disgusting.

Edwin, however, had more reason than most to feel empty and depressed at the interminable warfare, death and destruction. He had received a letter from his brother-in-law announcing the loss of his mother, two years to the day after his father's death; 18 June was now to be a dreadful day of mourning for him and his sisters. Edwin was the sole surviving male descendant; however, the house was left jointly to him and his four sisters where they would remain under his protection.

Elcano near Pamplona, August 2nd 1813 [Marked 'Received at Rhual 8th September 1813']

My dearest Charlotte

Since the arrival of Morgan's letter of the 23rd of June you have never been out of my thoughts, for what misery can equal that of parting for ever with those whom we respect & love most dearly. Alas my dear girls this blow has deprived us of our only parent, & a most heart breaking one it is; but, we must bow with resignation to the will of heaven; and instead of feeling discontent, or mourning at its decrees let us rather acknowledge our gratitude, & bless its providence for having had the best & tenderest of fathers & mothers spared to us for so many years as ours have been: let us hope, that lives spent in the practise of piety, & virtue such as theirs, cannot fail to meet with it's reward hereafter! It is some consolation to know that her last moments were peaceful, and that she appeared quite unconcerned of the change that was about to take place; this I know must have saved her many a pang on your account from what she has repeatedly said to me since the death of my father.

I have now only to beg you will all continue to be good about writing to me, & thank Morgan particularly for his letter which I will answer soon; it was put into my hands on the morning of the 30th ult when the French army & ours were drawn up within cannon shot of each other. Since that time they are again driven back into the Pyrenees, where our infantry are gone in pursuit of them. The cavalry were not much engaged, & as we were only an incumbrance among the defiles in the mountains we were sent back to occupy the villages between them & the plain surrounding Pamplona. I hope my uncle will make some stay with you; my affectionate love to him & every other member of your society, which I wish to God it was in my power to join.

Pray do you & Cony make every exertion to preserve your health & spirits. The hope & pleasure with which I have always returned to visit our dear old mansion, is, I fear, henceforth at an end, but my affection for you both must ever remain unalterable: would that I had it in my power to give you a more substantial & acceptable proof of it than mere profession. I hope Nina is well: I always include her you know as a member of our family. Ever yours,

E. Griffith

Direct to me in Spain not Portugal till further orders

While the hussars lay quietly in their cantonments, Edwin seems to have taken to long solitary rides lost in his melancholy, but did not fail to observe the people and comment on their ways.

3rd

I took a solitary ramble up the hills behind Auritz, when the day being fine I was gratified by an extensive prospect over a wild ragged country quite up to the huge craggy Pyrenean rocks. In the course of the last two or three days most of the unhappy villagers returned to Elcano. The Spaniards & Portuguese are a strange race, at least to Englishmen, they appear particularly so. On reaching their homes & finding them in the state of dilapidation I have already described, they began crying, tearing their hair, & clasping their hands in agony, invoked every saint in their calendar to assist them for that were cried for ever! In the course of half an hour this transport of grief & despair had resolved itself into a deep moaning melancholy; a short time after that, you saw them beginning to examine into their losses & put things to rights again; before night they appear to have quite recovered their spirits; & the next day laugh, sing & bustle about again exactly as if nothing had happened! What a happy disposition this, compared to the surly, discontented one of *John Bull*; who if his yields somewhat less than he expected, or the tax gatherer calls for the pittance he is forced to pay towards the securing to *himself* blessings inestimable; grumbles & growls at the hardships imposed upon him & inveighs with bitterness against his sovereign, his minister, and everybody in the country who has the rank of gentleman.

Wellington, having concentrated his siege guns to take San Sebastian, did not have the resources to mount two sieges at the same time, therefore the garrison of Pamplona were to be starved out. The hussars were stationed here as a covering force for the Spanish forces blockading Pamplona, which operation had commenced on 30 June.

From the 4th to the tenth nothing particular occurred. I rode several times to the very pretty little town of Huarte, & Villava, the former of which had been Lord Wellington's Hd. Qtrs on our advance from Vitoria, & the latter during the more recent operations. They are on two rivers, the Arga and another, which unite a little below them; and are the first towns you see on the plain of Pamplona at the feet of the mountains forming the pass of Roncesvalles.

I visited the Spanish batterys, & troops, (posted for the purpose of pre-venting the garrison foraging round the town) often. The information I could collect from them respecting the place, particularly from an officer of infantry, a native of America, who of course spoke English well, was that they did not believe the garrison consisted of more than 9000 men,* commanded by the Count le Gazan (a mistake),† (the run away general from Vitoria),‡ but that if they had provisions enough, it was sufficient force to defend the place for an immense time. The town, they said, *might* be taken by storm, but the *citadel* never; & that even if we were in possession of the former, the guns of the latter (reckoned the strongest in Europe) would knock it about our ears & level every building with the ground before we could possibly reduce *it*. This information added to my own observations leads me almost to despair of Pamplona. I have rode all round it within 4 or 500 yards, for they never thought it worthwhile expending a charge of powder at an individual, and certainly according to my ideas of fortification nothing can be more complete, particularly on the south & west sides of the town. The numerous outworks, the moats, & drawbridges, secure it from the possibility of any surprise, the immense walls

---

* The French force blockaded within Pamplona was actually in the order of 3,600 men and eighty guns.
† Edwin was correct in noting that the Spanish were mistaken, the French force in Pamplona was actually commanded by General Cassan.
‡ General Honore Theodore Maxime Gazan, Comte de Peyriere, commanded the Army of Andalucia in the 1813 campaign. The British attack on the centre of Joseph's army at Vitoria was helped greatly by Gazan's failure to hold his section of the line with any conviction. As soon as his troops came under fire, he commenced to retire, forcing D'Erlon to his right to retreat also as he became outflanked. Gazan's losses were minimal and his retreat made Wellington's victory easier than it should have been.

& glacis with which it is surrounded seem to bid defiance to the heaviest ordnance. A partial firing was kept up all day, by the Spanish batterys throwing shells at the foragers on the outside of the walls, which was returned by a few 24 pounders at the batterys. The cathedral & other buildings in Pamplona give it a very imposing appearance and I'm told the inside of the town corresponds in every particular of beauty & regularity to the out. Much would I give on every account to see the English in quiet possession of the place; but, as I said before, it is an event that I totally despair of. The blockade is formed with Spanish troops only, under Genl. O'Donnell,* meanwhile the British extend from Roncesvalles in the direction of San Sebastian; near which place Lord Wellington has re-established his headquarters, & we hope to hear the next assault upon that place will be attended with better success than the last.†

Forage being scarce, the hussars were ordered back into southern Navarre, a move which the regiment must have viewed with some trepidation, but the population of Artajona proved to be much more friendly than those of Olite had been when they were last in this district and provisions, particularly fresh fruit, were in abundance and they spent an enjoyable sojourn here.

11th Wednesday

The brigade marched this morning, the 10th & 18th for Tafalla & Olite, the 15th for Artajona. We halted this day at the villages of Salinas [de Oro] & Esparatz from which latter place I climbed up a high & very steep hill, the top of which commands a prodigiously extensive prospect. I counted thirty six towns & villages exclusive of Pamplona with my naked eye & within a few miles of the foot of the hill. The Pyrenean crags 'whose heads kiss heaven', stretched eastward from the neighbourhood of St Jean Pied de Port, as far as the eye can carry. The view was closed in this direction by the hills of Aragon, & southwards by those which follow the course of the Ebro. The sun was intensely hot, and the country round although very much cultivated, had a parched & barren appearance without a tree to be seen anywhere.

12th

Continued our march to Artajona where we arrived at eleven o'clock, and

---

* General Joseph Henry O'Donnell, Count of La Bispal, an officer of Irish descent, commanded the Spanish force of 11,000 men blockading Pamplona.
† San Sebastian had been assaulted on 25 July but it had failed with heavy loss; the main reason for the failure appears to be that the breaches could only be reached having filed passed the flank of a hornwork which was intact and well garrisoned.

I got well put up at the alcalde's house among kind & civil people. Artajona is a large village; it stands at the foot, & on the side of a sugar loaf hill, on the top of which is the church, the ruins of a large castle, & some old houses. We have all excellent billets here, the men & women at each house vying with each other in attentions & civilities to the *good English*. From the hill you see Lerin, distant 2 leagues, Larraga and Mendigorría. Puente [la Reina] is 2 leagues, Estella 4, & Pamplona six.

August

We passed our time pleasantly at Artajona during the remainder of this month; but the weather was intensely hot, with tremendous thunder occasionally. The grapes were getting ripe fast now; & towards the end of the month were brought to market, with figs, peaches, apples, pears & other fruits in great abundance.

Edwin took time to write to his brother-in-law regarding the death of his mother and for the first time economic realities had come to the fore. Edwin was painfully aware that the family could not continue to live at Rhual and in his absence he looked to Morgan and Sir Alured Clarke to do the best for his sisters by obtaining a smaller property from the proceeds of the great house and lands. Clearly this was a decision of some magnitude for the family and Edwin indicates a small chance that his uncle might wish to purchase it, but his hopes were not to be fulfilled. With regard to the war, Edwin still feared that a reported increase of French forces would drive them back into Spain and the war would continue ad infinitum.

Artajona Aug 18th 1813

Your kind letter dearest Morgan containing the afflicting account of my poor dear mothers death, reached me on the 30th of last month five weeks after you had written it. I cannot say that I was quite unprepared for the event, as neither my sisters, or her own report of herself for some time past had been flattering, & the moment I saw your handwriting with a black seal, I felt quite certain what the contents were. I know she suffered anxiety on my account which must have done her injury, and had vainly hoped she would have derived comfort & satisfaction at hearing I had escaped the dangers at Vitoria. That letter dispatched from Olite on the 1st of July, & another on the 14th have I suppose found their way to Rhual ere this does. I wrote a hasty scrap to Edward immediately (and a letter to my poor Chats & Cony) as soon as I had time. I think much of them, and am most anxious to hear what my good uncle and you propose with regard to settling our affairs: Rhual of course must go, . . . I hope not quite out of the family, but at all events I shall be perfectly contented with whatever you

& he decide upon. I trust there are letters on their way to me, as Frederick in his of the 12th says you were expected the next day or two at Rhual, and that Sir Alured desired him to tell me he would write soon. Edward is well, having unfortunately been sent to the rear with sick & wounded the day before the severe action, which continued from the 28th until the 30th of July. Never were troops so fairly, so completely beaten as the French on these three days. It was all on the sides of the steep hills forming the pass of Roncesvalles, where of course the cavalry could not act, but we saw most of it; the echo of the musketry & artillery among the mountains, with the repeated cheers of our brave infantry as they rushed to the charge with the bayonet, cannot be described, but it was the most heart thrilling scene I ever witnessed. Our brigade, & between 2 & 3,000 of Soult's finest cavalry looked at each other across a deep ravine & rivulet for 48 hours, exchanging a few canon shots, but both positions bid defiance against the attack of an adversary. On the third day, after they had pillaged all the villages near them, and were starving for want of meat & forage, they easily filed back through the Pyrenees to the place from which they came.

We remained near Pamplona till the 12th when we marched here on account of forage. The blockade of that place is continued, but I fear it is a hopeless business. Edward who is near headquarters, and the coast, will give you a better account of the proceedings in that neighbourhood than I can. We are in anxiety about the affairs in the north as upon them depends our future welfare entirely. Should Bonaparte be able to send reinforcements of any magnitude to Soult, we must retire to the south of the Ebro again, if not further, and the war will be as near an end, as it was at the battle of Vimiera. Adieu for the moment, I don't know what your party consists of, but a thousand loves to all. Yours sincerely dear Morgan most affectionately

E. Griffith

Officers who commanded regiments at Vitoria are to have medals I hear; I wish they would give us a step by brevet instead, it would be more to my purpose.

September came with no move for the brigade as the blockade of Pamplona dragged on interminably. Unfortunately one officer of the 15th had caused serious ill feeling with the 18th Hussars regarding their showing at Vitoria. As Cornet George Woodberry* recorded in his diary for 5 September: 'Croker†

---

* Cornet George Woodberry, 18th Hussars, rose to lieutenant at Waterloo but left the army when the regiment disbanded in 1817.

† Captain Richard Hare Croker, 18th Hussars, served at Waterloo and was made a brevet

brought us some very unpleasant intelligence from England; nothing less than that the report of our disgrace having reached England and that rascal Captain Dundas [15th],* who Croker saw at Vitoria, told him the 18th regiment run away at Vitoria and that the 66th foot fired at us; what a villainous liar. A meeting of the officers will take place immediately and master Dundas will suffer for his falsehoods.' The outcome of this meeting is not recorded.

On 21 September Sergeant Victor George was appointed to the 1st Portuguese cavalry.

Edwin wrote to Sir Alured regarding the situation in Spain and his thoughts regarding Rhual.

Artajona, Sept 6th 1813

My dear uncle

Your very acceptable letter dated Aug 9th reached me yesterday, & as an English mail goes to H. Qtrs tomorrow from hence, I lose no time in replying to it. The affecting account of the death of my ever to be beloved & lamented mother was put into my hands on the 28th of July, whilst we were drawn up in battle array opposite to Soult's cavalry & exchanging shots with them across a ravine; & as we continued in this position until the evening of the 30th I had hardly time to contemplate the calamity & consequently was spared much of the anguish which a sudden circumstance of that nature never fails to create. I was not prepared for the event so soon but like yourself had observed how deeply the loss of my dearest father had affected her, & feared she could not have long without him. To dwell upon their virtues & endeavour to imitate their bright example is alas! all that we have now left. Their trials throughout life have been great but under all the adversities of fortune they supported themselves with dutiful resignation in the practise of every amicable and endearing quality and in a parental tenderness that never was, nor ever can be exceeded. God for ever bless them! With regard to poor old Rhual I see but one thing to do. For even supposing Charlotte & Caroline had the whole of the income from the estate, it would be I am sure barely sufficient to support the expense of living there, let alone all idea of improvement, repairs, which every thing in & about it want to a considerable extent, & the delay of which not only decreases its value daily

---

major for it. He went on half pay in 1820 but rose to colonel on the retired list and died at Leamington in 1854.

* Captain Thomas Dundas joined the 15th in August 1812; he became a major in the 3rd Ceylon Regiment in 1816 and went on half pay. He eventually became a major in the 32nd Foot and retired by the sale of his commission in 1839 and died in London in 1860.

but must eventually reduce it to perfect ruins. In addition to these, Harriet & Morgan have families of their own, ought to have their shares of the property paid, and although the latter from delicacy may not press the sale of it just at this moment, you may depend upon it he will ere long.

I am therefore clearly of opinion that however mortifying it may be, it ought to go in the interest of Charlotte's daughter, should make them to live comfortably in a small house, which they can not do there; and their residence, wherever it may be, I shall consider my home & feel bound to contribute as far as lays in my power to its comfort & prosperity. You desire my sentiments on the subject, & I have given them candidly. I wrote to thank Morgan for his letter of the 23rd June, and merely observed, that I should be most ready to enter into any arrangement that you & he thought advisable for the settlement of our affairs, and this I beg to report to you.

We are leading peaceable lives at present, & are likely to continue so as long as Ld. Wellington can carry on the war in the mountains. My command goes on prosperously, & I thank God I have not had an hours illness since I have been in the country. I received a long letter from Charlotte with yours, giving a good account of themselves, she does not say a syllable about Rhual. I have not time to answer her letter by this pacquet [*sic*] or to add more to this than that I am my dearest uncle ever yours with the truest affection.

Edwin Griffith

Between 4 and 8 September the regiment was joined by Lieutenant Byam,* Paymaster Cocksedge† and Veterinary Surgeon Dalwig.‡ Edwin did make a note in his journal regarding the Spanish festivals and how much he enjoyed dancing – and he seems to have had a dalliance.

The 8th of this month being the Nativity of the Virgin was a grand holiday, or as they call it in Spanish, *Dia de fiesta*. I attended high mass which was performed in a small but particularly beautiful chapel belonging to a convent near Artajona; after the service I stopped to hear some ladies play the organ in a gallery adjoining & opening into the nuns apartments where I met & became acquainted with Annita Sennar, a young lady who

---

* Lieutenant Edward Byam had only joined the 15th in April 1813; he eventually rose to lieutenant general and died in 1864.

† Paymaster James Coppin Cocksedge was appointed to his position in May 1813; he served at Waterloo but went on half pay in 1816 and died in 1820.

‡ Veterinary Surgeon Conrad Dalwig was appointed in April 1813 and served at Waterloo; he transferred to the 2nd Light Dragoons KGL and went on half pay in 1817.

had come with her father & mother from Mendigorria to pass the holidays at Artajona.

The nuns, nine in number, were, like all others I have ever seen in Spain or Portugal, cheerful old, & ugly; we remained with them half an hour & I walked back with my new friends the Sennars. The remainder of this holiday week was spent the morning in bull fights, & the evening in dancing; the latter amusement was always at my house, it being the best, & the people the first in the village. The display of beauty was very good, & we generally mustered from ten to twenty couple every night. The Spanish country dance is much prettier than ours; instead of scampering up & down the middle of a set, pulling & jostling everybody about as the English do with great exertion, the figures of their dances possess both meaning & elegance, they dance them in excellent time & particularly easy & gracefully. Between the country dances waltzes were performed; & two or three times boleros & fandangos in the true Castilian style & spirit.

It would seem that at least Captain Wodehouse proceeded to San Sebastian to see the storm on 31 August (he had two musket shots through his cap during the storm) and final capitulation of the garrison on 8 September and was the means of saving the lives and honour of the two daughters of a local hotelier. On 14 September the 18th Hussars were finally removed from the brigade to Alten's brigade.

This very pleasant sojourn at Artajona was unfortunately ended with orders to move, Edwin with the right squadron and Captain Booth's troop to nearby Larraga, the others to Berbinzana and Miranda de Arga, but the loss of Annita Sennar seems initially to have been amply made up for by Senorita Azcona!

15th

The regt marched to Larraga, a large village situated exactly in the same manner as Artajona, on the south side of a sugar loaf hill on the top of which are the ruins of a Moorish castle. Although this was only five miles from the other, the difference in the appearance & manners of the people was very striking and I regretted the change very much until I began to discover the many amiable & fascinating qualities of my new patrona, Donna Dominica Azcona, whose very superior manners & conversation made ample amends for everything I had left behind at Artajona. She was married, by her father's orders, at the early age of 15 to a man every way unworthy of her, merely because he was rich. In proportion as she was sensible, refined, open & engaging, he was ignorant, vulgar, stingy and ill tempered.

Under the heading of October Edwin discusses his relationship with Donna

Azcona and the realisation that his advances will for ever be rebuffed and he seems to have rekindled his passion for Annita Sennar. His description of Spanish wine-making is grotesque, but he clearly enjoys the results. Pamplona was reported to be close to capitulation, with reports that the garrison was now forced to the extremity of eating cats and dogs, therefore a move to the front was expected.

It is manifest that such opposite dispositions could never possess a cordial affection for each other; a confession which I established from her with some difficulty after several weeks acquaintance, as her excellent sense and high spirit would never have made voluntarily such an acknowledgement to a stranger. Her friends live in Estella of which she is a native, & having rec'd an invitation from her sister Pepita, when on a visit at Larraga, to come to their house in Estella, I availed myself of this opportunity of seeing that place. It is a singularly pretty town, well paved & clean, there is a very handsome square in the middle of it surrounded by a colonnade with good shops under it, & several other smaller ones where a good market is held. The River Arga runs in a semi circular direction round one side of the town, along the bank of which there is a fine hard gravel walk between two rows of stately elms about half a mile in extent. There are also two noble convents & gardens adjoining this walk which contain (I was told) some *pretty nuns*. I was sorry not to have time enough to visit them as all the nuns I had ever yet seen were old & by no means pretty. The whole place is enclosed by hills & very high perpendicular rocks covered with trees & shrubs, with several chapels & other buildings stuck in the most picturesque & beautiful situations imaginable. Altogether Estrella is better worth seeing than most towns in the north of Spain. The women are *very pretty*, which added to its other recommendations makes it a desirable residence!

In my rides from Larraga I also visited Puente de la Reina, which for cleanliness, regularity & beauty of situation, on the Arga is second to none. The richness of the soil, & excellence of the wine at Puente is remarkable; there are also some manufactories of cloth & paper as well as at Estella, which give these two places an appearance of activity and industry very unusual in a Spanish town. The very pretty village of Mendigorria also claims notice if it was only from the circumstance of its being the residence of the sweet Annita. This is also a great wine place, and as it was now the season for making it I had various opportunities of witnessing that most simple & dirty ceremony. The grapes are brought in panniers & thrown down upon a tile floor, where they are spread even, to the depth of 8 or 10 inches. A few great dirty peasants are then brought in, who pull off their shoes & stockings & tread the grapes a mash. They are then put into presses, & all the juice squeezed out which runs along the floor into a pit, or trough sunk for the purpose which the liquor is carried to the barrels which are of immense size; here it ferments a few days, after which they are stopped up, & opened again for use in three weeks or a month. The inattention to cleanliness throughout this operation is quite in character with other Spanish customs. The men who tread the grapes walk in & out through all kinds of filth without ever thinking of wiping their feet, & the husks are swept along with the dirt of the floor, by a broom, which perhaps a few minutes before has performed the same office in the stable; but they tell you that the fermentation carries off *all*. I saw but one sort of grape, or wine; & the flavour & excellence of it depends entirely I am told upon the soil of the vineyard. Towards the end of this month orders arrived for the brigade to hold itself in readiness to march the moment Pamplona surrendered & as that place had now been closely blockaded for four months it was expected to fall every day. We accordingly made every preparation for an advance.

Edwin wrote a rambling letter to his sister, which was received at Parkgate on 15 October 1813; he describes his hosts and clearly still held out hopes that Sir Alured would buy Rhual.

Larraga 28 September 1813

I have to thank you my dearest Chats for two fishy letters of Aug the 5th & 29th and am made very happy by your account of everything and every body but yourself. I suppose you are at this moment at Parkgate, and hope the change of scene & air will have a good effect upon that tiresome headache you complain of and keep early hours, be out in the air as much as possible, eat heartily, & if you can fancy roast mutton & pudding in preference to carrots & pyecrust, so much the better.

You need be under no apprehension of my starving as long as we remain in Navarre, indeed excepting for three days when we were without bread before the battle of Vitoria, we have never been distressed for food. At present we lead easy lives, and the natives are such civil & obliging people that I begin almost to like them. I am in an excellent house, this family consists of a young husband & wife & her sister who is an uncommon fine girl, and so fond of battledore and shuttlecock that I get worked to death by her, but in return improve daily in speaking Spanish which she does remarkably clearly & distinctly. Although they possess a charming house with a variety of apartments in it, they generally breakfast upon the staircase, little cups of chocolate being ranged along the banister. They do dine in a room, but the meal is a scrambling sort of business, never in this world did people understand comfort so little as the Spanish.

Spain Again

The vintage has just commenced a fine amusement I expect it will be. It is impossible to describe the beauty of the vines and the foliage is so fine, & the branches bend to the ground with the weight of their large purple bunches; this perhaps you may imagine, but it is difficult to fancy mounting your horse after breakfast & riding ten or fifteen miles straight around without being able to get out of the sight of grapes. What would we English men make of such a climate & soil? We have had some intensely hot weather with such thunder as I never heard before; but it is now pleasant again. My friend Colonel Grant has got a brigade of light dragoons, so that although he is still in this country we shall seldom come in contact again, & never on duty.*

I was amused at Mrs Hutton writing to ask whether I should benefit by Col Grant's death. Oh her soothings how artful it is, among all our toils & troubles. I am sending you a very stupid letter but I am always hurried from one at one thing to another and have so many people bothering me about different things, that it is well if I write sense for any length of time let alone entertainment.

I am amused the speedy termination of the tourists tour, Gladdaeth or its owner, had perhaps more influence on the fair Emma than the weather. I hope Harriet is very happy with her; but can't help thinking it a misfortune that there is not some sisterly affection between her & the Indians. My affectionate love to dear Maria wherever she may be. I am very happy to hear she is so well again her faithful services & attachment to our ever beloved father & mother (to make use of Caroline's words) can never be repaid as she deserves. God bless her! You promise to be very good about writing & will I hope keep it; I apologise that you occasionally for a moment occupy the thoughts of a pretty woman. How amply does a man think himself paid for ever of hardships & misery if nature beauty smiles & approves – but before I get too romantic and stupid I will quit this subject. How fortunate you & Conny are my dear Charlotte in having made such very valuable acquaintances (friends I ought rather to say) as Sir Thos & Lady Hesketh seem to be; I quite rejoice in the prospect of their poor boy's recovery after all the anxiety they have suffered on his account. & hope some day or other to have the pleasure of offering my congratulations in person. Pray continue to mention them whenever you write.

Wednesday Sept 29th – this far I had written yesterday when my Sompery senorita insisted upon my leaving off & I knew it was in vain arguing the point. This morning I received Cony's letter begun at G[olden]

---

* Grant succeeded Long in command of a cavalry brigade consisting of 9th and 13th Light Dragoons but this appointment was very short-lived.

G[rove] on the 4th & ended at Rhual on the 7th inst for which I thank her very much & will not fail answering it in a shorter time than she took to answer my last to her. My beautiful Mrs Hutton! I share all Lord Hesketh's unhappiness on her account, and shall be particularly anxious to hear of her perfect recovery. She struck me as bearing strong resemblance to poor dear Lady Anna Maria, God grant she may not strengthen the likeness by a similar untimely end!

Remember me in the kindest manner to Mr and Mrs Pennant & tell him that Pierce of the 42nd is dead.* How, when or where I know not but the fact was communicated to me by the Lt. Colonel commanding that regiment. I heard from Edward yesterday, he is encamped among the Pyrenees which we have a distant view of only. All the knowing people say that the moment Pamplona surrenders we shall turn the long threatened invasion of England into practise against France. This I shall enjoy much, but hope Lord Wellington will temper his enterprising genius & daring spirit with a due proportion of prudence on this occasion. I received a letter from my uncle & answered it the 6th of the month, his letter was as affectionate as it could be but I wish he had told me what he thought best to be done with regard to making some sort of settlement of our affairs or whether he means to do any thing, he once held out a flattering hope to me when I was in London, but his means may have altered since. More of this another time, for the present a *Dias viva muchos ames mi queried* ever, ever yours.

E. Griffith

Sir Alured Clark also wrote to Edwin's sisters at Rhual to discuss the sale of the house as despite the clearance of some major debts there was little hope of retaining it. Although Sir Alured was certainly a wealthy man, it appears that he did not have the capital to hand to purchase Rhual, but it seems that he was involved in clearing some of the debts owing on the estate.

Hinchingbrook, Oct 1st 1813

My dear Charlotte,

I am to thank you for two letters, (the last dated the 29th ultimo was received yesterday), and express my satisfaction that the discharge of so many of the debts has afforded some relief to your mind; and I hope it may contribute towards removing the tiresome pains with which your head

---

* I have not been able to discover any Pierce in the 42nd Regiment at the time. However, I suspect that this refers to Lieutenant Donald Grant of the 42nd Foot, who died of natural causes at Maya on 6 September 1813.

has been so much affected of late. I received a letter from Edwin, dated the 6th of last month at Artajona, written with the good sense and those filial, and affectionate feelings that I knew both his head, and heart to possess. It is the first I have had from him since the death of your ever to be lamented mother. On consideration I think it is best to send it to you, that you may have the satisfaction of seeing, under his own hand, that he enjoys the most perfect good health; *and know his sentiments with respect to other matters of importance, in which you are all so materially concerned*; and about which I am very desirous to know the sentiments of each of you *four* individually, before I attempt to form my opinion, or offer any advice on the subjects. Do you know if Mr Morgan (to whom, and his amiable wife pray say every thing affectionate for me) has obtained any information as to the probable value of the estate, if the determination should be to sell it? For if he has, I should be glad to know it. I leave this place on Tuesday morning; but shall not be in town till Saturday the 9th: but if you copy your brother's letter, and return the original to me, *under cover to Lord Sandwich*, I shall find it in Mansfield Street when I arrive there, as his lordship will be in town before me. I am quite pleased at the favourable account you give of your young friend Mr Hesketh,* who I most sincerely hope may soon be restored to health, and thereby complete the happiness of his truly respectable and worthy parents. How unfortunate poor Harriet has been in adding to her *misfortunes*, by the fall you mention. I wish you had been a little more particular as to the nature of her accident, do give my hearty love, and good wishes to her, and to Emma; for though you don't mention her, I presume they are still together. I know by the newspapers of William Campbell's promotion;† but have not heard from him since it took place. I had however a letter from him dated the 24th of July, when he was in health, and spirits. I wish to have an account of the remaining debts, when you can ascertain them; and beg you will let it be as correct as possible. Mr Mostyn Edwards told me he had spoken to Mr Morgan about some land in Kiltyre?,‡ which he had reason to believe *belonged to your brother Edwin*; have you heard anything about it? Love to Caroline, and your nieces Louisa & Charlotte. I am in great haste, but always, and ever, your truly affectionate uncle, whilst

Alured Clarke.

---

* The Heskeths owned Gwyrych Castle near Abergele.
† William Campbell 36th Foot had gained the rank of brevet major in August 1813.
‡ I have been unable to locate Kiltyre, but there is a Kiltyrie alongside Loch Tay in Perthshire; a search of the local records did not find anything regarding the Griffith family.

On 20 October the right squadron under Captain Wodehouse marched back to Salinas, where Captain Thackwell joined it on the next day, to assist in the investment of Pamplona as it was feared that the garrison would launch a desperate bid to break out and escape into France. Three days later three troops of the 10th were also posted here. On 28 October a draft reached the regiment from England composed of Lieutenant Lane,* a troop sergeant-major and twenty-six rank-and-file with forty-two horses.

---

* Lieutenant Henry Lane had joined the 15th as a cornet in 1811; he served at Waterloo and eventually rose to lieutenant colonel in the Grenadier Guards, and he died in 1871.

Chapter 6

INVADING FRANCE

Rumours abounded of the impending surrender of Pamplona and with a thrust into France being likely, Edwin made a fond farewell to his Annita and prepared the regiment to move. It was not a moment too soon, as they marched the following morning.

On the 31st I rode over to Mendigorria to take leave of Annita Sennar; and as this is probably the last time I shall ever meet her, I must dedicate a few lines to her memory. She is rather above the middling size & perfectly well shaped; her features are regular & beautiful, particularly her forehead & eyes which are expressive of sensibility & sweetness and her light brown hair which she wears parted in front & hanging in thick curls on each side of her face heightens the natural transparent delicacy of her complexion. Her dress and ornaments were always chaste & simple, being generally a black silk, or coloured gown with long sleeves & made close up to her throat, with necklace, earrings, & bracelets of mother of pearl, or coral. A long black lace veil, which covered her head & reached below the knee was thrown over her other dress when she went to church or to take a walk, & added much to the symmetry of the form, it was meant to conceal, for she was modesty itself. She had been educated at Pamplona for the advantage of masters, & as she was an only child no expense had been spared in them, consequently she was mistress of the French language, of music, & painting, accomplishments, particularly the first, that are rarely to be met with in Spain; & she played beautifully on the guitar & pianoforte. As her father & mother with whom she lives are the first people in Mendigorria, general officers are often quartered upon them, and I was told by everybody that the heroic Mina,* commander of the Volunteers of Navarre, was her professed admirer. The difference of their ages is

---

* General Francisco Espozy Mina was a celebrated guerrilla leader.

however rather too great as he is 3 or 4 and thirty, while she has felt the warmth of eighteen summers only. Adieu Annita! accept the best wishes of a stranger; of one who is foreign to thy birth place, thy religion, thy laws, & thy manners, but who ever venerates female innocence & beauty wherever it may be found, & under all the disadvantages of different garb, customs, and ideas. And in proportion as thy course is mild & virtuous throughout this life, may thy happiness be perpetual in that which is to come!

In Mendigorria, the report of the surrender of Pamplona which had reached us the night before, was confirmed, and on my return to Larraga I found an order for the regt to march for France the next morning. The remainder of the day was spent in preparations accordingly.

November 1st

The regt. marched to Ibero, Echarri & Ororavia; villages on the Arga about a league from Pamplona. The day was wet cold & miserable & I sensibly felt the change from my clean warm room and amiable hostess Dominica Azcona. The French garrison marched out, & the Spaniards in to Pamplona about 12 o'clock. The weather & roads were both so bad that I did not go to see them, but several officers who did, reported that the French mustered about 3,500 men, who considering the short commons of bran bread & horseflesh they had been upon for many weeks looked very healthy & well.

Pamplona, one of the finest & completest fortress in the world, & the key of Spain, is thus in our possession without the loss of a single man!

2nd

Continued our march to Ascoz a mountain village to which we clambered up hills, & along paths through woods that were next to impossible. We had got into another climate; the wind was piercingly cold & the mountains covered with snow. Ascoz being a small place, I sent three troops to Etxaleku and Garran. My billet was at the curates, an enlightened & hospitable man who made me as comfortable as the ungenial nature of his home at this season would admit. In summer it must be delightful as it is surrounded with hills wooded up to their tops.

The regiment was destined to remain in this vicinity for five days.

3rd

It rained & snowed the whole day. Orders had arrived last night for the brigade to return to Ibero and adjacents, but counter orders for us to remain where we were, came at one in the morning.

4th

I visited my out quarters of Etxaleku and Garran, beautifully situated villages, but the residence of misery & poverty.

5th

Rode to Beunza it being the Hd. Quarters of the brigade, and on [the] 6th the regt moved to that place. It was at this village that I first found the little Spanish I had learnt of no use to me; the natives of these mountains talk Basqueyada [*sic*] only; a language as different to the Spanish, as Welsh is to English. Yesterday & today we had a sharp frost the first this year that we had seen.

Edwin was clearly still feeling the loss of his mother and wrote home regarding her will, which he felt made it imperative that they sold Rhual.

Ascoz in the clouds, Nov 5th 1813 [Marked 'Received Rhual Nov 22nd']
I reproach myself with having behaved extremely ill to you my dearest Harriett; I certainly had little to say, but *that* is no excuse for not having at least acknowledged my gratitude, and thanks for your letter received on the 24th of August, 25th of October and now on the 3rd of this month containing a copy of the will left by my much loved mother. I have perused and re-perused it with sensations not to be described. How clearly are her wishes expressed; how thoughtful and affectionate towards those she loved and had it in her power to notice as she wished! In short as you observe, it resembles any action of her life. What she so kindly terms a disappointment *to me,* I view in a different light, for *supposing* the whole estate of Rhual had been left *to me only*, what could I have done? I must have made provision for my unmarried sisters, which I could do only by selling the place: for it does not admit of a moments deliberation that the *income* is *very insufficient* to keep up the house, offices & grounds as they ought to be; and were Charlotte & Caroline in *possession of the whole*, and live there, they would soon find themselves involved in difficulties & the place must go to *ruin*. *Take* at this moment a *minute* but impartial view of everything in & belonging to it; beginning with the drawing room & ending with the hedges that skirt the premises, and tell me whether you think any sum under *thousands* could put things into that state of repair that they ought to be? And of course every day that this is neglected the evil will become greater. Heaven knows how dear to us all are the stones of our youthful joys and pastimes; & particularly to one like me whose profession dooms him to be a wanderer on the face of the earth, but where happiness was derived from the peaceful & domestic scenes of home. I love and venerate every thing about the place, but I would rather, infinitely rather

give it up at once, and live *in hopes* that some good fortune or other may enable me to recover it some years hence, than see it go to decay in our possession without benefiting anybody. You may depend upon it this is what we *ought* to do, and however the idea of quitting it may hurt poor dear Chats & Conny I *don't think* they will ever have *course* to *repent* so *doing*. You may show them this letter, & with my best love, beg them to think the matter over, as I have endeavoured to explain *my* idea & thoughts upon it. I am sure they will not only *agree* with me but come cheerfully into my way of thinking. I wrote to Cony on the 13th inst which I hope she will have received & reply to soon.

It is now about time to tell you that we are thus far on our route to France, according to the instructions sent to the general officers of cavalry. The whole were put in motion on the morning of the 1st inst. the day that the French garrison in Pamplona surrendered: and here we are; as the date of my letter shews enveloped in clouds & storms. We received orders to halt the day before yesterday but know not whether to wait for the infantry that has been employed in the blockade to get up with us, or that the Good Lord begins to think it too late in the year to commence a campaign in an enemy's country, as should any reverse make a retreat necessary it would be rather awkward having the Pyrenees behind us, which is impassable for man or beast from the end of this month to the spring. The scenery about us is wild and beautiful to the greatest degree, sugar loaf hills & deep valleys covered with forests & thickets form the face of the country; and now & then when the snow storms clear away you see a great white crag sticking into the skies; the whole forming a secure retreat for wolves & eagles innumerable. The miserable villages are stuck on the sides of the hills, & the communications between them are *roads* that when you travel you are continually either in a bog, or on a staircase! You may suppose what the *inhabitants* of such a region are. Nevertheless, the priest who I live with is an enlightened man, and comforts me with the assurance that we *must* all perish in snow if we don't get out of the Pyrenees, this month, and he is *right*; a few days must decide our fate, and before you receive this, we shall either be in Gascony or on the Ebro.

I hear from Frederick some times, & of him very often through my friend Dalrymple who constantly mentions him, in a way that would give you pleasure; he says he is all anxiety to come here to be estinguished [*sic*] & hopes that he shall be able to send him in the spring. Edward is encamped a few leagues on our left forward, and was well when last he honoured me with a state of affair in that quarter. What a glorious thing it is getting the strongest fortress in Spain without the loss of a single man! I had not time to go into the town, but the outside is magnificent & I am told the *in* is equally so. The domes & cupolas are in general covered with black tin, and a great many gilt ornaments, saints, crosses, weather cocks etc, &c. which when the sun shines upon them appear quite a blaze of gold and silver. The poor inhabitants were nearly famished and ran out to meet the loads of bread & other provisions coming in which they bolted like pointers.

Adieu make allowance for it's being eleven o'clock at night, and that I am writing with fingers benumbed with cold, by a blinking, stinking oil lamp. I shall direct this to Rhual as you desire. I have not light to read it over. My best love to Charlotte the younger, commonly yclipt [sic] the minx, and also to Emma who must think me very ungrateful for not writing to her but I seem to be writing so often to some of you that it would only be tautology. God bless you all my dearest Harriett and with the greatest affection

Yours Edwin Griffith

7th

Marched this morning to Aryce or Auza, a short league. The Hd. Qtrs of the brigade moved to Arraitz [-Orkin] on its way to Santesteban. The inhabitants of this place talk the Basqueyada language only, with the exception of the priest & my patron, who speak Spanish, & are considered very learned.

8th

Remained here all this day expecting orders to advance. Walked up a hill near the village from which I could see nothing but boundless forest of magnificent oaks, & a few peaks of snow. I fell in with a fine flock of sheep and goats, well guarded with shepherds & dogs, to defend them from the wolves with which the woods abound. In our march from Ascoz to Beunza we found a forest pony whose hind leg & haunch had been eaten to the bone by them, & his throat much torn by the fangs which had held him down. As he appeared to be in great agony & could never have recovered, I ordered a ball cartridge to be expended upon him to release him from his sufferings.

9th

Order arrived in the night, and in the morning the regt broke up its cantonments at Auza, Llaregi, Joarbe & Eltzaburu and marched to Donamaria & adjacents. This march which was about 4 leagues was I think without exception the most beautiful I ever saw. The road which was steep, rocky & bad past all description, was through forest the whole way, and as the day was particularly fine, and the heights we scaled immense, the view was proportionately sublime & beautiful. I would not have believed without seeing, that the whole of Spain contained so much fine timber as we saw between the great Pamplona road and this valley of Donamaria; and not the least extraordinary part of it is, that self sown beech & oak of gigantic size & luxuriant foliage, flourish on the tops of inaccessible mountains, whose summits, as I have before mentiôned are almost constantly enveloped in snow storms. If there were such things as gentlemen's country houses in Spain, what situations might be found for them in this part of Navarre, but the custom of all crowding into dirty villages is common throughout the kingdom.

The regiment was held at Donamaria while Wellington launched his successful attack on Soult's fortified positions in front of the Nivelle River. This mountain warfare offered no opportunities for the cavalry, who were forced to remain idle in reserve. On the 12th the regiment moved up to Santesteban, they were to remain there for ten days before shortage of supplies and poor weather forced them to return to the Pamplona area and Edwin had ample time to explore the area. It became clear to Edwin that the Spaniards actually preferred the French officers to the English.

10th

Soon after day light this morning a tremendous cannonade commenced in our front at the distance of ten or twelve miles. I mounted my horse and rode to Santesteban where I was told that the firing was caused by Ld. Wellington making an attack upon the French position *in France*. Orders were given for the brigade to turn out at a moments notice, & we passed the day in anxious expectation of being called upon. The cannonading however gradually decreased, & night closed in without our hearing any more of the matter. Santesteban is a pretty, compact little town upon the Bidassoa River, surrounded by [the] Pyrenees; there are several shops and a market place where many articles are sold, such as salt fish, chocolate, sugar, cloth &c &c. Altogether I was much surprised to see anything so good in such a situation.

11th

Rode again to Santesteban this morning in hopes of hearing the particulars of yesterday's action, none had however arrived.

12th

The regt marched this morning, the right squadron to Sunbilla, & the two others with me to Santesteban. A great number of wounded Spaniards passed through our quarters yesterday & today who all concur in Ld.

Invading France

Wellington having gained a decided superiority over the French, who they say have fallen back upon Bayonne. As the brigade is advancing right in front, the 7th Hussars are this day at Vera [de Bidassoa] & Sare & the 18th replace us at Donamaria.

13th

Poured with rain the whole day, & at intervals we saw that the mountains above us were covered with snow. Sat shivering in a great room with open windows without a fire, the French *they said* having destroyed all the brasuras, altho' the fact is I believe that *they* are stingy of their fire & hid them. The inhabitants of Santesteban are I suspect a very Frenchified set if one may judge from the difficulty we had in extorting our rations of straw, &c, out of them. If that is the case they were made a *proper* example of by the division of French which passed through the place after the Battle of Vitoria, as they broke open all the houses & robbed & plundered everything they could lay their hands on. I do not think gratitude forms any part of the characteristic *virtues* of a Spaniard. Oppressed by their enemies they receive us with open arms & open houses; but, the *danger past,* they, like the rest of the world, too soon forget their benefactors. They certainly are a poor, and oppressed people, & with the prospect of starving before them, it is not to be expected that they would give a portion of the little they possessed with a good grace, but then they should not have forgotten that what we took and paid for, the French would have taken without paying for. In answer to this, which I have occasionally taken the liberty to remind them of, they would reply, 'yes, but we cannot eat money, & if there is no corn what is the use of money?' Here then is another misery of the Spanish government that so fine a corn country as Spain is, & with such numerous fine sea ports all round it, should from want of roads, canals, and navigation, suffer in parts, all the hardships & privations that one would be exposed to in a desert; and for want of a stimulus being given by the government there is little or no communication between adjoining provinces, no conveyance for anything either by land or water to trade, no activity to be seen in any part of the country.

14th Sunday

I looked into the church, which had nothing particular about it; a priest was standing in the middle of it in his robes with a strap hanging over his shoulder; the congregation one after another all walked up to him, kissed the end of the strap, put a little loaf of bread into a bag that two boys were holding open by him, dropped a curtsy to the Virgin Mary & left the church. Small niggling rain fell the whole day but not enough to confine me to the house; I therefore mounted my horse & rode to the village of

Sunbilla where the right squadron was quartered. The road is along the right bank of the Bidassoa through a deep & rocky valley which widens a little close around Sunbilla; the whole is wild & romantic like every thing else in this neighbourhood, & there is a remarkably picturesque bridge across the Bidassoa which connect to the village with some very pretty houses on the opposite bank.

15th

Was a miserably cold & wet day, staid in the house the whole of it talking French to the young senora who told me that she had been asked by a friend, if she was *quite sure I* was an Englishman, and this same friend, who had an officer of ours billeted at their house who is of rather a serious turn, said in French, speaking of him, '*Ah, mon amie, il est truste et si stupide en un mot il est tout a fait Anglaise!*' from this I fear that my countrymen have not shone in the eyes of the fair sex at Santesteban; they thought they paid me a high compliment by asking if I was not a Frenchman; and the worst they could say of my companion in arms was that they thought him a thorough Englishman!

I have often observed that the French officers are more popular among the Spanish ladies than our own; and I should be much surprised if it was not so. They learn to speak the Spanish language perfectly in a quarter of the time that we do, they associate with the natives & conform to their manners & customs, they give balls to the ladies & captivate them with their polite riens, politesse & grimace; they help themselves freely to everything in & about the house, but by their extreme pleasantry and fagon le parler the owners are kept in good humour & almost forget the robbery committed upon them. An Englishman presents his billet, takes possession of the best rooms & stables, pays most scrupulously for everything, behaves with the utmost decorum but seems rather to avoid than court any communication with the inhabitants and to this circumstance may be attributed the character pretty generally given to the English all over the continent, that they possess more good qualities & make the most disagreeable companions in the world.

16th

Was as wet & miserable as yesterday & I did not stir out of the house the whole of it.

17th

It cleared up for a few hours this morning when two or three of us mounted our horses & rode up the valley of Bastan, so justly celebrated for extreme fertility & beauty. It is watered by the Bidassoa & other streams & ornamented by many quintas, or gentlemen's houses and fourteen villages the principle of which are Elizondo & Berroeta, the sides of the hills are well wooded and the whole is enclosed in then [by] a barrier of tremendous mountains.

18th
Was again a cold wretched day & it rained & snowed the whole of it.

Finally they were ordered out of their miserable quarters, back to the fertile plains of the Ebro. During this treacherous march through the mountains one man of the 15th was killed when horse and rider fell over a precipice.

19th
Orders arrived last night for us to return by the road we came to the neighbourhood of Pamplona. Accordingly this morning we set out much against the grain, to perhaps that most villainous of all mountain tracks, the pass of Donamaria. We arrived at Auza about 5 o'clock drenched with mud & rain & many of the baggage animals stuck in the sloughs & remained on the mountains all night.

20th
Marched to Beunza & the adjacent villages which we had occupied on the advance.

21st Sunday
Remained all this day in our quarters.

22nd
Marched with the Hd Qtrs of the regt to Ascain, a pretty but miserable village on the banks of the Arakil seven miles from Pamplona, the remainder of the regiment went to Ibero, Aldaba, Lete, Ochovi, &c. nothing could be more cheerless than the prospect of remaining in such quarters during the winter, but there was plenty of straw in them, & our horses soon made up for all the privations they had suffered at Santesteban. Fine weather & tolerable roads were also luxuries after what we had experienced among the Pyrenees.

The regiment was to remain here for a full month, refitting and regaining their strength ready for the coming campaign in France, which everyone knew would start as soon as spring arrived. Edwin found the time to write to his sisters from here; it seems that the receiver in Britain paid for post from the army as well as paying to post to the army. The fact that the army was now in the Basque region was clearly of some fascination.

From Corunna to Waterloo

Ascain, near Pamplona. Dec 7th 1813

Dearest Chats

I wrote to Cony on the 13th of October, Louisa on the 27th, and to Harriett from Ascoz on the 5th ult: since which I have rec'd a letter from Cony dated Park Gate Oct 26th. It is therefore now *your turn* to pay half a crown for a polisher. The date of this will show you that our mountain warfare is brought to a conclusion. We did not take part in the glorious business of the 10th November as the ground did not admit of cavalry acting; but after contending with the elements until the 20th we were ordered back to this neighbourhood which has nothing to recommend it except being a plentiful one, and close to Pamplona, the most beautiful city I have seen in Spain and indeed I don't remember any in England that can boast of better paved streets or handsomer buildings; *everything* is to be bought there, even to Windsor soap, & Smyth's Lavender water; & French nick nacks in abundance, but all terribly dear as yet. As soon as we have re-nailed and renovated our lean horse, & sorry habits we are to be advanced in front of the whole army to take the outpost duty; I shall enjoy this much as altho' being in an enemy's country will keep us constantly on the qui vivre yet any change from Spain must be for the better, the climate in France is much milder, and forage more plentiful & of a better description. I really expected we should have laid our bones among these confounded Pyrenees for there was nothing to be got but the very worst sort of Indian corn & little enough of that; and the passes dignified by the appellation of *roads* are beyond what you can form an idea of. We had several accidents but only one serious one which was a man & horse falling over a precipice by ground giving way. I saw this happen & can never forget it; the horse wonderful to relate escaped, but the poor man survived only a few hours. The sublimity of the scenery in some degree compensated for our *various* miseries. We had two or three clear days which enabled us to see great part of that range of snowy crags which stretches from Roncesvalles eastward, almost to the Mediterranean.

Eternal snows the growing mass supply, till the bright mountains prop the incumbent sky, as Atlas fixed each hoary pile appears. The gathered winter of a thousand years and the forests & vallies are as beautiful as nature can form, their principal inhabitants are wolves & eagles, there are not a race of mortals existing among us, the most wretched & ignorant think in Europe they are many degrees *worse* than the Spaniards, consequently can not be very many better than savages. They have a lingo of their own, called Basquenz [*sic*], and I might as well have attempted explaining myself in Spanish to the natives of Llanrwst. After this description you may imagine I was not sorry to turn my back upon such a region. I hope my dearest Chatts you improve in appetite consequently health & strength for altho' Cony informed me with much apparent self satisfaction that *she* was fat & blooming & that you was quite the reverse. I still hope that you will *get over this bout*, and that we shall all meet ere many months are over our heads to taste the delights that a united & happy family experience after a long separation never mind *where*. If we *could* have continued living at Rhual it would have been all very well, but as that is impossible I *shall* never give it a thought which will create uneasiness; my avocations would never have allowed me to domesticate much & I really cannot conceive anything much more melancholy than you and Cony setting down there by yourselves. I said a good deal more on this subject in my letter of the 5th ult. to Harriett which I dare say she has shewn you. Louisackles letter is as usual half filled with accounts of your friends Sir Thos & Lady Hesketh with whom you were going the day after she wrote to Rufford. How I wish I had the pleasure of being known to those *friends* of yours, for by all you both say of them they seem to be articles *of very peculiar merit*. Perhaps you have ere this got acquainted with Mr & Mrs Hulton: if so tell me if you ever saw a *nicer* couple, & whether you can wonder at my anxiety, that they should not be separated indeed her recovery has given me great pleasure both on her own account as well as his; I don't recollect ever taking such a liking to two people upon so slight an acquaintance as I did to them; and if I wished to give a foreigner a specimen of English *manners* & English hospitality I think Hulton Park is the house I should introduce him to.* I am all anxiety at present for the result of a brevet that is to come out, we hear in January and which will make Colonel Grant a Major Genl. and my friend Dalrymple (I hope & trust) Lt Colonel of the 15th.† This would make me first Major & give us the commanding officer that of all others on this world I should prefer for *I* cannot expect to retain the command of the regt on service after the appointment of a Lt. Col. in the room of Grant; by the bye that gentleman has left this brigade & gone home very ill.

I wrote to my uncle about 3 weeks ago asking him to send me out an almanack for 1814 in a pocket book & mentioned Peacocke's as the one Harriett gave me last year which I like very much. When you write to him pray ask if he rec'd such a letter? I made the request of him thinking he could have it sent me in our Adjt. Genl.'s cover, which will insure it coming

---

* The Hultons were based at Hulton Park near Bolton.

† Edwin was nearly correct as to the outcome of the promotion; Dalrymple was made a lieutenant colonel and Captain Cochrane became the junior major on 16 December 1813; Grant had to wait until June 1814 to obtain his rank of major general. Dalrymple's promotion led him to proceed to join the regiment in Spain, on his arrival he would take over command from Edwin.

safe & free of expense. Has the report about Hester Cotton proved correct? Sir Stapleton is not with *us* at present so I cannot ask him. I remember Lady Coghill & the Miss Cramers perfectly, both in Kent and afterwards at Weymouth; but to the best of my recollection; it was through Anson and Lady Beauchamp *then* Mrs Lygon that I became again acquainted with the St Albans set. My acknowledgements are nevertheless due to old Lady Hesketh, for honouring me with her remembrance. Well now my dearest Chatts this letter must begin to be as worrying as the blister you had upon your back when Cory wrote. I know nothing of Edward; the state of the weather & roads very much retards communication in this blessed country but if he had lost his head I sh'd most likely have heard it. *So no more at present* from yours till death.

EG

On 1 December Lieutenant Mansfield* joined the regiment to replace Captain Buckley, who left for England on 5 December to command a troop at the depot, having been promoted in the previous October.

It seems that Ascain was not a comfortable billet but Edwin did enjoy a number of visits to nearby Pamplona.

We remained at Ascain & the other villages on the Arakil till the 15th December when we again advanced for the purpose of taking the outpost duty of the army. The weather for the three weeks we halted was very bad particularly about the 9th & 10th when there was a deep snow, the nights were frosty & the mornings damp & foggy. People may tell of the sudden changes of the weather and unwholesome climate of England but I don't think any climate can be more changeable & more disagreeable than that of the north of Spain. I had a very bad billet at Ascain; very dirty people in it, with whom I was starved into the necessity of living a great deal, as my apartment had a mortar floor without a mat, no glass to the windows, & no fire place: altogether I never passed three weeks more uncomfortably. I visited Pamplona several times; it is the cleanest & handsomest town I have seen in Spain; the streets wide & well planned, good shops & handsome publick buildings. Happening to be there one Sunday I attended High Mass in the cathedral, nothing could be more impressive than the service, which was chanted by about four & twenty priests accompanied by a heavenly tuned organ. The circumstance of the churches in Spain being all open, instead of divided into aisles & pews as

---

* Mansfield would have rejoined the regiment as Grant no longer required his services as an aide-de-camp.

they are in England, adds much to their beauty & solemnity, & I never was more struck with the truth of this remark than in the cathedral of Pamplona.* The choir in which are placed the throne, the priests stalls & the organ, only, is in the center [*sic*] of the church; & from thence to the altar the people kneel upon the flags with their faces towards it, each with two or three wax tapers burning before them, from these apprised the principal light, as the narrow gothic windows of beautiful stained glass emit but a feeble ray. The women all wear black veils or shawls on their heads which hang long enough to conceal their persons and as the men generally dress in black or dark brown, the appearance is sombre in the extreme. The altar pieces present a striking contrast to this general gloom, for on them all the brilliancy of light, gold & silver is united to form a blaze of refulgent splendour.

Finally the long awaited orders to march into France were received and Edwin led the regiment forward with ill-concealed glee.

14th

Orders arrived in the night for the brigade to advance, and accordingly the 7th being the right regt, marched through our quarters this day for Lekunberri.

15th Wednesday

With infinite satisfaction I mounted my horse this morning to make a second attempt at getting out of Spain. God grant us better success & that we may never set foot into it again! The road we marched is the Camino Real from Bayonne to Pamplona, and as fine as any English mail coach road. It has been made with infinite labour and regularity through an extensive barrier of inaccessible mountains & stupendous rocks bearing the name of the Sierra de Andia. The man who planned & accomplished this vast work must have possessed more than an ordinary genius, & thinking from that circumstance, that he could not have been a Spaniard, I enquired, & learnt that he was an Italian Colonel of Engineers. We marched about five leagues, & got tolerably well put up at Lekunberri & an adjoining village at three o'clock in the afternoon. This ride reminded me much of the pass of Puente-Arenas, where we crossed the Ebro in June. In both the road & river together wind along the bottom of a deep trough overhung by wood, & jutting pieces of rock many hundred feet in height,

---

* The cathedral of Santa Maria is externally a rather unattractive gothic structure but the interior is very beautiful.

where numbers of eagles build their nests in situations that set even lords of the creation at defiance, in both are united the beautiful and the terrific, but *this* pass is as inferior to Puente-Arena as it is superior to any ordinary romantic road.

16th

After pursuing the same camino for one league & a half we came to the very pretty village Betelu & a league & a half further to the still prettier one of Lizartza where the left squadron halted; one league further on the road opens suddenly upon the town of Tolosa standing in the midst of some beautiful flat meadows & watered by the River Oria. Nothing can be more charming than the appearance of Tolosa, *without*; or more disgusting than everything within it. The streets are offensive with filth; the houses equally so, & the inhabitants an uncivil & frenchified set. The streets here as well as at Pamplona were crowded with Spanish officers, a sulky, self sufficient, dirty, ruffian like looking set of masters as any in the world. Having behaved ill in the battle of the 10th & worse afterwards in France,* Lord Wellington sent the whole of the Spanish troops back to their own sweet country; & here you saw them strutting about, smoking segars [*sic*], shrugging their shoulders and wondering (or rather pretending to wonder) what the English were doing here! Wretches! You know well enough that although *policy* gives you a share of the credit of having expelled the enemy from your country, that it is the English & the English alone that have accomplished it and that it is them that now prevent Soult's army of 50,000 men from again covering the whole kingdom of Spain. For the first time since my arrival in the Peninsula, I was here billeted at an inn; a place which bore the dignified appellation of hotel, and in which I was exposed to the combined miseries of filth & imposition. Tolosa is a very busy place, & a great thoroughfare, as the principal roads leading from Spain to Bayonne unite at it: There are also good shops kept by French, Germans, & Italians; everything is to be bought, chiefly, almost entirely, of French & English manufacture, and extremely dear.

---

* Edwin's comments regarding the Spanish army's performance at the Nivelle, which probably reflects army gossip, is unfair, as the Spanish attack was clearly meant as a feint and was never prosecuted with conviction. However, despite Wellington's orders to treat the French civilians well, it is perhaps not surprising that many Spaniards took their revenge for all the rapes and murders of their own people they had endured over the years on the first French people they encountered. Because of their excesses Wellington made the brave decision of depleting his numbers by returning most Spanish units back across the Pyrenees in an effort to maintain good relationships with the civilian population and prevent a guerrilla movement forming. This policy worked so well that the French appear to have felt safer and preferred selling their goods to the British army rather than giving them to their own forces.

17th

With infinite satisfaction we pursued our march this morning, every one hoping they might never pass another night in Tolosa. We went through Villabona, where the right squadron had halted, Elbarena and several other very pretty little villages & arrived at Oiartzun just at dusk & going over a hill about a league short of the town we got a fine view of San Sebastian, the Bay of Passages, Renteria &c. Oiartzun is a nice little town, there was a full market even at the late hour we arrived there & we found fresh mullet & other fish in great plenty; a treat we had not experienced since we quitted the vicinity of the Tagus. I had an excellent billet, my patron was a very gentlemanly old man & spoke French perfectly. He got me some very fine wine for dinner, & new milk for breakfast the next morning, and at parting begged I would always come to his house when I passed through Oiartzun; it seemed as if he was determined to give me a *lasting good impression* of his country; but long experience and acquaintance with the Spanish character, had already fixed it & it was not in the power of any individual however enlightened he might be, or however cleanly & comfortable his residence, to efface from my memory the bigotry & filth with which I had so long been disgusted.

The French border was reached on the 18 December and Edwin makes clear his excitement and pride at leading the regiment on to the very soil of that previously invincible country. His first quarters in France were certainly a great improvement on those he had so recently endured in Spain!

18th

At eight o'clock this morning we *romped* the march, I trust & hope for the last time within the Spanish territories. A league and half brought us to Irun, the frontier town; and about a mile beyond it we crossed the Bidassoa by a bridge of boats and entered France! The road winds up a hill from the top of which we saw several leagues to our front, the country green & level, & covered with houses, villages & encampments. I have seldom witnessed a more beautiful or interesting sight. The terrific barrier of [the] Pyrenees was visible on our right for an immense distance, the ever boisterous Bay of Biscay roared on our left; the cheerless hills of Spain peered one above another behind us, the lily'd fields of France smiled in our front. Her armies which had hitherto carried invasion & conquest into every part of the continent & been considered by all (England especially) as invincible, now failed, worsted & beaten everywhere, were rather to make a last effort in defence of her sacred soil destined in it's turn to become the seat of war, want & misery! Some part of our floating bridge having given way when the regt was about half over we were detained upon this hill nearly an hour until it had been repaired & the remainder of troops with the baggage had joined when we descended, & taking a road to the right arrived about 3 o'clock at the village of Ascain, where we got tolerably well put up considering the numbers & variety of troops by which it had so recently been occupied; a stately mansion was allotted me & I dined & slept in the same apartments which the great Marshal Soult had dined in for six weeks.

The weather now turned extremely wet, turning the roads into a quagmire and making the marches very tedious. The regiment now formed outposts on the extreme right of Wellington's army and was kept constantly on alert. Forage was scarce and difficult to collect, with many instances of ambushes being sprung on unsuspecting foragers by both sides.

19th Sunday

Marched to Laressore, the road altho' level was most rascally boggy; it was with difficulty the horses could get through some of the sloughs. We crossed the river Nivelle at St Pee [-sur-Nivelle] a pretty little town where Lord Wellington staid a day or two after the action of the 10th of November & from near which we had a good view of the positions from which the French were driven on that day. I was put up at the priest's house who was extremely civil, & assured me that I should find the English army would be received as friends and deliverers in every part of France.

20th

Was a cold & stormy day with the loudest thunder I ever heard. I had intended visiting the very pretty town of Ustaritz, but the weather prevented me, it stands upon the left bank of the Nive, which was much flooded today & about half a mile lower down than Laressore.

21st

Was again confined to the house all day by the badness of the weather, but the old parson was a most pleasing companion.

22nd

Marched early this morning to Bas Cambo which stands on the opposite side of the Nive to Cambo [les-Bains] Sir R Hill had had a sharp affair at this place with the French a few days before, the tête de pont they had formed was very strong but they were driven across the river & blew up the bridge which rather impeded our following them up. Bas Cambo although pretty was knee deep in mud & we were indifferently accommodated .

23rd

Rode with Lord Edward Somerset & Sir Stapleton Cotton round the outposts above Macaye, Mendionde & Gréciette; got wet through on my return to Cambo.

Edwin does not mention that on 23 December Trooper Barber and his horse were drowned while trying to ford the River Nive.

24th

Staid at home to write all day.

25th

The regt foraged in marching order in the valley of Macaye & we got plenty of hay which was a great treat to our horses after having lived all winter on straw.

26th Sunday

Staid at home

27th

Rode to Urcuray to visit my friend Hughes, who was wounded in a skirmish a few days before.*

A false alarm caused a very uncomfortable night.

28th

The regt. assembled on the brigade alarm post at daybreak in consequence of some move being made in the enemy's lines the evening before. We were kept shivering on the hill all morning & returned home just before dark at night having first foraged at Macaye.

29th

Staid at home writing letters all day & began to get tired of Cambo.

---

* The Spanish General Morillo had arranged an assault on Mendionde on 18 December, to support which Alten ordered two squadrons of the 18th forward. This advance prompted the French to attack with greatly superior numbers causing a speedy and humiliating retreat. During this short but sharp clash, Major Hughes of the 18th Hussars had been badly wounded, a musket ball entering his right side under his arm and lodging in his breast. The ball was eventually extracted by the surgeon and Hughes sent it home in a letter to his sister.

30th

Foraged again today at Macaye, a tiresome but indispensable operation. We had fine clear frost weather & the filthy streets of Bas Cambo began to dry a little.

The weather began to improve and the dry cold air began to firm the roads; it being New Year's Eve, Edwin wrote a short reflection on a very busy year which had seen much success but was also tinged inevitably with sadness, with the loss of his mother.

31st

The last day of 1813 was not distinguished by any circumstance to enter in my journal. It had been a year of great variety. Joy, sorrow, pleasure, ennui, comfort, misery, I had by turns experienced. It was an eventful year to me, and although, with the exception of one heavy domestic calamity, I had nothing to make me *unhappy*, it was too much a life of anxiety & change to be desirable. Memory will often revert to; & dwell perhaps with pleasure upon many of the hours I spent in Portugal & Spain, but I don't think I shall feel regret that they are past or, wish to experience them again.

It is presumed that Edwin continued to write a journal during the year 1814, but if so it has unfortunately been lost to us. However, many more of his letters from this period have survived, as have those of Rico who was soon to join the regiment in France, allowing us to follow their experiences throughout the remaining months of the war.

The first letter finds the regiment still near Cambo where on 16 January the regiment mustered 466 rank-and-file. Edwin seems to have been in good spirits, happily expounding his own excellence in the French language and how he had enjoyed a visit by Edward Morgan. He seems to have taken some enjoyment from hearing of the capture of Colquhoun Grant and shows pleasure at the news of the imminent arrival of Dalrymple despite the fact that he would thus lose command of the regiment.

Urcuray, Jan 21st 1814

[In] your letter my dearest Chats commenced on the 7th & finished on the 12th which reached me at Bas Cambo this day fortnight you are pleased to compliment me on my goodness in writing so frequently, but how much more ought I to express to you all on the same subject; your epistles being in general so much longer than mine, & the whole expence [sic] of the postage (which is not trifling) resting on your side; you may however imagine easier than I can express, the delight they always afford me, indeed the looking forward to the arrival of a mail from England as the greatest source of happiness we know, and although the newspapers are a neat treat, I invariably feel a disappointment when there are no letters for me besides. I wrote to Louisa last week, and after I had sealed my letter who should walk in but the Fusilier Captain, this was on the 14th & he staid with me till the 16th when I accompanied him back to his quarters. He is looking particularly well, & is perfectly sound. Pray communicate this to his father & mother as soon as you receive it. If he makes any report of me I have no doubt it will be equally good for I never was better; I am out all hours, night & day; oftener wet than dry, & experience no other great inconvenience excepting that of a voracious appetite. No movement has taken place lately, or is to happen I believe for some time. We (the 15th) have the outpost duty on the extreme right of the army; the French have a pretty strong corps of cavalry in our front about 3 miles & we have daily squabbles & skirmishes for what little forage there is left in the country between the two positions; but we are more hampered by our own commanders than the enemy. From the top of a hill near this village we look down upon the course of the Nive & Ardour, St Jean de Luz, Bayonne and a great extent of country as rich & beautiful as any part of England; it is extremely populous, and the houses being all painted white have at a distance the appearance of a vast encampment. The weather remains beautifully mild, but few days pass without rain; snow they hardly ever see.

The people are if anything too civil; they quite overwhelm one with kindness; the lower order speak in general the Pyrenean lingo, & you seldom meet a person who *speaks good* French; and they are apt to aspirate the *last* letter in a word as in lait, esprit, beaucoup, &c. and some are even so monstrous as to pronounce the 's' in substantive plural, as hommes, femmes and many others, which makes them sometimes rather difficult to understand. The priests are almost the only people who speak the language *pure* and *well* as *I* do, thanks to *Madame Durainville* and *you*.

Think of my stupidity a *few days* ago in standing for above an hour within twenty yards of George Greaves* remarking to an officer of ours what an uncommon fine lad he was, & that he must be a gentleman's son but never recognising my little actor acquaintance until my return home, when recollecting that Cony had mentioned his being in this army. I looked at the Army list & found his name in the 5th Foot. The regt. we had been standing with. The troops had assembled that day in consequence of some stir in the enemy's lines & what became of the 5th afterwards I know not: I have since endeavoured to find him out without success.

---

* Lieutenant George Frederick Greaves, 5th Regiment of Foot.

I expect Dalrymple daily, was ever anything so delightful as the capture of the little *Catherine*! Grant was onboard, & his having been taken prisoner gives us the Commanding officer whom *I* should have selected from the world.* Well my paper is full so 'adieu ma tres chere' Chatty. My uncle has sent me an almanack; mention my having received it when you write to him. A thousand loves to the Louickle and any other members of the family who may be present ever most affectionately

EG

The French strengthened their pickets in an attempt to gain forage but it was now very scarce indeed; Thackwell states that the 15th prepared furze with wooden mallets as an alternative which seems to have been quite successful. The weather in late January continued wet, cold and thoroughly miserable, and early February brought a cold snap which rapidly turned the interminable quagmire rigid. On 13 February orders were received to prepare to attack and the campaign duly began the following day. The 15th were involved in a push to the north-east and supported the 3rd Division who moved to Bonloc; the hussars lost one man and two horses wounded in a skirmish at Greciette. On 15 February the regiment moved with the 3rd Division to St-Martin-d'Aberoue, placing pickets to watch the road from Oregue, while Hill's corps took a strongly defended hill at St-Palais, killing and wounding five hundred. On 16 February the regiment moved on through Oregue to Arraute-Charritte and watched the road to Bidache. On the following day the regiment moved up to Came where they actually crossed the River Bidouze, but retired back across the river for the night. On 18 February the 10th Hussars took up the outpost duties, pushing out vedettes towards Peyrehorade, the 15th returning to Arraute-Charritte and then moving the following day to Arancou where they watched the enemy positions at St-Pé-de-Léren. The regiment retired to Ilharre on 21 February but returned to the front at Escos on the 22nd and maintained posts out to Sauveterre-de-Béarn; indeed all of the fords on the Gave d'Oleron were now watched by pickets.

On 23 February heavy firing could be heard in the direction of Bayonne which actually announced the commencement of the laying of the bridge of boats across the mouth of the River Adour; the regiment, however, moved to the east, arriving at Autevielle-St-Martin-Bideren and Osserain- Rivareyte. On the 24th the hussars joined the 3rd Division in a feint against Sauveterre-de-Béarn causing the French to blow the bridge which allowed Hill to cross the

---

* The capture of the *Catherine* by a French privateer does not appear in official documents but Colquhoun Grant among other officers was captured and held by the French until the termination of the war.

Gave d'Oleron successfully unopposed; losses were one man killed and two wounded.

The French retired from Sauveterre during the night and the hussars crossed the Gave d'Oleron at a ford and moved on to Salies-de-Béarn; the following day the 15th Hussars led across the Gave de Pau at a ford near Bérenx, losing one man, Private Faulkener, and found cantonments at St-Boés, the 7th Hussars putting out pickets.

Sunday, 27 February, was to be a memorable day as Wellington launched a major attack upon the defensive line held by Soult with 40,000 men at Orthes. The battle was, however, very much a clash of infantry in terrain far too rugged for cavalry operations: the hussars simply supported the infantry operations but were frequently under heavy cannon fire. Eventually after severe fighting the French were forced back to a second defensive location, but were removed from this position by a frontal attack combined with an outflanking march by Hill's corps, which threatened the French left wing. Soult commenced a precipitate retreat upon Saultes de Navailles and the 7th Hussars succeeded in capturing over 700 prisoners when they attacked their rearguard beyond Sallespisse. The 15th were ordered along the great road to chase the retreating French but the 13th and 14th Light Dragoons entered the road before them and they were forced to merely follow them. When within a mile of Sault-de-Navailles they came across the French left and centre in great confusion on the floodplains of the Luy de Bearn River as they sought to cross via the bridge. An immediate charge would undoubtedly have produced great results but they were ordered to halt by Sir Stapleton Cotton, reportedly because of the fading light,* and they were forced to watch the French escape. The minor part played by the 15th in these proceedings is clear by the casualty return which states that it lost one man and two horses killed, six men and five horses wounded. William records here an incident typical of Edwin, 'our humane commanding officer', on this day. He describes how, as the regiment moved their position during the action, they discovered a French artilleryman who had been shot in both legs, which hung by a few tendons only and was unable to move, lying in the middle of the road where he was liable to be ridden over. Halting the regiment momentarily, Edwin ordered some hussars to dismount and to carry the poor man to safety, off the road, before they continued. Edwin was awarded a bar for Orthes to add to his gold medal.

The hussar brigade continued to follow Soult on his retreat, the 15th arriving near St-Sever on 28 February. Proceeding across the river at a ford, the regiment moved towards Grenade-sur-l'Adour on 1 March. Here Captain Thackwell's

---

* Oman states that this action was terminated well before darkness fell; therefore indicating this was a poor excuse.

squadron which was leading discovered the French cavalry formed in line in the village square and drove the French before them after some skirmishing, capturing eighteen and killing or wounding about twenty. Sir Stapleton Cotton witnessed this small action and was highly pleased, putting Thackwell forward for brevet major.* The infantry closing up, the regiment continued towards Cazeres-sur-l'Adour, where the French infantry and artillery made a stand. A few shells landed near the 15th but luckily without causing any casualties. However, during the day's events they lost four men and six horses wounded.

On 2 March the 7th took the advance and the regiment rested at Borderes-et-Lamensans, remaining in the vicinity for three days. While at Borderes there were some reports of pillaging by members of the 15th and Captain Thackwell was required to produce a report for Wellington on one reported incident at the local church, proving the innocence of his men.†

On the morning of 5 March the regiment marched through Cazeres, passed round Aire-sur-l'Adour, through Barcelonne-du-Gers and halted at Arblade-le-Bas for four days. By 10 March it was very cold and heavy snow fell during the day but the regiment was still moved up and spread widely between Nogaro and Caumont. Wylly says that this day Lieutenant Colonel Dalrymple arrived with the regiment from England and took command. However, Edwin wrote a letter that evening recounting much of their late proceedings and reporting the news that Dalrymple was expected daily and two troops of the regiment were at St Jean de Luz, including Frederick.

Near Nogaro, 10 March 1814 [Marked 'Redirected to Downing near Holywell']
My dearest Chats
Since my letter of the 11th ult (I believe to Harriet) we have been marching, counter marching, making demonstrations, pushing forwards, retiring, fording rivers, driving in picquets, skirmishing & fighting day after day. A hasty letter written to Morgan the day after the battle of Orthes will I hope will have reached its destination, I have assured you of Edward & I being in preservation after the labours of that glorious day. Soult had drawn out all his force, & exerted every energy to defeat the plans and resist the further advance of our invincible Marshal. The position occupied by the French was strong by nature, & their defence of it, gallantry & obstinacy throughout the battle was such as has seldom been witnessed, but nothing can withstand the British troops led by Wellington,

---

* Sir Stapleton wrote to Edward Somerset that he should 'express to the officers and men of the 15th Hussars his gratification at witnessing the gallant and soldier-like conduct of that part of the regiment which was engaged with the enemy yesterday' (Wylly (1914) p. 215).
† See Wellington's letter of 7 March on page 559 of his *Dispatches*, Vol XI 1838 edition.

and their overthrow & defeat was complete. Had daylight lasted one hour longer we should have made mince meat of some thousands; as it was, our leading regiment (the 7th) got among them & killed & took about 700; the 15th was next but it was getting so dusk that Sir Stapleton would not let us continue the pursuit although I never felt so great an inclination to be savage and I know I should have been well supported. They retreated all night & at daylight on the 28th we continued the pursuit and pushed them across the Adour at St Sever. We forded the river at daybreak on the 1st and the 15th galloped after the rear guard towards Grenade where we got sight of them & charged them through the town killing & taking between 20 & 30 of their best cavalry. The next day we chivyed to Barcelonne & Aire, where Sir R Hill fell upon their flank defeated it & the chace [sic] was given up to rest the army & feed it, both of which we stood much in need of. I hope you have a good map of France otherwise this & all my future dispatches will not be very clear as to our movements. Edward has been living with me for the last three days; perfectly well. He is now at Grenade. We (the hussar brigade) are in front as usual where we live better although more hasseled than other people. The natives continue very civil & on our entering a new place frequently greet us with 'Vive le Roi George'. I saw George Greaves during the engagement and others & again the day before yesterday but not in high beauty as usual.

Poor Lord March was wounded* & fell in front of the 15th, every body thought he was dying, & his brother Ld. George,† Ld. Fitzroy Somerset, and all Ld. Wellington's staff collected round him: I never saw a more affecting scene or anybody disclose more heroism than he did on this occasion. What an example! the heir to three dukedoms mingling in the fight on foot with the meanest soldier! I am happy to hear he is doing well. Frederick is at St Jean de Luz, Dalrymple writes me word; I expect the latter daily. God bless you my dearest Chats excuse my haste & cold fingers; the ground is covered in snow. Yours ever most affectionately.

Edwin Griffith

Soon after this letter, Lieutenant Colonel Dalrymple and Captain Whiteford arrived. Dalrymple immediately took command of the regiment, Edwin taking the right squadron and Thackwell the left. On 15 March two additional troops

* Captain Charles Lennox 52nd Foot, the Earl of March, eldest son of the Duke of Richmond, was shot through the lungs at Orthes. He recovered and served at Waterloo but was forced to retire through ill health in 1816.
† Captain Lord George Lennox 9th Light Dragoons served as an aide-de-camp to Wellington in Spain and the Waterloo Campaign.

which had recently been added to the establishment of service squadrons, consisting of Captains Frederick Philips and Carpenter, Lieutenants Douglas* and Dixon,† ten sergeants, two trumpeters and 148 rank-and-file; 160 horses arrived with the regiment. Surgeon Gibney describes the excitement at the regimental depot when the news was received that two troops were to embark for France. He states that the colonel finding himself short of numbers sent both young men and horses little prepared for campaigning and they had eventually marched out in high spirits on the Portsmouth road in a thick snow storm. A very old and experienced officer, Captain John Bull, who had served in Egypt as an infantry sergeant, had been left in charge of the depot, now at Arundel.

One can only imagine the joy of the meeting between Edwin and Frederick after such a long time, but there was little time to settle in as the regiment marched the next day; Frederick and Captain Wodehouse led the two troops that made up the right squadron commanded by Edwin. This same day a private of the 15th got trapped in the church tower at St Mont by a French patrol, drew up the bell rope and, throwing it over the side of the church, slid down to his horse and escaped.

On 16 March the regiment advanced, driving in the French pickets; the centre squadron under Captain Hancox attacked a force of some 500 cavalry, driving them over the river at Tasque. The French loss was ten killed and one officer and thirty men captured, while the 15th only lost six men and horses wounded.

Frederick was quick to pen a letter home to his mother, to advise her of his safe arrival and to describe the trials of the journey.

St Germe, March 17th 1814

You will I fear begin to think I am very idle with my pen my dearest mother, but during our march up the country; I had no means of sending my letters so as to be certain of them arriving safe. We are now I am happy to say with the regt, we reached them the day before yesterday & found Edwin looking remarkably well: they were just changing their cantonments as we arrived so we took up our quarters together in a small village about four miles in the rear of where we now are. We advanced here yesterday in

---

* Lieutenant Sir John James Douglas had joined the 15th as a Cornet in 1813 becoming a lieutenant the same year. He served in France and at Waterloo, then became a captain in 22nd Light Dragoons in 1819 and went on half pay in 1820. He changed his name to Scott in 1822 and died in France in 1836.

† Lieutenant Henry Dixon had joined he regiment as a cornet in 1813 and became a Lieutenant the same year. He served in France and at Waterloo, becoming a captain in 1820 but retired by sale of his commission in 1822. He died at Inverness in 1838.

consequence of the French outposts having been driven back & I believe we shall move on to Plaisance tomorrow but before I proceed I must give you some account of our march. We went from Passages to St Jean-de-Luz on Wed 2nd in one of the most miserable days I ever experienced: the road passes through the Pyrenees &c is exceedingly bad; add to which, the rain fell in torrents & there was the loudest thunder & the most vivid lightning I ever yet saw – we were obliged to remain here three days (much against my inclination) owing to some of the horses being lame & unable to proceed; & during the whole of our stay the weather was tremendous – between 25 & 30 ships perished at the entrance of the harbour but I am happy to add that not many lives were lost. I was witness to three or four running on shore myself; & never did I see a scene so truly horrid – the surf broke entirely over the ships & most of them rolled their masts away: we saw the poor wretches clinging half drowned to the rigging, without being able to afford them the least assistance, they however contrived when the waves receded, to leap from the sides of the vessels on the sand & most of them scrambled on shore.

On Sunday 6th we marched from hence to Biarritz; a small village about three miles from Bayonne; & on Monday crossed the Adour over a bridge of boats which is thrown over between the town & the sea, & quartered ourselves at a place called Ondres: we passed this day in view of the blockading army: all was quiet with the exception of now & then a shot from the batteries.* The next day we proceeded to St Geours [-de-Maremne] the Hd Quarters of Gen. Vandeleur,† who was good enough to give us an excellent dinner.

Wednesday: went to [St Paul-les-] Dax a fine large town; & dined for the first time at a French hotel: our repast was famous; had they not given us our fish in the middle of dinner & crammed garlick into every dish.

Thursday: to Tartas, & crossed a branch of the Adour in ferry boats, the enemy having destroyed the bridge, it was sad tedious work as the river was broad & the boat only held 8 at a time.

Friday to St-Sever where we met with a division of Spanish infantry consisting of about 7000 men; they looked much more like soldiers than I expected to see them.

Saturday to Le Vignau about six miles from Aire [-sur-l'Adour] which is Ld. Wellington's Hd. Quarters; when I went on to report the arrival of the squadron; but did not see His Lordship. On my return I found myself

---

* The citadel of Bayonne had been invested since 27 February.
† General Sir John Ormsby Vandeleur commanded a brigade of light dragoons with General Graham's force.

established in a fine chateau, belonging to the Countess St Germain; who quite overpowered us with civilities. We were ushered into a very handsome salon surrounded by lemon & orange trees & opening into a beautiful garden & about six an excellent dinner of three courses was served up after which we had coffee noyeau &c.

We remained here Saturday, & on Sunday proceeded to join – it is getting too late for me to write more as the post goes early in the morning & this must go to Hd Qtrs tonight. I shall put another letter on the stocks immediately – Edwin joins me in best love to all & believe me my dearest mother, most sincerely & affectionately yours

Fred. C. Philips

We expect to advance to Plaisance tomorrow.

The advance towards Toulouse had now begun in earnest. On 18 March Edwin's squadron took picket duty as the brigade steadily advanced, reaching Plaisance this day. The following day the regiment marched south to Monfaucon where it linked up with Hill's Corps. The infantry were engaged with Soult at Vic-en-Bigorre and he was compelled to retire. Sunday, 20 March, saw a short violent action near Tarbes, (the 15th were not engaged) where Soult was again forced to retire. The brigade was attached to the 6th Division which moved to Tournay. They marched through country lanes and formed the left of the army on the advance. They proceeded through Galan on the Monday, through Castelnau-Magnoac to Thermes-Magnoac on the Tuesday, L'Isle-en-Dodon on the Wednesday, Samatan on the Thursday and finally St-Lys on Friday. Pickets from Edwin's squadron were pushed out beyond Tournefeuille, only a few miles from Toulouse. This was too close for the French, who launched a surprise combined attack of infantry and cavalry on 26 March which forced the squadron back. The 15th lost one sergeant, one trooper and eight horses killed,* and one officer,† five rank-and-file and one horse wounded. The following day the Light Division established the pickets at Tournefeuille and part of the 15th were stationed at St Simon les Mimosas to maintain communications with Hill's column at Portet-sur-Garonne, but were driven back to Cugnaux by incessant skirmishing from French infantry lodged in the houses and behind walls.

On 28 March the regiment was held ready to move as the Light and 6th Divisions performed a flank movement to the right. A pontoon bridge was to have been laid over the Garonne but was found to be two pontoons short and

---

* Neither man was killed outright, Sergeant Prigg died later in the day and Private Burden died on 6 April of his wounds.
† Lieutenant Barrett was severely wounded in the arm.

the 15th merely placed pickets forward at St Simon again. The main army was now in the vicinity of Toulouse but their delay in arriving had allowed Soult ample time to fully augment his defences.

The city of Toulouse was the great arsenal and storehouse of the south and was amply protected by nature and complemented by the art of man. The great river Garonne covered the western and southern sides and the fortified suburb of St Syprien to the west of the river formed a great bastion. To the north the city was protected by the Languedoc and to the east the city was covered by the long steep ridge of Mont Rave, which had been crowned with strong redoubts. At its foot the River Ers formed a wide expanse of marshy ground. All of the bridges were destroyed or commanded by cannon and outworks and it seemed that Toulouse was virtually impregnable.

While the regiment lay at St Simon expecting Soult to abandon Toulouse, Frederick wrote of recent events to his mother but played down his and Edwin's close escape on the 26 March.

St Simon [les Mimosas] *30th March 1814, 3 miles from Toulouse*
Your letter of the 2nd has this moment reached me my dearest mother; & as I understand we are not likely to make any movement to day, I shall commence an epistle to be ready whenever opportunity offers to send it. You will perceive by the date that we have not been idle since I last wrote to you, from *Avlar near Aire* [-sur-l'Adour]; we have been in full march ever since, following up Old Soult who has made a most rapid retreat; & is now with his army in Toulouse.

We arrived before the town the day before yesterday, & I believe it was Ld Wellington's intention to have attacked it immediately; but owing to some mistake there were not a sufficient quantity of pontoons to throw a bridge over the Garonne; which must be done before any offensive operations commence: the 15th were the first who appeared in sight of the town: Sir S. Cotton trotted on with us to an eminence called the *Pigeonaire* within about a mile of the gates; & no resistance was made to our approach; some cannon shots were exchanged but no damage done on either side.

The view of Toulouse from the place where we halted is most beautiful; there is a fine green plain which extends along the whole front of the town which is magnificent to a degree. It is the general opinion that the French will make no resistance to our entering it; & I hope they may not as it would be a sin to destroy it & it could not hold out more than three or four days; but I must now tell you our movements since I last wrote which I believe was on the 17th. We marched on the 18th to Plaisance, the enemy retiring before us the whole way; & got into comfortable quarters about four o'clock.

19th followed them again for about four leagues through horrid crossroads and got into wretched quarters after dark.

20th marched early & arrived within a league of Tarbes, about ten o'clock, when we discovered the French army drawn up in position upon some heights on the left of the road; their right was however soon attacked and turned by the Sixth Division, when they precipitately retired & were closely followed during the day; but you will most likely have seen Ld. W.'s account of the affair before you receive this.

The enemy retired during the night; & we followed the 21st, 22nd, 23rd, & 24th: without catching them; on the 25th however we overtook them again at a place called Plaisance [du-Touch] about three leagues from this; we did not however enter the town that night. On the 26th we drove them through Plaisance & the right squadron, (which consists of Capt. Wodehouse's troop & my own;) was ordered on picket in the village of Tournefeuille about a league in front; our reign there however was not long, for the French finding that we had no infantry to support us in the town; attacked us with theirs & forced us to retire. Poor Barrett was shot through the arm & there was a sergt killed; & seven men & nine horses wounded. Capt. Wodehouse was unfortunate enough to have one horse killed & another wounded under him.

On the 27th we went into cantonments between Plaisance & Tourne-feuille & Edwin & I dined with Sir S[tapleton Cotton] at the former place.

28th The enemy were again driven from Tournefeuille & we advanced as I before mentioned to Toulouse. Edwin has just been to *my chateau* to tell me that he has heard from Catty by the same mail that brought me yours; there is no news in the army; all is quite quiet, I shall leave this open as long as I can.

Thursday morning. I have just received intelligence that there will be a post go off this evening, so I must hasten to close this affair. I am going to try to find Edward who I hear is not far from this. Our weather for the last few days has been delightful & has every appearance of continuing. I trust you have received my three letters though I have some doubts about it as I directed them to no. *7* Bedford St. instead of *11 – stupid enough.*

Edwin joins me in best love & regards to all our friends & believe me my dearest mam, you're ever dutiful & affectionate

Fred. C. Philips.

The regiment remained at St Simon and was inspected here in marching order on 3 April, an uncomfortable duty as there was a cold biting wind. Finally on that night, in heavy rain, the regiment rode before midnight* through St Martin du

---

* Wylly (1914), using Thackwell, says at 2 a.m. in the morning, but Frederick and Edwin both agree that it was between ten and eleven that evening that they marched.

Touch and almost up to Grenade. A bridge of seventeen pontoons had been thrown across the Garonne and (although observed by many civilian spectators) the 3rd, 4th and 6th Divisions with Somerset's and Ponsonby's cavalry brigades crossed without opposition and encamped at St-Jory, while the 15th crossed at eight o'clock that morning and encamped near Gagnac-sur-Garonne. The French did try to destroy the bridge during the night, possibly in preparation for an attack on the forces then isolated on the eastern bank of the Garonne, but the attempt failed although bad weather did cut the communications for some time. The regiment was to remain here for four days, during which time a patrol commanded by Corporal Winterfield and two men fell in with a French patrol of the same strength and captured it.

Around midday on 8 March the regiment pushed the enemy's pickets back, and the regiment was bivouacking between Fenouillet and Toulouse when a corporal was wounded. Freire's Spaniards* crossed the bridge 8 March and after the bridge was moved nearer Toulouse to shorten communications, the Light Division passed on 9 March.

On 10 March, a beautiful sunny day, the army was prepared for a general attack and the columns were in motion by five in the morning. At eight o'clock the Spanish troops commenced skirmishing along the northern end of Mont Rave which completely commanded Toulouse to the east. Hill's corps demonstrated in the west threatening the suburb of St Syprien, while the 3rd and Light Divisions probed the bridges over the canal in the north. While all of these attacks were pressuring the French, Beresford marched 4th and 6th Divisions on a very tricky flanking movement, marching between the river Ers and the heights before turning to march directly up the slopes of Mont Rave to attack the redoubts which commanded them. The 15th and 10th Hussars advanced with Beresford's troops and proceeded a little further to the south so as to protect the left flank of the infantry and a brigade of artillery from the French cavalry stationed here. The cavalry were exposed to a heavy artillery fire throughout and took some casualties and it seems that part of the brigade passed across the southern end of Mont Rave in an attempt to cut off any French attempting to escape from the redoubts; Thackwell says that they became exposed to a heavy fire from six pieces of artillery near the canal and were forced to retire under cover of the ridge again. The hussars were mere spectators to the highland brigade's heroic storming of the French redoubts under a tremendous hail of shot and shell; and having eventually captured the two southern redoubts they then rolled the French northwards along the ridge line and forced them to retire over the canal into Toulouse. The fighting was virtually over by five o'clock but

---

*   General Manuel Freire commanded two weak Spanish Divisions totalling approximately 7,300 men.

the French continued a heavy cannonade from the guns positioned along the banks of the canal while Wellington suspended the fire of his guns to save the city from destruction. Eventually, at ten o'clock the brigade was cantoned at St Jean and the following day at Caraman. The losses of the 15th being only seven men wounded and seven horses killed or wounded,* Lieutenant Colonel Dalrymple received a gold medal for commanding the regiment at Toulouse.

Soult was forced to abandon Toulouse and escape to the south-east on the night of 11 April, but the regiment remained near Toulouse for a number of days, staying at La Point on the 11th and Bessieres on the 12th. On 13 April officers arrived announcing the capture of Paris by the allies, the abdication of Napoleon and declaration of peace, and the regiment remained in the Monastruc-la-Conseillere area. However, Soult declined to believe the authenticity of these accounts and Wellington, having replenished his supplies, marched rapidly to attack Soult again, the 15th reaching Puylaurens on the 17th; and it was here on 19 April that an officer approached the pickets of the hussar brigade bearing a notification from Soult that he now accepted the situation and that conflict was an end. The following day, when fully immersed in the joy and exultation following the announcement of peace, Frederick wrote again to his mother but finished the letter having moved nearer to Toulouse again. The regiment stopped at Monastruc on the 21st and Gargas and the surrounding area on 22 April, when Frederick and Edwin took the opportunity to visit the city.

Puylaurens, April 20th [and Toulouse 23rd] *1814*
You will begin to think me very idle my dearest mother, for not having written a line since the Battle of Toulouse; but you will have seen by the Gazette that we are *all safe*. I am not quite certain as to the date of my last letter; but I rather think it was from St Simon, about the 30th or 31st of last month. We remained quietly in our cantonments until the 3rd when the army was put in motion about ten o'clock at night; & marched down the left bank of the Garonne to a place called Grenade; about four leagues from Toulouse, for the purpose of crossing the river; we arrived about day break; & before nine o'clock the pontoon bridge was laid down; & the regiments began to move over without any opposition from the enemy. About dusk however they sent an immense barge laden with stones & other heavy things down the river, for the purposes of destroying the bridge; but it was fortunately perceived in time to prevent any very serious injury being done. L'd. Wellington then judged it expedient to have it taken up until morning, but owing to some heavy rain which fell during the night the water rose so as to render it impossible to lay it down again for two

---

* Oman says four men wounded, but I have followed Wylly (1908) p. 224, who quotes Thackwell.

days; during which time we were in continual expectation of an attack, as there were not above 15,000 men across & Soult's army was considerably above double our number; they however did not risqué [*sic*] it; & the remainder of the army came over on the 6th & 7th; the whole were encamped about seven or eight miles from Toulouse. We remained quiet on the 8th & on the 9th moved up near to the town preparatory to the action.

The French occupied an excellent position which commanded the town; & had been very strongly fortified for the occasion by three or four redoubts, & breast works which extended all along the heights. The attack commenced about nine o'clock upon the left of the French by the Spanish Division; they behaved tolerably well at first but as they approached the redoubt which was the object of their attack the French made a sally with about 1500 men & repulsed them with considerable loss; the battery was then carried by the sixth division; who behaved with a degree of gallantry that it is impossible to describe. Poor Campbell* you will have seen is wounded; but I am happy to say that he was doing well the last time I heard of him. Most sincerely do I pity the relations & friends of those who fell, their loss must be doubly felt; as the news of the downfall of Bonaparte must have been known in England long before the dispatch could reach it. Our brigade was not engaged but was most part of the day was exposed to a very heavy cannonade and part of the time to musquetry [*sic*].

Friday 23rd – My dispatch was here interrupted by an order to move from Puylaurens, much to my sorrow as I have spent my time there very pleasantly; the people were very fond of us; & gave us dances every evening. We are now in a small village on the high road from Toulouse to Paris; not very comfortably off; but I suppose the whole army will soon be on its way to Bordeaux for embarkation; at least such is the report here. Nothing could exceed the joy with which the inhabitants of Toulouse received L'd. Wellington & the English in general; nothing was heard but shouts of 'Vive l'Angleterre, Vive Louis 18!'. All the busts & pictures of Bonaparte were pulled down & trampled in the streets; & the white cockade was universally hoisted.

It is a very handsome town; but the appearance of it is a good deal spoilt owing to most of the respectable inhabitants having left it on the approach of the armies; they are now however returning very fast to their homes. I have only been able to get there one day, as we are generally quartered far in the country for the purpose of procuring forage. We live here quiet luxuriously; nothing can exceed the hospitable manner in which

---

* Major William Campbell 36th Foot was shot through both buttocks at Toulouse.

we are received by the people who are the most delightful race in the world. If anything could tempt me to leave England it would be this.

I get on tolerably with my French; & have even *once or twice had the satisfaction of being taken for a native*. I have seen a good deal of Edward since I wrote last, we have several times been quartered near one another; he is looking very well. I have likewise met with George Greaves, who is a very fine lad indeed. I have this instant read a message from Edwin to tell me that there is a mail going off & I must send my letter immediately. He joins me in best love to Emma & Girls, all our friends & pray remember me affectionately to my grand mother & aunts. I will write again in a few days – adieu my dearest mother, believe me most affectionately.

F C P

Edwin has received your letter.

Edwin wrote only a couple of days later with his version of the momentous events.

Gargas near Toulouse, April 25th 1814

My dearest Chats

I fear that by my late address in the epistolary way I shall have forfeited much of the credit you were pleased to bestow upon me for former good conduct but such strange events have crowded upon us during the last month, that I really have never had time to write any thing like a long letter. Little did I dream when last I wrote that this long & bloody war was so near its close, but still less that the downfall of the tyrant, the dismissal of his immense armies & their eagles with the restoration of the Bourbons & the lily, could have been accomplished in a few days without in the least disturbing the inward tranquillity of the empire! And that the act of depriving this one single individual of power should be the instant cause of restoring peace to the whole of the civilised world, & happiness to millions of his fellow creatures! His rise & fall is an event too extraordinary, too big for human comprehension in the contemplation of it one can only say; 'O God thy arm was there'.

My last letter went to Cony dated St Simon March 30th where I remained until the 3rd of April, at eleven o'clock that night we marched and at eight the next morning we crossed the Garonne 5 leagues below Toulouse, over a pontoon bridge. The following day the cavalry were pushed within two miles of the town, there we remained until the 10th when the whole army was put in motion at daybreak & moved in separate columns to attack the French who were in position to receive us. I will not bother you with a description of the operations of that glorious day; but this much I must say, that nature and art were combined to place the French army in a situation which would have been impregnable, to any but British troops, but they carried everything before them. The circumstances of the inhabitants of Toulouse, (the most populous city in the south of France) being eye witnesses of the complete defeat of one of their best marshals & finest armies by those of a nation whose military fame they had always affected to make light of, was not the least gratifying part of the business. Soult retreated towards Narbonne & I had hopes of getting a dip in the Mediterranean, but before we reached Carcassone, while we were all in full pursuit this most unexpected news came upon us like a thunder bolt & arrested all operations & almost all power of movement, so astonishing it appeared. From that time (the 13th) to the present we have only been marching about for the sake of forage which is nearly exhausted in this country; St Sulpice, Lavaur, Puylaurens, Monastruc &c have been our quarters; and I must not forget two very pleasant days I spent at the Chevalier Montcabrier's who lives at a magnificent chateau of the same name; he commanded the *Triomphante* a 80 gun ship in de Grasse's fleet on the 12th April 1782,* which added to his being a noble of the old school, rendered him a most interesting acquaintance. Dalrymple & I always go together and generally get put up at gentlemen's houses; by which we see much of the customs and manners of the people and have good practise in the language. I find I speak dreadfully ungrammatically but having once got over the 'mauvais haute' of that we go on pretty well. This part of France very much resembles England and notwithstanding all Bonaparte's taxes & conscriptions it is extremely populous & well cultivated and there is more general comfort & less appearance of poverty than any country I have ever been to yet. The houses are very pretty & well furnished with the exception of carpets which are not the fashion; but in the respects of neatness & ornamental grounds about them they are not to be compared to the English; the gardens are formal, and it is rarely, if ever you see a wood of timber trees. The market towns are well supplied & attended, meat, bread, vegetables, fowls & eggs much cheaper than in England but there is one article they are almost entirely deficient of and which we miss more than any other, there is neither milk or butter to be got for love or money.

I had almost forgotten to say that poor Campbell was wounded at Toulouse on the hill we were ascending at the time, and I met him going

---

* This of course refers to the battle of the Saintes, fought on 12 April 1782 between the fleets of French Admiral de Grasse and Admiral Rodney. Rodney was victorious capturing five ships including de Grasse's flagship the *Ville de Paris*.

off upon a man's back to the rear; he was shot through both parts of his bottom high up, a very painful and troublesome though not dangerous wound. I wrote to my uncle giving him an account of it and also to announce the health & safety of Frederick, Edward and me two days after the action which I begged him to communicate to both of you. I hope he received my letter and did so. Nothing ever was so fortunate as the 15th has been throughout *this* campaign. The 10th & us were formed up close together, being Lord Edward Somerset's Brigade, and during a most tremendous cannonade which we were exposed to, we suffered nothing scarcely while the 10th got knocked over terribly.* We are now all impatience & anxiety to know what is to become of us. It is quite impossible as vast an army can get home in a minute and I fear the last who embark will be here for three months yet. In the meantime I have nothing to do & I consider myself more as a young gentleman making a tour in the south of France than an officer on service. I got a letter from Harriet a few days ago dated March 29th, which is the latest intelligence I have had from home. I am glad to find you were on the mending hand at Downing; make my very best remembrances to Mr & Mrs Pennant. Harriet desires to know 'What division, brigade or what it is called, we belong to.' Pray inform her that the 15th belong to Lord Edward Somerset's Brigade in Sir Stapleton Cotton's Division. By the bye that gentleman was off two days after the news arrived leaving the cavalry to whoever chose to take charge of them; but however, there is a lady in the case. I wish I was going home to be married to a young lady, rich & beautiful, I would break her flirting.

The French dames are not beautiful, Spain and Portugal have more beauty to boast [of] than this part of France; they are however clean & good looking. I am going to Toulouse tomorrow to see the entrance of the Duc d'Angouleme.† I will give you an account of it in my next. Make allowances for having as usual; I have not time to read it over. Adieu my dearest Chats yours ever & ever.

Edwin

Edwin took the opportunity of writing to his sister, Frederick's mother, a few days later, full of praise for the actions of Frederick. He also described the triumphal entry into Toulouse and their hopes for a rapid return home.

---

* Oman states that the 10th lost one officer and four men killed and one officer and six men wounded.

† Louis de Bourbon, Duc de Angouleme, nephew of Louis XVIII, landed in the south of France to inspire a popular movement for the restoration of the Bourbons.

Invading France

Gargas near Toulouse, April 28th 1814

Your letter my dearest sister this day month claims my acknowledgement and best thanks. I therefore requested that Mr Rico would allow me to write to you by tomorrow's mail,

He having written, he tells me, by the last. I believe I have not yet expressed the pleasure it gave me seeing that young gentleman join the regt. In this country in such high feather [as] he did; and I do assure you (impartially speaking) the manner in which he brought his squadron from Passages a long harassing march through an exhausted country would have done credit to a much more experienced officer. Dalrymple left him in the entire charge of the squadron and considering that he had no directions given him & was, of course, unacquainted with the rules for rationing the men and foraging the horses in this country besides various other difficulties one has to contend with here, I confess I expected to see them joining in a very different condition to what they had but they all arrived in just as good order as when they left Arundel barracks & in the utmost regularity. I continue this as I am certain it will give you pleasure & you may believe it added much to mine on seeing him. This most extraordinary finish of the great emperor's reign gives us *reasonable* hopes of returning to England *soon*, though *when*, I can't guess as it may be some time before things are so engaged & determined upon that the army will be withdrawn. We were in full pursuit of Soult towards Narbonne when the news reached us, and it really was an event of such magnitude & so unexpected that we could hardly believe it. The French people would not. They shook their heads & laughed and said they wished it was so, but they were not so easily to be deceived as we imagined, and it was not until the Maire of the Communes had published officially the decree of the senate that some of them would be convinced. I had yesterday the satisfaction of witnessing a scene which I can never forget & still less attempt to describe; it was the entrance of the Duc D'Angouleme to the great & populous city of Toulouse. All the military authorities of this vast district, the generals of France, England, Spain & Portugal, with hundred of officers of each nation in full uniform formed a cavalcade a mile in extent at the head of which rode the royal duke and the Duke of Wellington. Thousands of country people crowded each side of the road for a league before we reached Toulouse, and absolutely deafened us with acclamation so that we could hardly hear the thunder of the artillery and the bells of the churches. The streets were all covered with sand or fine grass, the lower part of the houses hung with tapestry and pictures, the upper ornamented with wreaths of flowers and evergreens. Triumphal arches, the white fleur de lys, crossed the streets every twenty paces, the windows and even the house tops were crowded full of ladies, waving their handkerchiefs, clapping hands & calling with all their might 'Vive the roi! Vive les bourbons!' others with more expression held them towards heaven, clasped in silence; while hundreds of both sexes could only express what they felt by giving vent to their tears. You could see there was nothing affected in all this; it was genuine and sincere for it came from the heart. There was something so inexpressibly delightful, so *thrilling* in this whole scene that a stoic could not have helped catching the sympathy and I saw many an eye brim full whom I am certain were not remarkable for tenderness of their dispositions. To an Englishman it was not the least gratifying part of the ceremony to hear 'Vive Lord Wellington! Vive les Anglaise!' mixed with the shouts for 'Le roi' and 'les Bourbons!' I attended the theatre at night & at the entrance of the two great men the burst of acclamation was deafening and endless. The performance was very little attended & except some loyal songs between the acts, Henry IV and God Save the King, were alternately played. When the former first struck up I really thought the audience would have battered the walls, or at least the partitions of the house down: I am sure the chevaliers of the court of the Croix de St Louis must have used all their pocket handkerchiefs on this day. It was altogether a day to be *felt not* to be deserved and I will therefore have done with it.

This morning I went to hear [a] Te Deum in the cathedral which was particularly mystical and fine, and afterwards attended the levee and was presented in form by the Duc de Guiche.* There is a grand ball tonight which Frederick staid for, but as I knew it would be a *grand crowd* & my stock of finery not keeping any sort of pace with that of the French officers, Dalrymple and I withdrew from the city to our country seat where by very bad candle light I am thus endeavouring to give you an imperfect history of the reception of the Bourbons at the metropolis of the south. I leave it to you to make the reflection on these extraordinary circumstances which are come to pass! This time twelvemonth how quixotic & absurd the idea of an English army invading France would have appeared. How little better than a madman we should have considered anybody [who] could have expected we should be received as friends and deliverers not as enemies! You desire to know who we belong to? The 7th, 10th & 15th are the Hussar Brigade commanded by Lord Edward Somerset, but your interest in this of course ceases with the war.

I suppose Frederick told you how the *shells* cracked about his ears at the battle of Toulouse. We were much more fortunate than our neighbours on

---

* The Duc de Guiche, also known as the Duc de Grammont was a Captain in 10th Hussars but returned to French service in 1814.

that occasion although exposed to a line of French battery's, the cannon balls ploughing the ground about us in every direction. Poor Capt Gordon of the 10th was cut in two by one of them,* Campbell who was severely wounded is doing very well, I saw him walking about Toulouse this morning; he is however looking wretchedly ill.

I sincerely hope we shall not be detained very much longer in this country now that the fun is over; we eat up every thing like a swarm of locusts or caterpillars and must eventually sicken the natives of our presence, my joy at touching Ingleterra again will be great, for although we are in the latitude of Montpellier, and in a country as beautiful as nature & art can exhibit, *cleanliness* & *true comfort* can alone be experienced in England, and for an admirer of *female beauty* it is the only country in the world. Well God bless you my dearest Harriett my very best love to the minx, & Emma and accept the same yourself from your most affectionate

Edwin

Edward is at Condon a large town 8 leagues from Toulouse.

Frederick wrote again to his mother in early May while the regiment remained lodged in the villages around Gargas still awaiting its route home. Frederick gave further details of the triumphal entry of the Duc d'Angouleme and talks of a meeting between Marshal Suchet and Wellington.

Marked to: Mrs Phillips 25 Brook Street, Bath
Bazus 3 leagues north [east] of Toulouse, May 3rd 1814
My last letter was sent for[ward] in such a hurry my dearest mother, on account of a mail being about to be suddenly made up, that I had not time to finish it as intended, I shall therefore begin *another polisher* for the first [mailing] opportunity. The army still remains in the neighbourhood of Toulouse & nothing is yet known about its movement, but I conclude it will not be very long before we are off; report says, the cavalry are to march the whole length of France, & embark at Boulogne [sur-Mer], which I hope may prove to be true, it will afford such a delightful opportunity of seeing one of the finest countries in the world; the part we at present occupy, is charming beyond description, & the climate at the present season, exceedingly pleasant, but I dread the heat of the summer months.

I went to Toulouse on Tuesday last; & remained until Friday morning; when I returned with a heavy heart, to my stupid village, after having spent three of the pleasantest days I ever remember to have passed. Le Duc

---

† Captain Charles John Gordon was the officer killed.

d'Angouleme made his entree on Wednesday, & all the officers who were in the town rode out for about a league with Lord Wellington to meet him; he was escorted by a Garde d'Honeur, composed of the principal inhabitants, & Lord W. rode by his side; it was the finest sight I ever beheld; a royal salute was fired by a brigade of British artillery, placed at the entrance of the city; & Sir Rowland Hill's Division of infantry was drawn up on the bridge to receive him with presented arms; the bands of the different regts playing 'God Save the King'. The windows were crowded with beautiful women, who waved their white handkerchiefs, & showered down flowers as he passed with shouts of 'Vive le Roi' & 'Vive le Duc D'Angouleme'! In short, the greatest enthusiasm prevailed amongst all ranks, & I really believe the joy they expressed was sincere; for every countenance appeared to me, the picture of delight & satisfaction. Te Deum was sung in the cathedral, but the concourse of people was so great as to render it impossible for us to get in; Edwin & I were however more fortunate the following morning; when we saw High Mass celebrated with great magnificence before the Duke.

On Thursday evening the city gave him a grand ball at the Capitoleum,* which was also very fine, but the crowd was so great, as in some measure to spoil the dancing; there were however some cotillions, executed *even better* than those I have seen by the *famous Bath performers*; of course I could not attempt these, but I ventured to join in the 'many circles of the waltz'. Without at all wishing to depreciate the charms of my fair country women I must confess, that I never recollect to have seen a more beautiful, or elegantly dressed assemblage of females, whose fascinating manners *completely captivated me*; nothing would delight me more than being able to spend some months in France, so as to enter into the society of the country, which I hope at some future period to be able to manage. The dancing was kept up with great spirit until daylight. I rode out that morning to meet the French Marshal Suchet, who was expected to pay a visit to Lord Wellington, but he disappointed us all by taking a different route, & as my leave of absence was expired, I was obliged to return to my quarters without seeing him. I am happy to tell you that Campbell is going on well, I saw him several times, & he told me he hoped to be quite recovered in the course of a fortnight. General Robinson is with his brigade before Bayonne;† I have therefore sent his letter by post, & will

---

* The Place du Capitole was the hub of Toulouse life; it is so called after the Capitole, originally the office of the judges who controlled Toulouse, which stands on the eastern side of the square, now the Town Hall.

† Major General Frederick Philips Robinson commanded a brigade in the 5th Division.

make myself known to him, whenever opportunity offers.

Edwin has just been here to tell me of his having received a letter from Catty dated the 9th of last month, & I am quite disappointed at not getting one from you by the same post, as it's nearly two months since the date of your last, so I conclude some of them must have miscarried. I am delighted to hear a better account of dear Chatty who I was quite uneasy about since you mentioned her being so unwell. I am getting on famously with my French, I can now *jabber away* pretty fluently, & I take every opportunity of speaking the language. I am lodged here, *chez monsieur le curé*, who is a pleasant, well informed man. Tell Charlotte with my best love, that I hunted all the shops of *les marchandes des modes* in Toulouse in hopes of meeting with something pretty in the *lace* way for her, but since the arrival of the English army, everything has risen in price so extravagantly that I am sure it could be procured cheaper & better in London, add to which, I thought it most likely I should be *cheated, not understanding much* about it. How good it was of Emma to make that young *minx*, so handsome a present! I hope she will be more careful of *her* watch, than her brother was of *his*.

May 4th; Well, I think my news is nearly exhausted, & as I understand a mail is to be made up tomorrow, I fear I must soon come to an end.

You will have seen by the returns, that George Fitzclarence was wounded;* he is now I am happy to say nearly well; though at the time the hurt was severe, it was fortunate in its circumstances , the ball passed through the fleshy part of his thigh, without injuring either tendon or nerve; I have seen him several times since; he sets off in a day or two by water to Bordeaux, with General Packe,† & several wounded officers, from whence, as soon as he is able to travel by land, he has leave to proceed to *Paris*, lucky dog! I wish I had been hit under such circumstances.

I conclude that before this reaches you, you will be on your way to Rhual, as Catty mentions your intention of setting out, towards the middle of this month, I shall however direct of Bath, for the chance of catching you, & if not, it will be forwarded. I am very pleased to hear that my grandmother enjoys such good health, & looks so, pray give my best love to her, my aunts, & Eliza, & tell me whether they have heard lately from Fred. Noble,‡ how he is &c.

May 5th; I have just received a letter from Edwin through England, which I ought to have had previous to my leaving the country; provoking

---

* Lieutenant George Fitzclarence, 10th Hussars, was severely wounded at Toulouse.
† Major General Dennis Pack was severely wounded at Toulouse while commanding a brigade in the 6th Division.
‡ Probably Captain Frederick Noble, 67th Foot.

enough! As it mentions several things he wished me to bring out to him, such as hair brushes, tooth &c &c; one might suppose that such trifles might be easily procured *in France*, but even in the city of Toulouse, you cannot get them *tolerably good*. Well God help you my dearest *mammy*, Edwin & I, unite in kindest love to you all three & Louise & believe me your most affectionate &c

F.C.P.

I grieve to find that the sale of poor dear Rhual seems unavoidable; if so, it is the duty of us all to make up our minds to the loss; but for my own part I cannot help indulging a hope, that some means may yet be devised to save it; sincerely do I pray it may prove true. I have not seen Edward since my last, he is quartered on the other side of Toulouse; Edwin & I, had a good laugh at Catty's description of the celebration of his natal day at Canapa. John Lytons match surprised us much. Pray write oftener.

Despite so much talk regarding the necessity of selling Rhual, nothing was settled.

Chapter 7

FRANCE TO IRELAND

At the end of May Edwin was finally able to write from Toulouse with news of the start of their long journey home, one he was very keen to make. The eighteen regiments of cavalry were to march across France to the Channel ports in two divisions, the 15th leading the right column. Eighty dismounted men were sent to Bordeaux under Captain Booth to take ship to England and arrived at the regimental depot on 13 July. More importantly, Lieutenant Colonel Dalrymple sailed home claiming ill health, leaving Edwin to command the regiment as they marched across France.

Chateau Gargas at Toulouse, May 30th 1814 via Paris
To Miss Griffith Park Gate Chester.
At length my dearest Chats we have received orders to turn our faces homewards, and the day after tomorrow we commence our march for Boulogne; six hundred miles! But the distance would be trifling even were it twice as much when every step takes us nearer to our dear island, & to those we love. Our route lays through the finest part of France, & I promise myself great pleasure from it. You will be able to trace it on a map by the following principal places which we halt at as follows. June the 4th Cahors; 7th Souillac; 12th Limoges; 17th Chateauroux; 19th Vatan; Orleans on the 23rd; Etamples the 27th and Mantes the 1st of July; where we shall receive another route for Boulogne or Calais. If therefore everything goes on prosperously we may reasonably hope and expect to touch British ground before the 20th of July; I will write to you during the march whenever opportunity offers of sending my letter. I am sorry to find by a letter received from Harriet a few days ago that you had not yet received my letter to you from the 24th or 25th of April. Although she had received mine of the 29th; the reason I did not write sooner after the battle of Toulouse was that I knew the Gazette would show you we had not been killed on that occasion, & as poor Campbell *had been* [wounded] I addressed my letter to Sir Alured who I knew would feel anxious about

him, & begged if he was writing into Wales he would tell you he had heard from me.

Harriet says that she had just been *copying* my letter to send to Rhual, this is rather unfortunate as my epistle to Cony written a few days afterwards was descriptive of the same scene & consequently could not vary much in substance or expression. Harriett gives a good account of herself, I hope her Bath doctor & your Chester one will be able to *fettle* you up a bit so that we may look forward to a merry meeting in the course of the autumn, which I dare say my uncle will be tempted to join. His purchase of the swndwr, after all he has said to me, appears rather odd; but he is odd himself, and I'm sure he had no other object in so doing than thinking it a pity (which it was) that the ground so close to the house should not belong to it.* So my friend John Eyton has sold his freedom for a mess of pottage. Poor fellow! Pray tell him that I wish every happiness may be his portion throughout life, which I would have written to him on purpose to express had I not thought that you could do it better for me. You need not add that although I hope we shall always consider ourselves as *neighbours*, *he* may depend upon it, I shall never break the two first sentences of the ten commandments.

Souillac June 7th. I have never had time to finish this since I left off writing at Gargas, but however I shall commit it to the Post Office at this place and will take its chance. We have had had weather for our march hitherto; much rain, violent thunderstorms and two intense hot *sunshiny* days, we have a charming road & the country is in general rich & beautiful in the extreme & very populous. Excuse a stupid letter but we have had a tedious business to day in ferrying across the [River] Dordogne. I am very hungry & Dalrymple has already commenced an attack upon the dinner which consists of boeuf al la mode fricassee cats & dogs and two or three other very filthy looking dishes (At the Lion D'or). Adieu for the present. Frederick is in the town very well and writes in 'beacoup d'amitie' &c &c. yours ever my dearest Chatty, most affectionately

E.G.

Frederick also wrote regarding the journey to his mother and found time to describe the scenes he witnessed en route.

St Germain [du-Bel-Air], *June 6th 1814*
About 40 leagues from Toulouse.

My dearest mother,
Your letters to Edwin & myself, arrived by the same mail, three or four

---

* It would seem that Sir Alured Clark bought this plot of land near to Rhual house to make the sale of the property a more attractive package.

days before we commenced our march for embarkation; I did not hear of
his, until the morning after I received mine, & you may imagine I was a
good deal vexed at your not having got the first letter I wrote after the
battle of Toulouse, so late as the 12th of May; I have two others on wing,
which I hope will be more expeditious. The assurance you give me that you
have benefited by the prescriptions of your new doctor, was a great comfort to me, as I have not been happy about you since the shabby account
you gave of yourself in your last; let me beg that nothing may tempt you
to leave him until he says you may safely do so, as the want of a little
perseverance may perhaps prevent the permanent cure of your complaint.

We commenced our march from our quarters in the neighbourhood of
Toulouse, on the 1st, much to our satisfaction, we were all getting tired of
them, & I believe the *natives* were not less so of us, as we put them to great
inconvenience by eating up all their forage, & taking possession of their
stabling, & houses. We have received our route as far as Mantes, where we
wait for further orders; I will copy out the stages, with the days we are to
arrive at each, so that if you have a good map, you will be able to follow
our movements; we have as yet, been uncomfortably off in point of
quarters, as we have been passing through towns which were occupied by
Soult's army, & for the last two nights, three parts of the horses of the
brigade have been '*en bivouac*', but in the course of tomorrow or next day,
I hope to leave all the French troops behind us. We are passing through a
charming country, the town of Montauban is particularly beautiful; it is
situated upon the River Tarn, & is one of the cleanest, & best built places
I have seen; Cahors, is likewise a handsome town, we were to have
remained there as today, but being unable to procure a sufficient quantity
of stabling, we were ordered on, to make one halt here instead, & I am not
sorry for the change, as I was billeted at the house of an old lady, who so
overwhelmed me with *civility* & *garlick*, that I quite dreaded remaining a day
in her house; this is a very small town, about two miles to the left of the
main road, so you may perhaps not find it on the map, it is about half way
between Cahors, & Souillac, where we march tomorrow morning. Edwin
is very well, & desires his love. I have not seen Edward these six weeks &
of course we shall not now meet again in this country, as the infantry
embark at Bourdeaux.*

Limoges June 13th, I did intend to have dispatched this from Brive [la
Gaillarde] my dearest mother, but was so occupied, that I never could sit
down to finish it; the last few days march have been delightful; it really is

---

*   The infantry were loaded on to transports at Bordeaux, many destined to sail directly for
    Canada to take part in the war with the United States which still rumbled on.

impossible to describe the magnificence, & richness of the views & the beauty of the situation of almost all the towns through which we have passed, they are chiefly built upon rivers, & surrounded by rocks, & woods; I quite envy them & the French, as according to their idea of a fine country, it ought to be perfectly *flat*. This is a very large place, & we are comfortably put up. there was a grand religious ceremony yesterday, & in the evening a fine procession passed through the streets; it was very extravagant & absurd, as those ceremonies generally are; a quantity of penitents brought up the rear with their *heads tied up in sacks*, which must have been pretty severe I think, as it was one of the hottest days we have had. I will write again from Orleans. Give my best love to Emma, Catt & our friends in Bedford Street &c & believe me my dearest mother your ever dutiful & affectionate

F. C. P.

Pray write to Mantes if you think it will catch me, but fear the English mail will not overtake us.

Route for the march of the right column of cavalry to embark for England from Toulouse, June.

Grisolles	1st of June
Montauban	2nd
Caussade	3rd
Cahors	4th
St Germain[du-Bel-Air]	5th
Halt	6th
Souillac	7th
Brive [la Gaillarde]	8th
Halt	9th
Uzerche	10th
Pierre St Buffiere	11th
Limoges	12th
Halt	13th
Bessines [sur Gartempe]	14th
St Benoit [du Sault]	15th
Argenton [sur Creuse]	16th
Chateauroux	17th
Vatan	18th
Vierzon	19th
Halt	20th
Salbris	21st

La Ferte St Aubin	22nd
Orleans	23rd
Halt	24th
Artenay	25th
Angerville	26th
Etampes	27th
Halt	28th
St Arnoult [en Yvelines]	29th
Montfort [l'Amaury]	30th
Mantes [la Joile]	1st July

Where we halt for further orders, & I think you may venture to direct a letter to me there; we don't yet know where we are to embark, but believe it will be Boulogne or Calais. You will perceive that we shall not be very far from Paris, but fear I shall not get there, as everybody will want to go of course. Adieu!

Edwin wrote again from Limoges; clearly his duties on the march were far from onerous allowing much more time to write.

Limoges, 13th June 1814 to Mademoiselle Griffith, Parkgate
My dear Chatty
My letter began at Gargas & finished on the 7th inst. I put into the Post Office at Souillac on that day, and a jeune mademoiselle assured me you would get it within a week; but not feeling confidence in French parts or French affections, I shall fly you another from this place, but to say that we are safe & sound thus far on our route to Boulogne. Our march is very tedious as from the quantity of live head lumber we have it is not feasible to advance above twenty miles a day on the average, and the heat & dust are both very offensive, we are however in some degree repaid by the variety of scenery and in some parts (particularly in the neighbourhood of Brive) by the extreme richness and bounty of the country. This is the next town next Toulouse. I have been in, but it has nothing to recommend it except charming promenades under avenues of elms along the banks of Vienne* which were yesterday covering crowds with all the fashionables of the place, the band of a French regt quartered here played till ten o'clock. it seems very odd walking without hats which almost all the gentlemen do – not so the ladies, a straw hat the size of a drum, with a full grown gooseberry bush stuck at the top of it would not be at all out of the way,

---

* Actually the River Vezere.

but I believe I have before noticed this preposterous taste. Our next halting day is at Chateauroux on the 24th at Orleans, 28th at Etamples, and on the 31st we arrive at Mantes & wait for orders. It seems uncertain yet whether we shall embark for England at Boulogne or Calais, or at Havre de Grace or that neighbourhood. I shall hail the event with rapture wherever it happens. There being no chance of any more English letters or papers overtaking us in this country is very provoking & I think might have been better contrived; I suppose rejoicing for peace, and the arrival of such mighty potentates as the Emperor of Russia, & King of Prussia will have driven all the people in London nearly crazy.* I had no idea that the French could make themselves quite as ridiculous as the Portuguese & Spaniards in religious mockery but really there was a procession here yesterday that was nearly equal to anything it ever was at Lisbon. The penitents walked barefooted & covered themselves with enormous red or white extinguishers with holes cut out to see through as in a mask. They looked like huge radishes and parsnips walking along the streets upon their heads. Frederick is very well & exactly the colour of nutmeg. I have been out of order for three or four days by drinking two glasses when hot, of stuff called biere & which was, made of every thing *but* malt and hops. I am now quite shank again, but thought much of poor John Slack & the excise man all the time it was *working* me, for I'm sure there was *wormwood* in it.†
Goodbye, God bless you dearest Chats. Love to Cony from yours ever

EG

Edwin wrote again from Orleans, explaining that the cavalry had marched across France to embark at Boulogne. However, Frederick had been taken ill and Edwin had proceeded ahead with him in a carriage to Orleans. Edwin had clearly not been impressed with the French posting system. He was also planning a visit to Paris with Rico.

Orleans, June 24th 1814

My dear Chatts
'Cec vient saclant d'eu l'esperance de vous trouve en bon sante, comme il me quitte a present, grace a dieu pour le meme'. ['I hope this finds you in good health, which at the moment I am not, thank God all the same.'] I wrote to you on the 7th from Souillac & on the 13th from Limoges, both

---

* The Emperor's of Prussia, Russia and Austria and their most renowned generals all travelled to London to celebrate the great victory over Napoleon.
† Wormwood has hallucinogenic properties; it is perhaps most famous as an ingredient in absinthe, which is thought to have caused Van Gogh to cut off his ear.

which letters I hope you will have received. they like this were merely to announce our gradual but incessant progress northwards & much hope we continue with equal success until the 12th of July when we arrive at Boulogne, when we shall be detained there for want of sufficient transports for England, for the whole [other] column (the cavalry marches in two columns, one on *this*, the other on the Poitiers road) will arrive three or four days before us; & each column consists of about six thousand making a total which I should think will take some weeks to convey from shore to shore unless, which is not likely, they have every cavalry transport employed in our service. Frederick wrote to his mother yesterday, to Bath, as we thought there was a chance of her not having yet quitted it. The extreme heat & constant work gave him a slight degree of fever which the day after we left Limoge threw itself out in a rash all over his body & rendered it advisable for him to go a few days marches in a carriage which I was not sorry to accompany him in & we pushed ahead of the brigade so as to get to Orleans on the 21st in the morning. These few days halt have completely set him up & he is now doing his duty again as usual. The posting in the country is dreadfully tedious, expensive & a person intending to travel far ought to lay in an *ample* stock of patience & money, the extreme ridiculousness of the carriages the miserable jades that draw it, the shreds and patches of the rope harness, together with the postilion in a huge laced hat, great greasy fronds and queue, nearly sans culotte and a pair of boots that at the very best weigh twenty pounds each, are altogether nearly sufficient to repay you for the delays and impositions you are subjected to. I had expected to find Orleans a handsome city & my expectations have been fully realised; the Loire which is as large as the Thames at Westminster & the bridges over it are magnificent, the streets, houses & shops beautiful, and the cathedral without exception the most beautiful pieces of external workmanship I ever beheld. In the middle of the principal square upon a pedestal of white marble stands a statue in bronze of the heroic Joan of Arc brandishing her sword and bending forward, her beautiful countenance highly expressive of the wildness & enthusiasm with which she was possessed. The four sides of the pedestal represents likenesses in brass of her introduction to the French king; her defeating the Earl of Shrewsbury & raising the siege of Orleans, the coronation of Charles the 7th and lastly her horrid death, which however politick it might have been in those days reflecting in my view nothing but shame.

On the 22nd peace was proclaimed here, a ceremony I never before witnessed; the decorations, illuminations &c were very like what I saw at Toulouse on the entrance of the Duke of Angouleme, by the bye how tired you cannot have been of that subject; as Harriet sent you a copy of my letter to her which could vary but little from the accounts I wrote Cony and family afterwards. A mail from England through Bordeaux, contrived somehow to overtake us here yesterday & by it I got your letter of the 24th ult. which claiming my very best thanks. I hope you are both quite well but you [did] not mention yourself. I shall not easily forgive the panorama people. Mr Hayes does me honour, but as I have not the slightest recollection of *him* it is *particularly* flattering his remembrance of *me*. We are to arrive at Mantes on the first of July & on the following day Frederick & I start for Paris, please God we hope my next will therefore most probably to be from that famed city. Adieu excuse great haste but I have much to see here.

Yourselves ever Edwin, best love to Louisa.

Edwin's next letter did indeed announce their safe arrival in Paris. They had only just arrived but Edwin was clearly impressed with the little that he had seen.

Hotel de Wagram, Rue St Augustin, July 3rd 1814

Me voici a Paris ma chere Chatty. We left Mantes last night, slept at St Germain [en-Laye], dined at Versailles and arrived in this wonderful City between six & seven o'clock. We took two or three turns in the gardens of the Tuilleries [*sic*], & the boulevards des Capucines, & then indulged in a luxurious warm bath, which I am just returned from and while our supper is getting ready write to you a few hasty lines. You may suppose I have not time to describe any thing suffice it to say that they all exceed the expectations I had formed.

Versailles is the only *palace* I ever saw. What can the Emperor Alexander &c &c think of our king's residences coming from Versailles & the Tuilleries? The road from St German goes over the Malis height from where I got the first view of it, & have been fancying myself 'John Bull for pastime' ever since: the Palais Royale really strikes one dumb. It is Sunday evening & everybody was on the Pavee; but I am too tired & sleepy to write any more to night.

Monday morning. I am just going to make a start in my *fiacre*, and shall finish this to take with me. My plans for the day are, first, Notre Dame, 2) the Palais Royale & the celebrated gallery of paintings & statuary in the Louvre; the Napoleon museum, & finish with the opera or theatre Francaise & so you see I have enough upon my hands. Adieu excuse the scrawl & believe me ever most affectionately.

Yours E. Griffith

I hope you got my letter from Orleans.

Edwin wrote again at the end of his six-day stay in Paris. A party of his fellow

232

officers from the 15th, including Rico, would now catch up with the regiment at Boulogne by the diligence. It would appear that Thackwell had commanded the 15th en route to Boulogne in Edwin's absence as he does not mention Paris.

Paris July 9th 1814

My dearest Chats,

I wrote to you on the 3rd to announce my arrival at Paris and have now to acquaint you with my intended departure this night at nine o'clock by the Boulogne diligence, which we have taken amongst us of the 15th, & fine fun the journey will be I expect.

I never passed a more delightful week than I have here, & I believe have seen all that it was possible in the time. I cannot attempt to describe any thing till my next. Frederick has enjoyed himself as much as I have, & we have almost come to a determination to pass a month in Paris some time hence; the expense is the only thing against it as Monsieur les Anglais pay at least double for everything; I mean at the hotel and those sort of places.

I went to the Tuilleries the day before yesterday to see the King receive the various petitions that are handed to him, the old fellow hobbled about the room speaking to everybody & seems so happy that it does one good to see him, at the same time I cannot help fearing that a very great proportion of the people would be glad to see that arch villain Boney back again. He certainly has done wonders in Paris & has contrived to leave his name, or deeds, so completely into every palace, church, bridge, monument &c &c throughout the whole place that it would be impossible to efface it without destroying half their beauties. Well my dearest Chats I hope my next will be written in Ingleterra, all my anxiety now is to know where we shall be quartered and when leave of absence will come out. Frederick who is at my elbow writes in best love & esteem to all your party. Ever & ever yours dear Chats.

E. Griffith

At Boulogne Major General Fane inspected the regiment, who expressed 'his entire approbation of the appearance of the regiment'. Edwin wrote from Boulogne of his excursion to Paris, while he waited for the transports to arrive.

Boulogne, July 14th 1814

Well my dear Chatts, I have nearly brought the journal of my movements to a conclusion. We left Paris the night of the day I last wrote to you. Breakfast was at Beauvais, lunched at Abeville & arrived at this place early on the 11th & after a pleasant a journey as the nature of a diligence will allow & before the whole I am highly delighted with my trip to the French capital, & would not for the world but have seen it if it was only to convince me of it's inferiority to our own. I don't think it covers more than half the ground that London does & the Seine being about the same proportion to the Thames; Notre Dame is a parish church compared to Westminster Abbey & the theatres & public buildings will still less bear any comparison to our own. There are no handsome squares & very few good streets, the equipages & well dressed people are in the proportion of about one to ten. On the other hand the palaces & gardens are beyond description superb; the gallery of the Louvre is an inexhaustible delight to a lover of the arts; it is above a quarter of a mile long & hanging closely with all the most rare & valuable paintings of the Dutch, French, German & Italian schools, one of these alone, by Raphael is estimated at 1 million sterling, so I leave you to guess at the value of the whole collection, the ground floor is divided into separate apartments containing all the most exquisite performances of the chisel among them the celebrated & inimitable Apollo & Venus, which (particularly the former) absolutely rivets me to the spot. Next to the Louvre the Palace of the Tuilleries is the best worth seeing of any thing in Paris one can no longer wonder at Bonaparte murdering the Duc d'Enghien* or half a hundred Dukes, to ensure his keeping possession of & receiving the homages of 30,000,000 Frenchmen *in* so glorious a pile of richness & magnificence. All our astonishment is that he could not be satisfied with the peaceable possession of such power and luxury. In the Royal Treasury are deposited Bonaparte's and the Empress's coronation paraphernalia on which splendour has exhausted its devices, the lining of the robes alone is composed of eleven thousand ermine skins. The Empress's crown is the most beautiful thing I ever saw; His is nothing more than a simple wreath of gold leaves in imitation of the Caesars. In the same room are kept the crown, sceptre and sword of Charlemagne, which I contemplated with greater veneration than Boney's and as the love laid no *bloods* here every thing is open to the touch as well as view and therefore you cannot be deceived as to the reality of the jewellery &c &c.

---

* Louis Antoine Henri de Bourbon-Conde, Duc d'Enghien, had fled France like many during the revolution and he eventually settled at Ettenheim in Baden. Royalist attempts on his life caused Napoleon to order the Duc's arrest despite the fact that he resided on neutral territory. Napoleon ignored the illegality of the act; the Duc was arrested and swiftly returned to France, where he was hauled before a military tribunal at Vincennes with little opportunity to defend himself and immediately condemned and shot. This one act lost Napoleon the support of reformers throughout Europe and he would regret it till his death. As Fouche reputedly said '. . . it was more than a crime – it was a mistake.'

France to Ireland

The 15th boarded transports at Boulogne on the evening of 15 July. Edwin and Joseph Thackwell sailed on the *Kingston* Transport with fifty-four horses. The regiment landed at Dover on 16 and 17 July 1814 in heavy rain and proceeded to Canterbury, where they hoped for some rest and a spot of leave. Edwin wrote a short letter, clearly delighted to have returned safely and gave thanks for his deliverance.

Dover, July 17th

Thanks to the God of armies, the God of navies, the goddesses of wisdom, prudence, health & every other God or Goddess concerned in it. I am once more safe & sound in the tight little island! On the 15th having no prospect of immediate embarkation I put myself into a cabriole & drove over to Calais; on my return at night I found orders to embark at daylight, which I did, sailed at nine and at half past two was moored off Dover pier. Oh my dear Chats what a blessing it is to an Englishman to find the cleanliness & comforts of a little fishing town like this superior to every thing foreign. There are only three transports arrived yet, Frederick not one of them but I expect him tomorrow. We have got a route for Canterbury, but I believe it is only to assemble the Regt preparatory to our going to some other quarter; in the meantime write me a line to that place as it is quite an age since I heard from you. I must superintend the disembarkation of the horses therefore excuse great hurry. God bless you most affectionately your

Edwin.

Write by return of post pray; to Canterbury.

The regiment was to remain at Canterbury for ten days of rest and recuperation after the long march. They now proceeded to Hounslow where they were reunited with the regimental depot which had marched there from Arundel on 22 July. The regiment now numbered twelve troops totalling 910 rank-and-file and 746 horses and, Hounslow being too small to accommodate them all, the troops were spread around the Brentford and Isleworth areas. It is clear that a projected peacetime reduction in troop numbers, which was not to become official until 9 August, was already known to Edwin and that the regiment was due for a tour of duty in Ireland. He was obviously looking forward to a spot of leave to travel home to Rhual.

London Aug 1st 1814

My dearest Chats,
Here am I; and I have hardly time to tell you more in the midst of the row which pervades this vast metropolis today. We left Canterbury on the 27th

& arrived at Hounslow yesterday when we remain a few days to be reviewed & reduced, & then proceed for Ireland. I don't know whether to be glad or sorry at going to the land of potatoes; but am determined to make myself happy & comfortable wherever we go. Our good uncle is looking particularly well I think, & not the least altered during the two years that have elapsed since I last saw him. He leaves town on Wednesday for Hinching Brook where he stays a few days & then proceeds with his own horses for Rhual, Frederick was there (Mansfield Street) with me & he (Sir A.) compliments us both on our good looks although we are both darker & older than when we left England, very natural this. The march to Ireland shall not interfere with my intended visit to Wales; I hope to be with you very soon after my uncle. Let me hear from you at Hounslow; I will write when we move from thence. You can have no idea of the enormous mass of population assembled in the park; what must foreigners think of London! I fear they must think us crazy & indeed every thing wears the appearance of disorder & folly; I hope this will be the last of all rejoicings for some time. Mrs Daniel has got something for Cony, but I desired her to give it to Illy. Adieu- best love to all from yours most affectionately

EG

On 3 August the regiment was inspected in marching order on Hounslow Heath by the Prince Regent and the Duke of York as part of the Grand Jubilee, they were reported to be 'much delighted' with the 15th. Following this, the officers were occupied in identifying the men and horses which were to be turned out at the reduction and on 9 August 350 men were discharged and 288 horses cast. William is very critical of the way it was done, claiming that the fresh-faced youngsters of the depot squadron were retained at the expense of those hardened veterans returning from France. With this process complete the regiment was reduced to eight troops of sixty-nine men and fifty-six horses. Finally on 11 August the regiment commenced their march to Liverpool in two divisions, Edwin leading one via Amersham and Thackwell the other via Rickmansworth. The regiment re-combined at Liverpool, remaining there and at Warrington between 25 August and 7 September, then sailed for Dublin in the transports. Frederick had been allowed to remain in London and at some point, possibly once the regiment was at Liverpool, Edwin was allowed time to visit his family at Rhual and then proceed independently to Dublin. The fact that Edwin's first letter from Dublin was quite clearly written shortly after his arrival there indicates that his period of leave amounted to some three months. He writes of his adventures by coach and ship, the stormy crossing and the after-effects of a great party!

France to Ireland

Dublin 22 Dec 1814

Miss Griffith, at David Pennant's Lodge, Downing, Hollywell, Flintshire

Arragh be now my jewel for sure aren't we quite safe & snug in the nate [*sic*] little City of Dublin. To begin from the day I set out; you must know that I got to Pontifrith about three o'clock to which was pretty well considering the tremendous storm we had to face the whole way & that two trees, one near Vecclos and the other below small gate had fallen across the road & obliged us to drive through a farm yard. I did nothing but rejoice the whole way that I had not taken your chaise & the poor old blacks out in such weather. At Pontifrith they were all civility as usual and the old lady more speechifying & tiresome than ever, about my kindness in giving them a day of my company before I left the country &c &c. I never attempt to answer hers you know; as after letting her go on for exactly 25 minutes by a watch that laid on the table, I merely observed that her stream of compliments had so entirely wrecked me on the rock of silence that I had not word to say. I had asked Madge & Edwards to arrange a chaise from Denbigh to take me on to St Asaph on Saturday, but she shipped it & insisted on my taking hers which was indeed particularly thoughtful and kind of her; I tried to argue it with her but she again beat me easy and I was obliged to accede to her proposal.

I left St Asaph at 12 & got to Conwy ferry at ½ past 2, waited till three for the boat and was upwards of an hour crossing. The storm was so furiously against us; the rain fell in torrents & the sea broke over the boat every few minutes, so that had I swung across* I should not have been at all better than as it was. I got tolerable quarters for the night at the Harp, proceeded in the coach at seven the next morning; my companions were a Liverpool merchant going to visit his family at the Head; & two sons of Sir Wm Hughes, particularly nice lads going home for the holidays; the rough weather no ship could or packet sailing for several days (and the inns at Holyhead were crowded; I however got a bed at Spencers and a plentiful though not a very cleanly dinner in the *travellers room*; there were specific occurrences, vulgar gentlemen of the party, but they were very entertaining. As soon as we sat down one of them asked the waiter for a little eel, which I thought inexcusable as there was a fine codfish & plaice on the table. The waiter however understood him & brought a glass of cwrw. The next morning Frederick arrived, and a packet sailed in the evening; but the wind was contrary, the sea high & we not prepared for timing &c, thought it would be better for us & Ben to wait till the next day

---

* As well as the ferry, there was also a rope across the river by which passengers could cross suspended in a basket.

and as the writer had by that time recognised us & made tender enquiries *after you* & *Caroline* we got a comfortable letting room to ourselves, his name is *Walker,* he lived at Gly about ten years ago. On Tuesday the 20th we easily walked at seven in the morning on board *Pelham,* Capt Judd and at a ¼ past weighed anchor, there were upwards of forty passengers but none that I knew the face or name of except Sir Charles Saxton,* Colonel Burgh (one of Ld Wellington's ADC's)† and Capt. Verner of the 7th Hussars.‡ The night was clear but there was hardly air enough to fill the sail. We paraded the deck till near seven & then returned to our berth & I went to sleep. At half past four I was awoke by a noise made by nearly a dozen people at the same moment for the steward, to bring them basins & warm water, a pretty stiff breeze from the south east had sprung up and its effects upon the cabin inmates was irresistible for they were calling in all directions; I thought I should have died of laughing at the uncouth noises & miserable figures some of them exhibited. At seven I went on deck preferring starvation to the hot stink of the cabin which I found I should not be able to *stand* much longer. The Howth & Black Rock lights were then in light, & at a little after eight we came dashing into the bay of Dublin at the rate of *eleven knots & a half an hour.* Landed at the custom house & walked up to Tuthills Hotel in Dawson Street (where I am now writing) to breakfast. The entrance to the bay is very beautiful. The shore on the right & left being covered with villas and woods. The town handsome & clean looking and a fine background formed by the Wicklow & Kildare mountains. The Clonmel mail is full for tomorrow so we have taken our places for Saturday the 24th, I will write again soon after my arrival at that place. I shall direct this to Downing according to your desire, pray give my very kindest regards to Mr & Mrs Pennant. I was very near saying love, but recollected that if Mr Pennant has a fault it is that he is prudish. If David is at home I include him of course. Well my dearest Chatty I will bid you adieu for the present, write on the receipt of this to Clonmel and believe me ever & ever yours most affectionately

Edwin.

Let me have a return of the killed & wounded in action with the forces under mounted Eoleus on the 10th as soon as Adjt. Genl. Jarvis has made it out. There were some fierce fellows laid low before I left the field, and

*   Sir Charles Saxton was the son of the late commissioner of the Navy at Portsmouth.
†   Lieutenant Colonel Sir Ulysses Burgh KCB, 1st Foot Guards.
‡   Captain William Verner 7th Hussars, his memoirs were published in Special Publication no. 8 of the Society for Army Historical Research in 1965.

tell me if any more shells struck the house besides what fell when we were at breakfast! Adieu encore. It snows fast, and the jaunting cars and rattling like fury along the street, apropos fury *still keeps up* but is enormous.

Edwin and Frederick spent only a few days in Dublin and Edwin was writing home on Christmas day 1814, confirming his safe arrival at Clonmel. He reports his adventures on the mail coach and that his dog, Fury, had finally produced only one pup. The regimental headquarters were at Clonmel, with squadrons based at Fethard, Cappoquin and Kilkenny where the 42nd Foot were also based. It seems strange that when the army generally consisted of a disproportionately large number of Irishmen, the 15th could not boast a single one! Assistant Surgeon Gibney puts this down to the fact that the regiment had never sent a recruiting party into Ireland.

Clonmel Dec 25th 1814

My dearest Chats,

I hope you will have received my letter from Dublin of the 22nd. I have now to announce my arrival at my journeys end & heartily glad to have got there. It has been upon the whole as prosperous a one as could reasonably be expected at this time of year but uncomfortable enough too. We left Dublin on Saturday night by the Cork mail which to our horror was discovered carried six insiders instead of 4 & was loaded with luggage like an English heavy coach. Only one of the doors would open and upon our asking the gentleman the reason he said 'is it the spring broke over loaded which makes the coach lean too near the wheel for the door to open too well', and we were squeezed to death & jolted to mummies almost, with great success till we got near Naas when we came to a walk, which was accounted for by one of the passengers saying we were near a very lonely place where carriages were easily fired at & that our coach was waiting for the Waterford mail, accordingly when the coach of the Waterford hove in sight a good allowance of oaths & ship cord got us into a trot again & we reached Naas in safety: the coachman there told us that they had all received orders to be more [than] usually vigilant that night as the Post Office had notice of a strong gang being upon the road & that the coaches were to keep company as far as possible. In going down a little hill near Carlow the coach made two or three very odd twists first to one side of the road & then the other & at length came to a stop the horses all huddled together in a heap. We asked what was the matter? 'Shure wasn't the fowl looke' said coachee, 'and its great odd we'er not turned over'. Out we all got as fast as we could through one door, & after sliding till they had fetched the pole of a chain from an inn near the place, & which was a mite too small every way, when it did connect we proceeded to Carlow. Added to this one spoke had been knocked out of its socket some weeks before and was now kept in by a few nails only which did not prevent it clattering all the way. So much for Irish mail & you may guess from this what the other coaches & chaises must be. The country that we passed through was very ugly & bleak, totally destitute of trees & nearly so of hedges. The gentlemen's houses look deserted, which indeed most of them are & the poverty & wretchedness of the peasantry & their mud huts is great in the extreme. Clonmel is the only place I've seen with the exception perhaps of Kilkenny that I could bear to live at. We got here at two o'clock yesterday & found Dalrymple all our friends as well as can be expected; my horses also in high condition. The barracks are old & dismal, but tolerably comfortable; just out of town, with a fine river in front, & a very high mountain behind them. I shall take possession of Dalrymple's apartments when he goes which will be in a few days; at present I am living in the hotel. I saw as much as I wished of Dublin for that sort of thing & like it much; the part of the town where the college & the bank stand is particularly handsome, Dame Street, Westmorland and Sackville are superior to any I think in London; Merrion & Mountjoy Squares are also very pretty but won't bear comparison to Grosvenor & Portman. By the bye I hope this will find you at Downing, but whether it does or not remember me most kindly to Mr & Mrs Pennant & tell him that I enquired at several libraries in Dublin but could only find one copy of 'Beaufort's memoirs of Ireland' belonging to *his* map;* but that as it is a very thin quarto and costs 2 guineas I would not buy it; the man however promised to keep it till he heard from me. If Mr P wishes to have it let me know soon as it is a very scarce book.

Pepper† is quartered at Carrick on Suir about 14 miles from here, he dines here today. We have already talked *Acton* over; and I'm sure by what he *says* he did not escape with impunity from all the dangers which surrounded us there. One of our captains Dundas has been caught in this neighbourhood by an English lady of the name of Boultby who is very charming I hear. The forlorn situations in which some officers are placed is likely to make them marry in a fit of *desperation* and therefore don't be surprised if I bring a Mrs G back with me. Frederick is quite well & desires his love. Fury produced one child on the road and no more; but I think they must either have jolted out of the gig or been eat by wild beasts in the

---

* The Reverend D. A. Beaufort had produced a new map of Ireland in 1792.

† Lieutenant the Honourable Richard Pepper-Arden 15th Hussars transferred to the 2nd garrison battalion in April 1815 and hence missed Waterloo. He eventually became a major in 84th Foot and retired by sale of his commission in 1829. He later became Lord Alvanley and died in 1857.

stable as she was immensely big & Fletcher* is a sleepy fellow & perhaps did not *see* more than one. Well My paper is full so God bless you and believe me always yours my dearest Chats most affectionately.

Edwin

In early January Edwin was writing home again, clearly bored with his enforced exile from any form of social life. He complains of no news from home, but has little to give in exchange. William, however, states that the men were not so bored, being regularly called out on long exhausting night marches in an attempt to surprise and destroy these robber bands, from which they did gain some success.

Clonmel, January 12th 1815 [Marked 'Received 23rd March']

Written to Downing, Holywell

Thankyou dearest Chatty for your two letters; it is very odd you did not receive my [letter] sent from Dublin, sooner, but I suppose that little ferry renders the arrival of a letter at its destination quite uncertain. I calculate that this will catch you this day before you set out for Peover.† When I left home I really did intend writing from the Head, but when I thought you would most probably hear of me from Harriett or Louisa both of whom Frederick wrote to & that, even if you did not the disappointment would not be *fatal* to you, & postponed it until I got to this side of the water. You were indeed very considerate for getting the chevalier to trunk that very uninteresting affair which came to Rhual after I had left it. I wish in return I could find a franker for this but Clonmel does not abound in such likes of *ton*. I had seen poor Mrs Fortescue's death in the Bath paper before your letter arrived;‡ it seems to have been somewhat sudden but really at four score, one has no rights to expect much warning. Write me the particulars when you know them. My life at this place is not likely to furnish much matter for letter writing. I took possession of my barrack room the day Dalrymple set off and neither the country, roads or weather are such as to tempt me far beyond our boundary wall. I do not much encourage visiting as it is not the fashion in these parts to make the offer of a bed; riding home in the dark is a bore & chaise here is expensive to say nothing of the certainty you undergo of being robbed & murdered every

---

* Private Thomas Fletcher obviously served as a servant to Edwin.
† Peover Hall, five miles south of Knutsford in Cheshire.
‡ Mrs Fortescue was mother of Viscount Clermont of Louth in Ireland. She died at Ketton Cottage, Rutland, aged 80. I must thank Philip Haythornthwaite for this information.

time you attempt these, not only the dispositions of the people but even the names of all places about this takes something with Knock or Kill. Lord Donomaugh's* & Col Greene; who have both called on me live the former at Knocklofty & the latter at Kilmaccuragh castle; there is a range of heights called Knockmealdown mountains on one side of the valley, & Killallon ridge on the other; and in order to carry the affinity still closer between in some of the villages & their inhabitants, there is Clonmuck, Rathgormuck, Sleivenamuck, &c &c. I wrote to my uncle yesterday which I thought right although I had nothing particular to say to him; if Sir Murray's court martial is not put off it will find him in a fine fuss,† & he will wish me at old nick for plaguing him; as he called it; he must be stiled a Grand now‡ but I dare say not half pleased at the order of the Bath being made so common I assure you. I was quite vexed at it; some other order might have been instituted as a reward for ordinary services; but the most honourable military order of the Bath should have been kept sacred and bestowed only on the highest merit. What think you of *Sir Colquhoun* Grant by way of a pretty sounding title?§ Frederick is persevering as usual with his *gun* and has killed a few cocks & snipes. I have not yet unpacked *mine* as the weather has been too open for shooting from comfort in these bogs. We have had no frost or snow at least for not longer than one night, it generally begins to rain after dark, fogs & humidity being the order of the day.

I never heard of a narrower escape than the Despard family had, it would have been a great pity if that poor little harmless girl had been crushed to death by a great chimney. Old Whitehall Davies having been once started which I dare say to be married in turn to all the spinsters in North Wales; what a charming interesting couple he & Charlotte Cunliffe would make. If you have not written before this reaches you, pray do so from Peover and of course remember me to the Barnett & his lady. How idle Harriett has grown with her pen, Frederick has only had one letter

---

* Actually Lieutenant General Richard Hely, 1st Earl of Donoughmore, who became Viscount Hutchinson of Knocklofty; he died in 1825 when the title descended upon his brother, General John Hely Hutchinson, commander of the British forces in Egypt in 1801 following Abercromby's death. I have been unable to identify Colonel Greene.

† This refers to the court martial of General Sir John Murray, for his failure at Tarragona, which commenced sitting at Winchester in January 1815, although it is unclear why this would be a bother to Sir Alured as he was not a member of the court.

‡ Sir Alured Clarke was appointed a Knight Grand Cross of the Order of the Bath, having previously only been a Knight; hence Edwin's 'Grand' comment. Wylly (1914) says that Edwin became a member of the Order of the Bath, but there is no evidence for this.

§ Colquhoun Grant was appointed Knight Commander of the Bath.

from her since she got to Bath. He writes with me in bouquets of love to you both ever adieu dear Chatty most affectionately yours.

Edwin.

I was glad to hear that Mina gave a good account of herself. My best love to her. How could Cony or David suppose me silly enough to my waiting after supper at Acton?

Edwin seems to have become embroiled in a major dispute between a bankrupt firm of outfitters in London and some of his officers, including Frederick. The thinly veiled threats provoked a stinging reply; it is strange, however, that this odd document has managed to survive.

23 January 1815 To Major Griffith

Sir,

It seems very singular that Lt. Mansfield's memory should be so bad as to forget he had a pair of mixed casamere [*sic*] pantaloons dated 1812 value 2–2–0 & that Capt. Philips had the following articles

Great coat repairing	0–2–0
Sash repairing (it looks like)	0–4–6
Jacket repairing & bid	0–5–6
	0–12–0

However permit me to say that the assigner of the estate of Messr.'s Finn & Johnson bankrupts has not forgotten it is in their books legal debts & as such they will lay it before the Commander in Chief on oath as valid. It is of little use denying the name when there is ocular demonstration of the debt.

Your obedient servant

M. Barnett

Lt Carr's* father has this week paid the debt without denying any knowledge of the parties.

Clonmel, February 11 1815

My answer enclosing the above back to him.

---

* Lieutenant John Carr, 15th Hussars, served at Waterloo but was placed on half pay in 1816.

Sir,

Why you should have addressed the enclosed to *me* I am at a loss to conceive. I never had, *or intend to have* any concern with Finn & Johnson or yourself. Your letter is extremely disrespectful & your signature so difficult to decipher that I fear this will never find you. Every similar production addressed to me shall be returned to you in like manner.

Edwin Griffith, Major Commanding 15th or King's Hussars.

Edwin was able to write with a little news towards the end of February.

Carrihmore, February 28th 1815 Waterford March 2nd 1815

My dearest Charlotte,

I have not time to write a dozen lines but will endeavour to do that merely because I have an opportunity of sending you them free. I have been here since Saturday & return to Clonmel either today or tomorrow for Lord Waterford is very civil in preparing me to stay: as for the marchioness I am quite in love with her, & their children are dear little clever riotous things as ever were seen. It is a charming place, I don't know that there is one more so in England even; at least on so large a scale, for you can ride a circle of eighteen miles within the grounds. There is a pleasant party in the house, and if they would only keep better hours it would be delightful; but breakfasting at ½ past eleven, dining at seven & going to bed at two don't suit my fancy at all. I hope to hear soon from you again with favourable accounts of David, I received Cony's last letter tell her I shall answer it ere long. I should not be surprised if you were still at Downing but shall direct this home.

Everybody in this country has been lamenting the picturesque death of the young Duke of Dorset; – so striking an instance of the instability of all worldly grandeur and happiness certainly rarely occurs. At one o'clock he was in possession of health, youth & vigour, the highest rank, a splendid affluence & every virtue & good quality which gives prospect to long enjoyment; at three he was a corpse. While millions of his fellow creatures are permitted to decay through a tedious length of years in want, disease & wretchedness. What a theme for a moralist! I have time for no more so God help you both. Ever & ever most affectionately

Yours Edwin.

Edwin wrote again in March and spoke much of tenant problems with the Corn Laws, the lawlessness in Ireland, and more practically on saving money on the postage. William says that not a week went by without a murder being committed.

France to Ireland

Clonmel, March 11 1815 [Marked 'Received 29 March']

My dearest Chats,

I wrote you a short letter on the 28th ult at Curraghmore & left it for Lord Waterford to frank; if however that great Marquis is as irregular in his epistolary as in every other department the letter is still lying on his Escritor untouched, and you must be in perfect despair of ever hearing from me any more. Yours of the 4th arrived in due time & I was very happy to find by it that poor David [Pennant] *was* gaining ground by *certain*, tho' slow degrees and sincerely hope he will continue to do so. Frederick & I think & talk of him a great deal which pray tell him with our best remembrances and regards. Pepper also makes constant enquiries after him whenever we meet & bids me say he hopes we shall *all* meet again in October. He is quartered at Carrick on Suir but almost lives at Curraghmore which is within 5 miles. I have had a long letter from Louisa the older written in excellent spirits. It was dated the latter end of February which I should think would be about the same time that she wrote the desponding one you mention to Mrs Pennant (but as you observe) I don't much mind what she says either way: in my answer I gave my opinion pretty freely about Madam Oliver, which I suppose won't be very well received but I *don't mind that either.* You seem to be in a bit of horrible mess with your tenantry; but you must bully them well, assemble them on the pavement. Tell them through the front room window, that you will hear no more of their methodisical whining, that the land is considerably under let; that they never knew when they are well off; then give them a few extracts from the debates on the Corn Bill & bid them get home & be damned to them all. If you will do this properly depend upon it you will hear no more complaints on the subject. I think Wynne must have managed badly the meadows or surely they might have been let for *something* as it is they will be an expense to you & if you don't look sharp there will be no *crop at all* upon them, for they are in wretched order. The assizes begin here on the 18th which I suppose will give us something to do as they always attempt to rescue their innocent relatives; there are one hundred and ninety six prisoners in the jail, but only 143 for trial, which is reckoned very little. You think Robert Lloyd having been wounded by this, by his son a shocking circumstance but it would hardly attract notice *here*. I take the Clonmel Herald &c, I give you my honour three columns out of the 16 are always filled with 'Inhuman murder' 'Brutal rape', 'Daring robbery' &c &c &c; and it is published twice a week too. A few nights ago one of our officers who slept in the town heard as he was going to bed, the report of a pistol under his window; in the morning he asked the waiter what it was? 'nothing at all plase your honour' said he but added 'the coachman who drives the Cork mail would not stop at the whisky shop over the way there so the guard fired at him *that was* all' You will perhaps say, a good story but 'it *can't be true*'. I pledge my self to its being an *historical fact*! No less than, a more entertaining circumstance occurred at one of the counsel hall. Mr Douglas of ours was dancing with a young lady, who not being very amenable in getting out of the way, was seen again nearly pushed over by a gentleman going down the middle 'ach! says she to Douglas. 'Did you see what a great powlt that fillow gave me' Douglas said he believed it was quite accidental, Och returned the lady, 'for the matter of that it's no odds, for the *baste* he knew no better' you may be very sure that this story was not long in circulating amongst us & that the lady will never be known by any other name than the *Powlt* while, we live, I thought Frederick would have died of laughing, when told it. By todays paper which I have just seen *we* seem to be in the most quiet country of the two; I fear the Corn Bill will occasion serious riots in the large towns in England. The Post Office at Holywell always charge you letters 2/4 instead of one & seven pence; I recover it at this office on every letter; if you would tell them of it you would save me much trouble. I hope you don't pay more than 1/7 for my letter, mention this when you write. Your account of Sir Stephen gives one great concern; I have always been in fear for him since we met at Canterbury in July last whenever you hear of him pray repeat it in you *letters*. I shall direct this to Downing as you do not talk of going home my kindest remembrances as usual will therefore await your host & hostess and if Cony ever writes to the fair Lucy I hope she will say something pretty from her friend Edwin. There is no immediate prospect of our changing quarters unless perhaps to Caher next month if the new barracks there are finished. I don't dislike this place at all, for there is capital salmon fishing within a walk, & I have got acquainted with every body worth knowing in the neighbourhood. Remember to tell me whether Lord Combemere ever came to any agreement with John Lytton about the gates? It is about time I should think for milady to pay, I am glad to hear so good an account of Maria. Give my best love to the old lady when you write or see her. And now good bye. I began this yesterday but was interrupted. Frederick joins in all *my good wishes* to *everybody*. Yours ever and ever most affectionately.

Edwin

Chapter 8

WATERLOO

This peaceful sojourn in Ireland was to end abruptly in March 1815. Soon the news reverberated throughout Europe of Napoleon's escape from Elba on 26 February and his rapid march to Paris where he successfully reclaimed the throne on 20 March. The entire diplomatic corps of Europe which very conveniently had been sitting at the Congress of Vienna condemned Napoleon's actions and Europe declared war, not against France, but against Napoleon. Lord Wellington was to command a conglomerate force of British, Dutch and German troops in Belgium, where he was to work closely with the Prussian army under Prince Blücher. The government was embarrassed by the sudden change of events; it had as usual reduced the size of the armed forces drastically at the end of the war and many of Wellington's Peninsular troops were still in Canada where they had been engaged with the Americans until a recent fortuitous peace treaty had brought the fighting to an end. Units were hurriedly ordered to Belgium to bolster Wellington's force and it was clear to Edwin that the 15th would very soon receive their orders to march. Orders were received to work on increasing the number of troops from eight to ten immediately. Lieutenant Colonel Dalrymple had returned from leave and would lead the regiment. Frederick was relieved to hear that he would not be required to remain with the depot squadron this time.

The expected order arrived on 19 April for six troops to prepare for foreign service and Edwin wrote home to apprise his family that by the time they received his letter he would once again be at the seat of war. Assistant Surgeon Gibney records that the men knew war was inevitable but that there was no enthusiasm for it. It is clear that Edwin did not fancy the sea voyage, fraught with dangers around the Scilly Isles and requiring favourable winds to avoid a very long passage in cramped transports. The total embarking was twenty-eight officers, thirty sergeants, seventeen corporals, six trumpeters, 372 privates and 399 horses.

The six troops selected for service were:

A Troop   Captain Wodehouse
B Troop   Captain Philips
D Troop   Captain Booth
E Troop   Captain Thackwell
F Troop   Captain Whiteford
H Troop   Captain Hancox

The depot squadron which was to be commanded by Major Cochrane was initially quartered at Fermoy but was then sent by sea to Portsmouth in the June and was stationed at Arundel to await the regiment's return.

Clonmel, April 23rd 1815

My dearest Chatty,

It was not to be expected that while almost all the troops in Europe are in motion the 15th would be suffered to remain inactive; and although we feared we should not be present at the opening of the ball in Belgium we flattered ourselves that we were much too accomplished a corps not to receive an invitation. It has accordingly arrived; & the probability is, that when you receive this we shall be on our march to Cork for embarkation.

I would give a months pay to have gone through England, the voyage from Cork to Ostend is such a long one and requires all the winds in the compass to make it in less than a fortnight or 3 weeks. I hate it very much on my own account as I detest a transport, but more for my poor horses who will suffer much I fear from the confinement, & the buffeting which we shall be sure to get till we have cleared the Scilly Islands & we are fairly in the channel.

Since my last I have been on a fishing expedition to the mouth of the Suir. We slept two nights at Waterford, went to Passage [East], New Geneva, & all along the western coast of the beautiful bay formed by two promontory's of Wexford & Waterford; the weather was delightful, & I was altogether much gratified with the trip. Dalrymple & I had intended to make our first visit to Killarney in May; but this Belgium party will rather interfere with our plans. On my return I found Cony's Volume of the 14th; and participated fully in dear old Mina's affliction at parting with you: poor soul, if my prayers are of any avail she will be spared all further sufferings; but in her situation & time of life, happiness can hardly be hoped for on this side the grave.

'From the grief of my friendships all dropping around till not one that I loved in my youth can be found' is a wish that all occasionally feel, although there are few who do not hope to attain a good round age before they die. I will write again as soon as we receive orders to move; in the meantime let me know if you have fixed upon any plan for your summer's campaign. Cony sent me a favourable report of David, & the reverse of his mamma; I shall be glad to have the one confirmed, & the other contradicted, & pray as usual, say every thing most kind for me to her & Mr Pennant. I am sending you a shabby letter my dear Chats but you may believe I have plenty to do. Frederick is quite well; and happy that he is not to be left with the depot this time. He enjoyed Conny's history of the Papillion as much as I did myself. God bless you both, yours ever & ever most affectionately.

E. Griffith

The regiment, having marched to Cork on 4 May, was now destined to suffer the vagaries of awaiting transports and a fair wind. Edwin fired off a further short note while busy preparing everything for embarkation.

Cork, May 7th 1815

My dearest Chatty

The hurry & confusion that one is always in at this point of embarkation must excuse me from writing more than just to say we go on board our ships tomorrow morning & sail the moment the wind suits. We had a pleasant march from Clonmel to this place which is one of the handsomest towns in His Majesty's dominions. It was quite an agreeable surprise to me finding any thing so good in Ireland. Dalrymple & I go in the same ship & we heartily pray for a short passage for our horses sakes.

Your letter from Rhual of the 28th inst. reached me yesterday. I hope this will make a speedier journey to Peover where I shall direct according to your desire. The illustrious Pepper we left at Clonmel, he has had a week on his knees for which good advice is deemed necessary & he goes through England for that purpose; I much fear he will not join us again as he expects to be gazetted to a company directly* & his finances will not allow of his returning to cavalry.† He says Frederick is here quite well, I

* Edwin was right; the Honourable Richard Pepper-Arden did receive his commission as a captain in the 2nd Garrison battalion on 26 April 1815 and thus missed serving with the regiment at Waterloo. It would appear that this is the gentleman whom Assistant Surgeon Gibney refers to previously as the cornet of a Scottish Baronet who gave 'insufferable airs' and while in Ireland as the future Lord who sold out because 'he couldn't abide the smell of pigs.'

† Edwin's comment regarding Pepper-Arden's limited means, in that he would not be able to remain in the cavalry, needs some explanation. The post of lieutenant in a cavalry regiment which Pepper-Arden would now be vacating and which he could sell on, was worth approximately £997 to him. A captaincy in the infantry would cost around £1,500 requiring therefore a further sum from him of £503. A captaincy in the cavalry was a

don't like your account of dear pod, always mention her when you write. Remember me kindly to Sir Harry & Lady Mainwaring* and believe me as usual your most affectionately.

Edwin

I suppose '15th Hussars, British army, Belgium' will be the proper direction to me. Adieu.

On 8 May the regiment was inspected in marching order by Lieutenant General Lord Forbes,† who expressed himself 'highly gratified'. Maintaining his normal practice, Edwin commenced a journal with the start of a new campaign. The campaign was not to start well with counter-winds but this did not stop the men enjoying themselves while the officers dined ashore. The first entry reads:

May 12th 1815

Dalrymple, Mr Griffiths,‡ Mr Dalwig§ & I embarked onboard the *Mary* transport,¶ Capt Daniel Monro, & sailed at eight o'clock in the morning. A heavy squall with rain coming on we could not get out of the harbour but returned to our anchorage off Cove. The Captain & the mate, Mr Lillie joined our party at dinner. The evening became fine & as there was a fiddler onboard, the crew & our men danced reels & jigs upon deck till dark.

With a fair wind finally appearing, Edwin despatched a short note home.

---

great deal more expensive at around £2,782, requiring a much greater payment of £1,785, which was clearly beyond his means.

* The Mainwarings lived at Peover Hall.

† Lieutenant General James Lord Forbes, colonel of 54th Foot.

‡ There is some mystery regarding this person who joined the 15th Hussars as a cornet and adjutant in 1814. He appears as Joseph Griffith in the army lists throughout his career (1814–29) but the 1815 Gazette notifying of his lieutenancy (vice Pepper-Arden) has his name as Henry Griffith. This could be put down to a clerical error, but intriguingly Thackwell in his journal seems to indicate that this person's surname may actually have been Jackson rather than Griffith. It is clear, however, that this gentleman had no family ties to Edwin or Frederick.

§ Veterinary Surgeon Conrad Dalwig had been appointed to the 15th Hussars in 1813 and went on half pay with the 2nd Light Dragoons KGL in 1817. Strangely Beamish records his name as Henry Hogreve (number 166).

¶ Gibney indicates that both he and Surgeon Thomas Cartan also sailed onboard the *Mary*. Gibney actually records the surgeon's surname as 'Carson' but I have followed Wylly and the Army List.

Waterloo

Onboard the Mary transport,
Cove of Cork, May 12th 1815

My dearest Chats

We have been on board since Tuesday, but the wind has been foul till this moment, when the whole fleet is getting under weigh. Such rowing & swearing from right to left as you never heard. I meant to write the last minute & I have now really run it so that I have only time to say adieu. I am sorry to make you pay for such a thing, but thought you would rather, than not hear at all. Ever & ever yours.

E. Griffith

Edwin continued his journal, describing a very rough passage, just as he had feared, but at least it was rapid.

13th

At daybreak the agent made signal for sailing again, & we ran out of Cove with a fine breeze at west. There was what the Capt called a 'nasty chopping sea' which tossed us about & made all the landsmen as sick as death. We lost sight of land about one o'clock; & soon afterwards the breeze freshened so much that one of the fleet carried away her foretop mast, & appeared in distress. Went to bed early.

14th

We had a fine run all night, & early this morning made the Scilly Islands which are, mostly, frightful & barren. This is a very dangerous spot but we passed within half a mile of the shore along the north and east coast. The circumference of this assemblage of ruin to ships is about 30 miles yet there is only one lighthouse upon them, & that difficult to see from the fogs & thick weather which almost always prevails here.

About noon saw the Lands End at a great distance, & before dark made the Lizard Point. The wind was nearly south west, but we ran at the rate of seven or 8 knots all day.

15th

This morning we going up the Channel at nine knots, but out of sight of land. Towards evening we made the Isle of Wight, & it soon afterwards fell mainly calm. There were four frigates, & many sail of different sorts in sight at this time.

16th

Was a fine clear morning with a light breeze from the south west. Spoke a brig of war who advised the Capt to carry more sail as privateers were expected, & war was to be declared in London this day. Beachy Head was then in sight, distant 6 or 7 miles. Ere soon afterwards saw the lighthouse at Dungeness, & dined off Folkestone where we were fired at several times & brought to by the *Nightingale*, gun brig, Capt. Nickson who sent for our Capt. on board to row him. At sunset we were within a mile of Dover & heard the drums of the garrison beating the retreat. We glided quietly through the straits, & at bed time were just under the South Foreland lighthouse. This was altogether a charming days sail: we passed numerous vessels, bought some fresh macarel [*sic*], & were never a moment without something to interest one.

17th

Was a dead calm; the ship however continued to move on slowly with all her studding sails, royals, &c set. At noon we made the land, saw Dunkerque, & Nieuport churches. Spoke some transports from the Downs, & a breeze springing up in the evening we took a pilot on board, who ran us into the harbour of Ostend at eight o'clock; having been only five days & four nights from the Cove of Cork. Several other ships of the fleet came in before & after us the same evening; & Philips drank tea in our cabin.

While laying to in the roads of Ostend, Edwin wrote another short letter to announce his safe arrival.

My transport off Ostend sent to Rhual, redirected to Lady Cottons, near Nantwich.
May 17th Evening

The hurry'd scrap I wrote at Cove near Cork on the morning of the 12th will have reached you my dearest Chats by this time & as the tide will not serve for entering the harbour of Ostend for two hours I shall avail myself of the delay to communicate the particulars of our voyage. We weighed anchor soon after eight on the 12th but after beating against a heavy gale & torrents of rain for a couple of hours we were ordered back to our anchorage, to the great joy of all fresh water sailors. At day break on the 13th the signal was again made for sailing, the wind at west, & blowing fresh, we soon got into the Atlantic and at ½ past one lost sight of land. The sea was very rough, and both Dalrymple & I suffered much from sea sickness, we had a fine run all day & all night, though we were pitched about a good deal & at nine the next morning we made the islands of Scilly & stood in close along the shore. Never did I see such sterility in His Britannic Majesty's dominions, as these islands present; or so frightful a collection of rocks as those which surround them. They really appear to be of no use for anything but to wreck ships upon. Towards the evening we saw the Lands End in Cornwall at a great distance & the next morning the 15th we were fairly in the channel, but out of sight of land as there was a strong gale from the south west with dirty weather, which made our Capt desirous of keeping a good offing. It moderated towards night & we had a view of Blackgang Chine, Culver Cliff & many of my old haunts in the Isle of Wight. Yesterday was clear & beautiful, & we ran close to Beachy Head, & all the headlands of Sussex & Kent near enough to distinguish objects with the naked eye; at sunset we were in the Straits of Dover, & heard the drums of the garrison beat the retreat; at nine o'clock we were abreast of the lighthouse on the South Foreland, from whence we took our direction to this coast; making Dunquerque, Neiuport, &c, in succession all day & here we are rolling off Ostend waiting as I before said for the tide. Altogether we have had a charming passage & if I can by keeping this open till tomorrow tell you of the arrival of Frederick, & the safe landing of my horses. I think I shall have communicated all you wish to hear in my first letter. Bonsoir. Thursday morning 18th we got into the harbour last night & I had soon after the pleasure of shaking Frederick by the hand. We are about to disembark & as we march for Ghent the next moment, have only time to say God Bless you. Yours & yours my dearest Chatty most affectionately.

Edwin

Rico also left a few notes of the campaign; he wrote:

We arrived in the harbour of Ostend; after an excellent passage of eight days.

Edwin records the process of disembarkation and the immediate march into Belgium.

18th

Soon after four in the morning we were roused to commence disembarking. The horses were lowered into the sea & towed on shore. My stud landed about 12, and it was not till near ½ past four [p.m.] that we were ready to set out on our march to Bruges. Before starting we eat our farewell dinner with Capt Monro, whose obliging & accommodating conduct during the time we were on board his ship entitled him to our gratitude & thanks. Ostend is a good sized place; the streets wider & cleaner than the generality of sea ports, & the people all spoke or understood English. The fortifications are not at present strong, but are undergoing improvement; the canals & ditches are however sufficient to repel any force invading by land if properly defended. The road we went from Ostend to Bruges is sandy & must be nearly impassable in winter; it is by the side of the Grand Canal the whole way, through rich meadows, woods & cornfields. The spires of Bruges were visible the moment we got out of Ostend, but it is full fourteen miles distant.

Several barges full of people passed us; it is a commodious, cheap & delightful way of travelling. Two horses draw them at a trot; although the barges are some of them as long as a gun brig.

It was dusk when we arrived at Bruges, but light enough to see that the town was extremely handsome; perhaps the most so of any country town I ever saw with the exception of Orleans & Oxford. I was billeted at a charming house belonging to Madame Moerkirke, who invited me to sup with her, her son & daughter; after which & a dish of politicks I went to bed.

Rico simply records,

> Disembarked and marched to Bruges; a fine handsome town; distance about five leagues from Ostend.

19th

Marched at eight for Eeklo; the ride was beautiful the whole way; more so than I thought it was in the nature of a *flat* country to be. The only fault it has is *that* & its being so intersected with dykes that you cannot get off the road; consequently is a capital country for a retreating army.

A squadron of the Royals having occupied Eeklo before us, part of the 15th, went on to some other places in the way to Ghent. Madame Moerkirke's wine had not agreed with me & I was very unwell all this day: I also suspect that the bed she gave me was not aired, as I had much pain in my bones. My billet was at an ironmongers; the cleanliness & elegance of whose house exceeded any thing of the kind that is to be seen at the most fashionable watering place.

Frederick again simply records,

> Marched through a fine rich country to Eeklo where we were cantoned for the night.

20th

At seven we continued our route through the same rich country for four leagues which brought us to Ghent, where we halted a few hours for rations, & proceeded on to the village of Sleydinge. Unfortunately this was pre-occupied by the 23rd Lt. Drags. & we had to wait until the return of Philips from Ghent for fresh orders. These were that the 23rd must make room for us that night & move the next morning. The officers of the 23rd were very civil in assisting to get us under cover, & gave us an excellent dinner at the inn where they messed. I still suffered much today from the effects of Madame Moerkirke's wine & bed.

Rico does not mention his ride to Ghent but states:

Proceeded to Sleydinge a beautiful village two leagues from Ghent. Dined with officers of the 23rd, here we remained until 26th.

They found a real welcome here and were delighted with how cheap it was.

21st

The 23rd marched & we got possession of their quarters. I changed my billet from the priests to the widow Dykes, where I got comfortably put up. We dined together nine in number at the inn, got an excellent dinner, plenty of wine, beer &c &c, and the amount of the bill was only 25 francs. Less than 2 shillings & four pence a head! The very uncommon cleanliness & beauty of every house, from the chateau, to the smallest cottage, & the apparently contentedness of every individual we had seen in Flanders, struck us all. There was no appearance of overgrown wealth, nor at the same time a single instance of poverty & distress. Surely these must be the happiest peasantry in the world.

22nd

Nothing particular occurred, the climate & weather is very like it is at the same season of the year in England.

23rd

I rode to Ghent, which is a handsomer looking town than Bruges although not quite so large. It however contains the most numerous population by some thousands. We went into the cathedral which is extremely handsome; & contains many very superb monuments. Also six enormous candlesticks brought from England by ... [left blank by Edwin]*

---

* Although the exterior of St Bavo's Cathedral is particularly unimpressive, the medieval artwork within is extremely beautiful. The four huge candlesticks in red bronze date from around 1500 are the work of Benedetto Da Rovezzano. The Italian master intended them as pillars for a canopy over the tomb of Henry VIII. During the Civil War they were sold to Bishop Triest, Bishop of Ghent 1621–57 and the pillars, changed into candlesticks, were placed near the altar in 1669. I must thank Canon Ludo Collin, Rector of St Bavo's Cathedral, for this information.

From the top of the tower which we ascended there is a prodigiously extensive view of the surrounding country uninterrupted by anything like a hill; we saw the churches of Bruges plainly, & the person attending us said that with a spying glass on a clear day those of Antwerp and Brussels were also visible. Of the town of Ghent we had a bird's eye view & all the gentleman's gardens which are full of fruit trees and give a rich, snug appearance to the whole. It is not fortified, but some thousand workmen are employed in throwing up works round the suburbs. The beautiful canal of Bruges which comes up to Ghent is a great convenience to the people, & gives the place almost all the bustle and appearance of a sea port.

24th

After muster, I rode round some of the men's quarters in the Parish of Sleydinge; with every lane & cottage in which I was delighted. All are clean, neat & comfortable; buried in the shade of their orchards, with a little garden on one side, & a farmyard on the other in which are two or three beautiful cows & horses, poultry, &c &c. when you have seen one of these residences you have seen all; an instance of poverty or misery is not to be found.

25th

Was a holiday among the villagers though we could not ascertain the occasion of it. The peasantry after church service was over amused themselves the remainder of the day, in playing at bowls & other rural sports in the shade of their orchards & avenues.

They were not pleased to receive orders to move further, especially when their new quarters proved to be so miserable.

26th

We had indulged a hope that we might be left in the charming village of Sleydinge till the regt was all assembled (for there is still a ship unaccounted for) & the army had commenced active operations. Our vexation this morning was great on receiving orders to march immediately for Oordegem; six miles on the road from Ghent to Brussels. We could not assemble till near eleven o'clock from the men being much scattered, & before we reached Oordegem we met an Aid De Camp who gave us fresh orders to proceed to Sint-Maria-Oudenhove, [Sint]-Goriks-[Oudenhove], Elst &c, three leagues & half further.* The consequence was

---

* These villages lie between Zottegem and Brakel.

we did not get in quarters till dark & found them all very indifferent.

Rico records,

> We received orders to move to St Marie Oudenhove, Elste &c, the regt was miserably cantoned.

Edwin appears to have become a little frustrated with the peasants in these more rural settings.

27th

I rode round the quarters of the regt which I had some difficulty in finding, the country is so woody & the people so very dull of comprehension that if you do not pronounce the name of a place exactly as they do themselves, they cannot guess at all what you mean. We occupied the villages of Goriks, Sint-Maria-Oudenhove, Elst & [left blank, Michelbeke?] all very beautiful, but not near so clean & comfortable as the quarters we had quitted at Sleydinge.

28th Sunday

Dalrymple & I rode to the very pretty little town of Zottegem, the Hd Qtrs of the young Prince Frederick of Orange,* where there were a few Dutch troops. I saw & bought a little black mare to carry baggage for 20 Napoleons. The day was extremely hot; we returned to dinner having a party to dine with us.

Wellington and Blücher held a great review of the British cavalry and horse artillery which was clearly very impressive as every memorial of the period describes it in detail. Edwin is no different.

29th

The British cavalry & horse artillery were reviewed by the Duke of Wellington in the meadows near Schendelbeke, 4 or 5 miles from Grammont. We had to march about ten miles to the ground where we arrived at ½ past nine.

The cavalry were drawn up in three lines; the first composed of the 7th, 15th, 18th and 10th Hussars; the second line of the 1st & 2nd

---

* Prince Frederick of Orange was brother to William Prince of Orange of Peninsula and Waterloo fame. On 18 June Frederick actually commanded a Dutch Corps stationed around Hal to protect the allied right and did not take any part in the battle.

Lifeguards, the Blues (two squadrons of each) the King's Dragoon Guards, the Royals, the Greys, & the Inniskillings. The third line was composed of the 11th, 12th, 13th, 16th & 23rd regts of Light Dragoons, amounting altogether to 46 squadrons, & about 5000 men. The artillery were posted at intervals between the lines, consisting of thirty six pieces of different calibre besides a brigade of rockets.*

The Duke was accompanied by the Hereditary Prince of Orange, & his brother; the Duke de Berri,† Marshal Blucher,‡ and an immence [sic] train of big wigs, & staff people. The heat of the day was very great, not a cloud in the sky, or a breath of air stirring, all of which added to the brilliancy & beauty of the scene though it roasted us all to death. After they had passed along the different lines, we marched past by half squadrons and filed to our quarters where we did not arrive till between 7 & 8 in the evening. It being King Charles's Restoration day all the troops wore a sprig of oak in their caps which had a very good effect as we had no feathers with us.

Frederick noted

It was a magnificent sight the whole being in the finest possible order.

30th

Dalrymple & I took a quiet ramble to ride off the fatigues of yesterday. We went to look at a Chateau near Sint-Maria with an idea of taking up our abode there, but found it so dull & out of the way that we changed our minds. The day was much cooler than yesterday, & the evening turned out wet. The more we see of this country the more we find to admire. This day we rode through some rye that was high enough to conceal one on horseback: I brought home a root of it & found one stalk measure[d] seven feet nine inches and this was by no means uncommon.§ Every other species of vegetation was proportionably [sic] luxuriant.

---

* The horse artillery were equipped with either 6- or 9-pounders, Whinyates's battery having both cannon and rockets in addition.

† Charles Ferdinand, the Duc de Berry, was the son of the Comte d'Artois, Louis XVIII's younger brother.

‡ Gebhard Leberecht von Blücher, Prince of Wahstadt, commanded the Prussian army, he had proven to be Napoleon's most implacable enemy.

§ The height of the crops was to become a major factor in this campaign, particularly at Quatre Bras, it is perhaps easier to understand how difficult it was for infantry to protect themselves from surprise cavalry attacks, when even horsemen were able to hide themselves within the crops.

Waterloo

31st

Took my usual morning ramble. The heat which had been rather oppressive for several days had left us, & this evening I enjoyed a good fire & the Vicar of Wakefield.

June 1st

Several of us rode to see Oudenaarde, the scene of one of Marlborough's victories.* It stands in a flat country & is watered by the River Scheldt or Escaut, which runs through the town. There is a good sized square, on one side of which is the Stadt House, or Town Hall; a very curious old building; on the other sides are tolerably good shops. We dined at the Head Inn where the dinner, stables garden &c &c resembled an English inn more than usual. Oudenaarde was once a fortification, but dismantled like most others in the Low Countries during the reign of Joseph II of Germany.† People are now employed in throwing up works & batteries on the principal roads leading into it. The ride was beautiful all the way, and I think I saw more good looking people, particularly of the fair sex in & near Oudenaarde than in any other part of Flanders which generally speaking has not much female beauty to boast.

Unfortunately at this point, probably because of the sameness of the days, Edwin seems to have ceased writing in his diary. He did however write to his uncle Sir Alured Clark in early June.

Gorikx‡ near Oudenaarde June 2nd 1815

My dear uncle,

I have intended writing to you for several days but something has always interrupted me. The first principal purport of my letter is to thank you most sincerely for your kind attention to my wishes about a map which I received safe & like very much. From the little experience I have already had it appears correct & for its scale contains a great number of small villages. You have not told me what it cost or I would send it to you as I have a few bank notes with me that are of no use here. We had a prosperous voyage from Cork sailed on the 13th & landed at Ostend on the

---

* Marlborough and Eugene won a great victory against the French at Oudenarde 11 July 1708.

† Joseph II was Holy Roman Emperor from 1765–90. He tried to bring in many radical reforms during his reign including the enforced distribution of land to serfs but failed having caused major unrest in Holland.

‡ Edwin spells the town as Gooritz, but this is almost certainly a misspelling of Gorik as in Sint-Goriks-Oudenhove, where the regiment had been stationed for some while.

morning of the 18th. Marched to Bruges that day & to Ghent the next, in the neighbourhood of which place we remained till the 20th & then came to the villages we now occupy.

The Duke of Wellington received the cavalry & horse artillery on Monday last on some meadows near Gramont, we were drawn up in three lines; the first composed 24 half squadrons of hussars, the second of 19 squadrons of heavy dragoons & the 3rd line of 15 squadrons of lt. dragoons. The artillery was posted at intervals between the lines. It was a beautiful & gratifying sight as we are all in excellent order; the day was very fine & a great concourse of spectators attended. I don't think the Duke looks well or in good spirits. I trust however I may be deceived & that he is both. Blucher, Marmont* & number of big wigs accompanied him & dined afterwards with Lord Uxbridge at Ninove.

Flanders is without any exception the finest country I ever saw, richly cultivated & wooded, & full of houses & cottages every one of which could serve as a model for convenience, cleanliness & comfort. Living is cheap, as it abounds in all the necessaries of life & the people so universally well disposed that the enemies for which hundreds are tried annually & so get to swing in the unfortunate country we have just quitted are perfectly unknown in this!

We are quite in the dark respecting our future operations but the question of peace or war with Buonaparte having been decided at home, I suppose a few days more will let us into the secret here. I saw Campbell at Cork looking better than I thought he ever would again. Frederick unites with me in best love &c. to you with yours my dear uncle ever most affectionately

Edwin Griffith†

Luckily for us, Frederick continued with his diary although it is often brief and to the point.

Went on visit to Oudenaarde then occupied the above cantonments until the 16th.

On 9 June the Fifth Brigade, which consisted of 7th Hussars, 15th Hussars and

---

* Marshal Auguste Frederic Louis Viesse de Marmont, duc de Ragusa had shown some skill in dealing with Wellington in Spain but he was severely wounded at the Battle of Salamanca and did not serve in Spain again. With the return of Napoleon, he went into exile with Louis XVIII.

† This letter has had a note added, presumably by one of Edwin's sisters 'The last letter written from him, alas'.

2nd Hussars KGL, were inspected at Schendlebecke by Colquhoun Grant, who seemed to enjoy finding fault with everything, but it seems that when Lieutenant General the Earl of Uxbridge, Commander of all the cavalry, arrived he proceeded to compliment everybody on their turnout, which did not please Grant.

This pleasant but mundane life of leisure was shattered in the early hours of 16 June 1815. The order arrived at five o'clock and the 15th were on the march by 7 o'clock to Grammont.

June 16th

When we received orders at day break to turn out; marched through Grammont, Enghien, Braine-le-Comte, & Nivelles; & bivouacked about two miles from Quatre Bras; where the action had been fought that day.

According to Gibney's account, the original order simply called them to the brigade's alarm post at Grammont, with the rather alarming news that the French were only eight miles away. As soon as they arrived at Grammont the brigade marched on towards Enghien without stopping; where on their arrival they halted for thirty minutes to feed both horses and men if they had a morsel in their pockets. At Enghien they received news that the Guards infantry brigade had marched from there early that morning. Further orders arriving, the regiment continued to march a further five leagues to Braine-le-Comte which they reached by late afternoon. They were not permitted to halt, but continued to Nivelles, which they reached at ten p.m., and rode on a further two leagues, passing great numbers of wounded on the road, until they reached the crossroads of Quatre Bras at midnight. They had marched fifty miles that day, according to Gibney's estimate, virtually without a halt. The regiment encamped near the houses on the crossroads and after feeding the horses they rapidly sank into a deep slumber, only to be awoken to form up before daybreak, as usual when in presence of the enemy.

17th

Were on our horses at five o'clock, marched to Quatre Bras where we remained dismounted until three p.m. when Ld. W. commenced his retreat to the position at Waterloo. We accordingly retired before the enemies cavalry & bivouacked in rear of the position.

Unfortunately any journal or letters written by Edwin or Frederick regarding the vital three days of the Waterloo campaign are missing; however, from letters and journals of other men of the 15th, it is possible to reconstruct their involvement. The regiment was moved up in front of Quatre Bras in the early morning to form part of a cavalry screen, where they were obliged to remain throughout the morning while Wellington drew off his infantry and artillery to a position just in front of the forest of Soignies. As the 2nd Hussars KGL still remained on the Franco-Belgian border near Mons, the 13th Light Dragoons were added to Grant's brigade in their place.

The cavalry retired at three in the afternoon in three columns. The 13th, 15th and 2nd Light Dragoons KGL formed the right column which passed the River Genappe by a ford and retired to the ridge at Mont St Jean with little molestation. The central column, however, was at times forced to retire at speed to avoid being overwhelmed. Unfortunately the regiment lost some wounded as prisoners and some baggage in the retreat, when a small force of light cavalry broke into the column and made off with them. Captain Wodehouse' squadron forced them back taking a few prisoners in their turn.

The regiment seems to have bivouacked for the night to the left of Mont St Jean farm. The men settled down on the boggy ground amid pools of filthy water with no food or drink to quell their severe hunger pangs; a lucky few found a little comfort from smoking their cigars. Like everyone else they suffered dreadfully from the incessant heavy rain and many lay shaking from the gnawing cold.

Again they were roused before daylight for fear of a dawn attack and they moved to a position just in the rear of the Hougoumont chateau and farm complex; but once the light was good enough to prevent surprises, the men settled into their routines of feeding the horses and checking their equipment, loading pistols with dry powder, drying and cleaning their rusty swords and gaining warmth around a fire, while if they were lucky, preparing their food. The 15th were luckier than many that fateful day as their wagons had found them and food was distributed to the men and forage for the horses. Water, though, was a serious problem as there were no streams nearby and the Guards, who were preparing to defend the nearby chateau of Hougoumont, were ordered to refuse all access into the chateau grounds, where there was a well which could have easily supplied their wants.

18th

The memorable Battle of Waterloo ...

The position of the hussar brigade was just behind the ridge at the rear of Hougoumont farm, where they protected the right wing of the army. During the attack against Hougoumont which heralded the commencement of the battle, the hussars remained under this cover only to be occasionally troubled by roundshot which overreached the farm and bounded over the rise.

The brigade remained in this relatively quiet position until 2 p.m. but had recently begun to suffer from the fire from a battery placed upon a height on the Nivelles road and protected by a large force of lancers, which enfiladed their position and began to cause some casualties. Lord Uxbridge ordered the brigade to prepare to march across the ground which intervened between them and the guns. The movement was rendered unnecessary, however, following a great cry from the French lancers, after which the guns retired.

Looking back towards the allied lines to discover the reason for their jubilation, they saw masses of cuirassiers cresting the ridge and charging the infantry squares stationed in its lee. Grant left two troops (those of Wodehouse and Frederick Philips) of the 15th on the right wing to watch the valley leading to Braine l'Alleud for any French turning movement. Once again Frederick was destined to be side-lined and although given an important task, little happened; indeed his troop did not record any casualties at all during the battle.

The 13th Regiment formed to the front and charged a force of cuirassiers forcing them over the ridge and back some 300 yards. The two squadrons of the 15th supported them on their left and made a brilliant charge upon a regiment of lancers. Ney had launched his great cavalry attack and wave after wave of cavalry were launched against Wellington's centre in the clear ground between Hougoumont and La Haye Sainte. No one can be sure how many charges were made by the French cavalry. They were stubbornly resisted by the allied squares, and it seems that they lasted virtually without respite from 3 p.m. until nearly 6 p.m. The 15th was fully involved in this contest, forming behind the infantry and advancing to engage the broken remnants of each attack on the squares, driving them back over the ridge before calmly returning to their original position where they would await the following wave.

Some time between six and seven p.m., when the cavalry attacks had finally failed, the 15th were called forward and stationed immediately to the rear of the road, the banks of which they hugged tightly for protection from the heavy artillery fire. Near seven o'clock they were ordered to charge a strong column of French infantry, supported by a large body of cuirassiers, which seems to have advanced in support of Ney's successful attack upon La Haye Sainte. William Siborne states that a massive skirmisher screen was pushed out by the French, consisting of the remnants of Donzelot's and Alix's Divisions, but many, including the 15th, claim that the French infantry were formed in solid columns rather than deployed as skirmishers. The version as described by the 15th seems more likely, as even a dense screen could hardly be mistaken for a solid column by experienced soldiers. Further evidence comes from the fact that when charged, the French had time to take up a defensive square formation before the 15th could close with them.

The 15th, numbering about 240 men in four troops* prepared to charge the

---

* A manuscript in the regimental records and initialled by Colonel Dalrymple shows the following distribution: present in the brunt of the action: eleven sergeants, eight corporals, three trumpeters, 217 privates and 239 horses; detached on the right wing: ten sergeants, seven corporals, three trumpeters, 105 privates and 125 horses. Absent with the baggage: nine sergeants, two corporals, fifty privates and sixty-one horses.

infantry, but as they crested the ridge they became a target for the French gunners and began to suffer dreadfully. Surgeons Gibney and Cartan were ordered back to Mont St Jean in preparation for any casualties, but had not left when Colonel Dalrymple was struck as the charge commenced. I believe it was likely that he was struck early on, as once they drew near the infantry, the French cannon would not have dared to fire for fear of hitting their own. A ball of roundshot had killed his horse and shattered Dalrymple's left leg, leaving it suspended only by a few muscles with the bone in splinters; the shot had then continued on to kill Grant's horse which was nearby, one of five horses he lost at Waterloo. A door removed from a nearby outhouse was quickly turned into a palliasse to carry him to the surgeon for amputation.* It would appear that Lieutenant Buckley was mortally wounded at about this time.†

Edwin took command and led the charge home, but the infantry were fully formed in square and took deliberate aim, particularly singling out the senior officer riding out in front. Such a charge against formed infantry was rash if not suicidal, but orders were orders and Edwin led the regiment bravely forward. A number of shots rang out, emptying a few saddles and both Edwin and his horse, Forrester, crashed to the ground never to rise again. Edwin had received five musket balls in his chest and died instantly; later that evening he was to be buried by his brother officers at the same spot.‡ The fateful date of 18 June had struck the Griffith's family again, first his father, then his mother, now Edwin himself. Indeed, the family stone erected by Edwin's sisters near the baptistry of the church of St Mary the Virgin in Mold records:

---

* Gibney in his memoirs written many years later, states that Dalrymple was brought to him at Waterloo, but Dalrymple who kept a journal on the spot records that Surgeons Gibney and Cartan were with the regiment when he was wounded as he states, 'Dr Gibney bound up the wounds and assisted by Dr Cartan, carried on a plank to Waterloo. I was placed in a room with an officer of the 33rd desperately hurt in the neck. He died in the course of the night before which his groans were most melancholy. Particularly to a person in my situation . . .'

† Gibney arrived at Waterloo village with Dalrymple and recalls 'I came across my dear young friend Lieutenant Buckley of my regiment. He had received a bullet wound in the stomach; the missile had passed through his liver and come out through his back, causing great haemorrhage. I hurriedly dressed the wound and gave him all the hope possible, but did not conceal my misgivings.' He died of his wounds the following day.

‡ The various accounts describing the death of Edwin Griffith are very confusing; some claim the 15th were charging cavalry, others infantry, and they all usually describe him as simply receiving five wounds but not specifically how caused. However, Dalrymple's journal says 'Hancox called on me at night and communicated the sad account of poor Griffith's death by 5 musquet [sic] wounds, one instantaneously mortal.' I must thank Ralph Thompson, Assistant at the Hussar Museum, Newcastle for providing this information.

Waterloo

Sacred to the Memory
Of Thomas Griffith Esqre of Rhual
who died,
June 18th 1811.
Of Henrietta Maria his Wife, who died
June 18th 1813.
And of Edwin their youngest Son,
Major in the 15th Light Dragoons
Who, on a day so Fatal to his family
June 18th 1815
fell, in the thirtieth year of his Age
pierc'd in the breast by five honourable wounds, while
gallantly leading his Regiment, which he commanded
to a charge of a body of French, in the sanguinary
and ever memorable battle of Waterloo.
His remains were inter'd by his afflicted Companions
in Arms on the field of arduous conflict.
Peace to the Good and Brave!*

The command of the 15th now devolved upon Captain Thackwell who, it seems, drove the regiment to the attack once again, charging the square of infantry. As he led them on he was shot through the left hand then seconds later received another ball in the left arm that shattered the bone and he fell to the ground. He too faced the surgeon's knife before dawn.†

For the third time in a period of no more than a quarter of an hour, the command of the 15th changed hands again, Captain Hancox now being in

---

*   It will be noted that my version is a little different from that printed by Wylly (1914) p. 246, but its veracity can be confirmed by the photograph of the stone printed in this volume. Wylly wrongly inserts the word 'cavalry' after '. . . a body of French . . .' which may be a cause of the confused writings on the death of Edwin (see note * opposite).

†   There is quite a lot of confusion in the various accounts of the 15th at Waterloo as to when exactly these charges and losses occurred. However, piecing all the available evidence together it is clear that the 15th charged and forced back the French infantry column just prior to the advance of the Guard. From the position given to this infantry column on Thackwell's plan in his letter to Siborne dated 20 December 1834 (The Waterloo Letters No 68), their position would be completely in the way of the Guard and must have been removed before they advanced. This premise is proven by Thackwell's statement in the same letter that 'This square was charged by . . . the 15th Hussars, . . . a little before or about the time of the advance of the Imperial Guard; but as I was then severely wounded . . .' This also proves that the portrait of Thackwell charging at the head of the 15th at Waterloo is in error when it shows the French square to have been composed of the Imperial Guard.

command, and it was he that brought the regiment out of the battle a little later.

The 15th then retired to the rear of the infantry while keeping some skirmishers out and took no part in the defeat of the attack of the Imperial Guard. However, immediately their retreat was known the French army visibly wavered, Wellington launched all of his forces to overwhelm them and complete the victory. Grant's brigade joined fully into this pursuit, the 7th Hussars overthrowing a large force of lancers and the 15th charging through the infantry.

The regiment continued to harry the French fugitives as the retreat now became a complete rout and rode on about three miles before exhaustion forced them to halt and allow the Prussian cavalry to take over the pursuit. It is clear that some French units put up a stiff resistance to the 15th even during the final retreat, as many of the regiment's casualties occurred towards the close of the action.

Total losses for the 15th at Waterloo were three officers killed or died of wounds and seven wounded,[*] two sergeants killed and three wounded,[†] twenty-three rank-and-file killed or died of wounds and forty-five wounded[‡] and forty-three horses killed, thirty-two wounded.

Frederick had been stationed on the right throughout the day and would have been unaware of the death of Edwin until the regiment reformed after the battle. His grief would undoubtedly have been great and he would surely have formed one of the party who must have searched the battlefield the following morning to discover Edwin's body and bury him where he had fallen. It is certainly recorded that Edwin's possessions were put into the hands of Frederick.

It would have been Frederick's painful duty to write to his mother and aunts to advise them of the loss of Edwin before the official lists were published. Soon after the battle, an epitaph to Edwin was published by his sisters:

> Weep not; he died as heroes die,
> The death permitted to the brave;
> Mourn not; he lies where soldiers lie,
> And valour envies such a grave.

---

[*] The officers were: killed, Major Griffith, Lieutenants Sherwood and Buckley; wounded, Lt Colonel Dalrymple, Captains Thackwell and Whiteford, and Lieutenants Mansfield, William Byam, Edward Byam and George Dawkins.

[†] The sergeants killed were Hubbard and Monro.

[‡] The privates killed or died of wounds were Bailey, Black, J Brown, Budd, Carnell, Coggins, Collins, Curtis, Dollman, F Drake, French, Knapp, Milton, S Morgan, Moss, Napier, Phippard, Shelmerdyne, D Smith, Stewart, Townsend, Whitehouse and T Williams. It should be noted that a number of names differ in their spelling here to Wylly (page 247–8). I have followed the Waterloo Medal Roll spellings, which are more likely to be correct. It should be noted that Townsend is not recorded as 'killed' in the Roll and it is possible that the discrepancy of one which Wylly mentions, may well be this man.

Waterloo

He was the love of bold emprise,
Of soldier's hardships, soldier's fame!
And his the wish by arms to rise,
And gain a proud, a deathless name!

Later when recovered from the amputation of his left arm, Joseph Thackwell, who had been made the regimental major in lieu of Edwin on the spot, rode from his quarters in Brussels to Waterloo village, where he arranged for a stone tablet to be placed in Waterloo church on behalf of the regiment, to the memory of Edwin and the other officers who had died. It reads:

To
The Memory
of
Major Edwin Griffith
Lieutenant Isaac Sherwood and
Lieutenant Henry Buckley
Officers in the xvth King's Regiment of Hussards
(British)
Who fell in the Battle of
Waterloo
June XVIIIth MDCCCXV
This Stone was Erected by the Officers
of THAT REGIMENT
As a testimony of their Respect
Dulce et decorum est pro Patria mori*

The 15th, led by Captain Hancox, advanced towards Mons on 19 June, leaving the injured in the care of Surgeon Gibney at Waterloo and Assistant Surgeon Jeyes† at Brussels. Frederick continued to note the bare facts of their movements in his journal, but not surprisingly there was no joy or care taken over them.

19th
Followed up the retreating army & bivouacked near Nivelles.

---

* It will be noted that my version of the tablet is a little different to that produced in Wylly (page 254) but has been recently re-checked for accuracy at the church. I must thank Mr Paule Van Kerkhove for checking this for me, when I recently discovered the discrepancy.
† Assistant Surgeon Samuel Jeys had been promoted into the regiment from a hospital mate in 1811. He was to become a surgeon in 1822 and surgeon to the forces in 1838. He seems to have altered the spelling of his surname in later life.

20th
Bivouac near Ville sur Haine. [6 km east of Mons]

21st
Proceeded at daybreak; the cavalry assembled under the walls of Mons. We were quartered for the night at Nouvelle.

22nd
Proceeded through Bavay to a small village in front of Le Cateau-Cambresis. Bivouacked.

The 15th was ordered to join the 4th Division commanded by General Colville*
who was to invest the fortress of Cambrai.

23rd
Marched to Cambrai: remained under the walls the whole day. Bivouacked at Forenville.

24th
Cambrai stormed and taken.

Colville ordered an assault on Cambrai and after a short resistance from the French garrison, the fortress capitulated. It is strange, however, that Frederick did not record an incident that occurred this day, one indeed that was very close to causing his own death!

Family tradition, which is confirmed by William, recounts that during the day of the storming, the 15th patrolled the suburbs. When riding through some gardens, the ground suddenly gave way beneath Frederick's horse. Luckily he was able to extract his feet from the stirrups and propel himself to safety as his horse plummeted all of one hundred or so feet to the bottom of a hidden well or mine shaft where it was killed instantly.†

---

* Lieutenant General Sir Charles Colville had commanded the reserve force stationed at Hal, who remained unaware of the great battle throughout the day despite their proximity.

† William recounts this incident in detail on pages 259–60 of his Jottings. I quote 'His [Frederick's] troop was on the extreme left of the extended line, and he was directed to open a communication with an infantry post stationed on our left, and at a windmill on an elevated spot. I accompanied him on this duty, and after cantering through a field of very high-standing rye, I suddenly lost sight of him, being a few yards in his rear; but on clearing the field found him standing on the brink of a well into which his charger had precipitated himself, and deposited his rider harmless on the margin. It would be difficult to give expression to the mixed feelings of horror and joy I felt on this occasion.

Frederick continued laconically:

25th

Remained at Forenville

26th

St Quentin; bivouacked.

27th

Marched through Nesle to Roye.

28th

Passed the River Oise and remained at Arencon.

29th

—

30th

Arrived at Epiais [Rhus]

1st

Halt

2nd July

Herblay

On 3 July Paris surrendered to the allies and was occupied by their forces on 6 July. It is possible that Frederick and his fellow officers revisited their favourite haunts in Paris, which they had discovered the year before; but perhaps Frederick was not in the mood to enjoy it and stayed away. Unfortunately Frederick gives us no clue.

7th

Chatou [north of Versailles] where we remained until . . .

The spot was revisited on the following morning, and a peasant was lowered down by a rope, who cut off the valise and brought up what else was valuable or useful. The well proved to be a dry one, of about forty yards in depth; the mouth had been masked by some slight material, whether for a hellish purpose must be left to conjecture. The poor animal, a noble charger, lay at the bottom crushed and doubled up. And what an escape for the owner, whom the slightest hitch of his spur in any of the numerous trappings, must have caused to be dragged into the abyss!'

From Corunna to Waterloo

31st

When we proceeded to Pontoise.

Aug 1st

Magny-en-Vexin

2nd

Lions le Foret where the regiment remained until the 3rd of October when we received orders to move to Gisons. Was quartered at the Chateau de Boisdenuent.

An unexpected order for a change of quarters was received on 3 October but their new quarters in the villages near Fauville-en-Caux proved to be very comfortable indeed.

On the 10th;

moved to Rouen

11th

Fauville. I was quartered at St-Aubin-de-Cretot. Afterwards at Rocquefort.

The first letter after Waterloo to survive was sent to Frederick and was posted from Rhual by his mother, giving full details of Edwin's last will and testament, which it seems, had only just been found by luck in Edwin's writing box which had obviously been returned to the family with his possessions.

Rhual Oct 9th 1815

If you receive Charlotte's letter, which went two days ago, much before you get this, you will be anxious my dearest Frederick, to know the particulars of our beloved Edwin's will, which she mentioned our having found; I shall therefore copy it for you on this side of my paper, to prevent all chance of its being torn in opening; but must first observe, that I found it in the writing desk, which my uncle looked over himself, on his first arrival here 5 or 6 weeks ago, & though he seemed to examine all the papers accurately, (for I sat by him though I did not touch any of them) the only one we so anxiously wished, & expected to find, unluckily escaped his notice; which was very extraordinary but I conclude, it must then have got slipt [*sic*] into some other paper with the jumble of the journey; but I found it in nothing particular, merely laying at the bottom of the desk, which I never should have looked into again, as you may suppose it a most melancholy employment for me, but just before our good uncle left us last Monday; he said it had occurred to him that he had not opened the packets

270

of letters, & that as such a paper as we wanted might be tied up in some of them, he begged I would open every one carefully, & see nothing was enclosed, & then he thought they had better be burnt; so accordingly last Friday, Charlotte & Caroline, being gone out on horseback I took the opportunity of fulfilling my promise, without any chance of interruption, & I was soon fortunate to see, what we have all been so anxious to obtain, as we could hardly doubt, of a will having been made, after your opinion on the subject, what the surgeon told Col. Dalrymple, & above all, the full conviction we felt of our dearest Edwin having provided to the best of his power for those sisters who wanted it most, his excellent heart always suggested to him to do the thing that was right, his life was consequently, a life of the most exemplary virtue, & he is now I humbly hope in the full enjoyment of such happiness, as 'passeth mans understanding'.

The will is written in his own hand on a sheet of paper, which was enclosed, sealed up, & on the outside written as follows.

'My last will & testament, to be opened by any kind friend who will be good enough to see my wishes attended to. E Griffith, Major 15th Hussars'.

'I Edwin Griffith of Rhual, in the county of Flint, being in a sound state of mind, do hereby declare this to be my last will & testament; dated at Buenza in Spain the 6th day of Nov 1813'.

'As the house & estate of Rhual is left between me, & my four sisters, Henrietta Maria Philips, Louisa Morgan, Charlotte Griffith, & Caroline Griffith, share & share alike, (as specified in my father & mother's marriage settlements), I do, in consideration of my sisters Charlotte & Caroline Griffith, not being so well provided for as my sisters Philips & Morgan, give & bequeath to them, Charlotte Griffith & Caroline Griffith, the whole, & every part of my share of the aforementioned estate of Rhual; & if that estate shall have been sold for the purpose of dividing the amount between us, then, whatever sum, or sums my share may be, either paid, or owing to me for that estate, I give & bequeath in like manner to my sisters Charlotte & Caroline.

Also the whole of the furniture of the house of Rhual, all the plate, books, linen, & all the live & dead stock, which may be on the premises, or anywhere else belonging to me at the time of my death, (& which have been left to me by my ever honored & beloved mother) I give & bequeath to my sisters Charlotte & Caroline Griffith; save & except my bay horse*

---

* Presumably his horse Forrester killed at Waterloo and subject of the painting at Rhual.

which I bought from my nephew Frederick Charles Philips, which I leave to him; & my grey charger, & baggage animals which I leave to my other nephew Edward Morgan Captain in the 7th Royal Fusiliers, if he thinks any of them worth his acceptance. My gold watch & seals the late property of my ever honored & beloved father, I give also to my nephew Frederick C Philips, & every part of my regimental appointments, which he thinks worth his acceptance.

Edwin Griffith, Major 15th Hussars
Buenza in Spain Nov 6 1813

One copy of this will I keep in my own possession, & give the other in charge of Mr Cocksedge Paymaster* of the regt; who will oblige me in case of my death by sending it by a safe conveyance to my sister Charlotte Griffith of Rhual in the county of Flint'.
E.G.

This is every word of the will, & the only omission in it is there being no witness's as *three* are necessary in the strictness of law where landed property is left; but in this I suppose it can make no difference, as only our own family are concerned, & it's very unlikely we should any of us find a fault with what was so well meant; I sent Mr Morgan a copy of it yesterday, but owing to the tediousness of the post, we shall not hear from them for some days; I fear the intelligence will not be pleasing to him, as he had long given up all idea of their being such a thing, & was consequently making arrangements for *an equal division of everything* here, which is not quite at an end, as poor Charlotte & Caro have all between them which is very right & proper, what would the books, plate &c be divided amongst *four*? But it will [mean little] for them for their lives; as to me, I am not satisfied with a fifth for my share of the estate [nor] of the personalty, but am most thankful that [it is clear] whose right it is; I will let you know how [it] is arranged, as things occur, but take [care of my] comments, I mean relating to your uncle, [it is] extraordinary it seems that the Paymaster [retains] the copy he has of the will; if you know where [he is, you] had better write to him *immediately* for it, for if you keep it, it will be the same I suppose, but it ought to be taken care of; how sadly vexatious it will be to you my dearest Frederick, to find that the two principal things the dear fellow left

---

* Paymaster James Coppin Cocksedge, served with the 15th Hussars from 1813 to 1818. If indeed he retained a copy of Edwin's will it is far from clear why he had not presented the same to the family.

you, are gone, & never can be yours; & I much fear you have sold several of the horses & things that were to be for Edward & you, so what can be done for him I know not; I grieve above everything that the watch is gone (which my uncle told me you mentioned being the case) for that, having belonged to your dear grandfather before, would I am certain have made it even still more valuable to you; the poor horse would also have been a great treasure to you, from having been such a favourite of our dearest Edwin's; but though both of these are gone, I hope you will have something to keep for ever for his sake; you had better write to the depot, to desire all the baggage &c &c belonging to him may be left safe & untouched till your return!

I think I requested in one of my former letters that you would take particular care of all the papers, memorandums &c that you found, that we may have them some time, & particularly if there is any journal, Charlotte says there certainly is one, of a year or two's standing, but that might have been left at the depot in some of the packages; pray mention this, poor Charlotte is so anxious to know its safe. I have hardly room left for more than to thank you for your last letter dated the 20th of Sept which contained a very interesting account of the country, place &c you now inhabit, I fear you must find it dull enough though you seem to have met with a good deal of attention & civility, particularly from your acquaintance Mr Maupasse.

I am glad you have been at Rouen, as it must be a place well worth seeing; your father stayed there many months, to learn French; I hope you are constantly improving yourself in the language, I should make a point of learning to write it grammatically & fluently if I was you, as it certainly is a great advantage to know languages, particularly to an officer; whenever you answer your sister's letter, I wish you would do it in French, & I will make her continue the correspondence in the same way as well as she is able; it would improve her more than anything. We were all very glad to hear of poor little Fury having gained you once more, after all her perils & dangers, & the *1000* chances there was (after we lost her) of her ever getting back to you; her life would be a curious one if she could write an account of it. Charlotte says she told you of our good uncle's departure, I never saw anything so low as he was, which was sure to be the case, for he certainly always doated [*sic*] on this dear place & which he has now quitted for ever! & alas! So must we all in the course of a few months; which I quite dread the thoughts of. The two girls, myself & Charlotte unite in affectionate love to you my dearest boy, & believe me ever your very tenderly attached mother. Emma is gone to Mostyn for the hunt.

Alas! & alas! How happy were we all attending it this time last year. Answer this directly pray. I got your last on the 28th or 29th of Sept only a week after it was written, so I am now in daily hopes of another. God bless you!

My uncle was to reach home today. I wrote on Saturday & sent him a copy of the will, which I know will afford him the *greatest* satisfaction, he all along felt so certain there must be one somewhere.

The only major change to their routine occurred on 24 July when the emperors of Russia, Austria and Prussia reviewed Wellington's whole army of British, Hanoverian and Belgian troops arrayed along the Champs Elysees.

Orders were finally received on 13 December to proceed to Dieppe, where the regiment formed part of a new brigade commanded once again by Colquhoun Grant, consisting of the 11th and 13th Light Dragoons and 15th Hussars and Lieutenant Colonel Smith's troop of horse artillery. Frederick went into cantonments in the neighbouring village of Arques-la-Bataille. While near Dieppe the regiment received a draft from the depot of three officers and 102 men to make up their losses at Waterloo.

Dec 13th

Dieppe

16th

Arques

A letter from Frederick survives giving news that the 15th were rumoured to remain in France with the occupying forces for three years.

Dieppe January 6th 1816

My dearest Charlotte & Caroline,

My correspondence has been so frequent with my mother since the melancholy event with which it has pleased God to afflict us; that I have heard of you constantly; but as you will be separated from her for three months, I must beg that one of you will now and then, let me know how you are: the longer and more frequent your letters, the more pleasure I shall have in receiving them; I need scarcely add that the most trifling circumstances connected with yourselves, can never ceace [*sic*] to be a source of the greatest interest to me. It has made me very happy to hear that my mother and yourselves have taken a house that is likely to suit you. I remember the name of the place perfectly; but do not think I ever was at it. I trust you are improving in health and spirits; it gave me great pleasure to learn that you were engaged to spend some time at Downing, the society of such kind friends cannot fail to be of service to you. Pray remember me most particularly to them; and tell David, that when he has nothing better to do I hope he will pay me a visit for a month or two; we are generally in comfortable quarters, and can find room for himself & horses; add to which we should in most places be able to show him some good shooting. Dieppe is dirty and miserable enough; as most seaports are: but I fancy our stay will be short; for we are in constant expectation of receiving orders to take up our cantonments on the frontiers. You will probably have heard that the 15th is one of the regiments destined to remain in the country for *three* years; I should have had no objection to *one*, for the purpose of perfecting myself in the language; but I suspect we shall be heartily tired before the period that is fixed is over.

I have just received a letter from my mother dated the 21st; she seems to have been tolerably lucky in her lodgings; though her journey was rather disastrous for the two first days – the Morgan's she says are in Margaret's Buildings – how utterly unaccountable *his* conduct upon a late sad occasion has been! But the subject is too disagreeable to dwell upon & you will probably have heard my *opinion* of it from my letters to my mother. His own reflection must be a severe punishment. Well I shall now release you from this scrawl which I dare say you will hardly be able to read. *Pray write* & believe me, my dear aunts ever most affectionately yours

Fred. C. Philips.

My love to Mina who I hope is well.

On 12 January the regiment marched through Eu and Abeville to the vicinity of Frevent, where they arrived on 14 January, Frederick being quartered at nearby Bonnieres.

Jan 12th

Eu

13th

Abbeville

14th

Bonnieres

The regiment continued its slow progress towards the channel ports, Fredericks's final entry in his diary reading simply:

21st

Avesnes le Comte.

On 2 February the regiment moved to the Bailleul area, where on the 20th of that month they were inspected by Colonel Doherty* of the 13th Dragoons, who temporarily commanded the brigade in Grant's absence. During February two sergeants and twenty-five men transferred from the regiment to the cavalry staff corps.

On 29 March the regiment marched again, this time to Bourbourg near Dunkirk. This was to be their last station in France. It had been decided to reduce the size of the Army of Occupation and at the end of April the 15th received their orders home. On 5 May Lord Combemere, the Sir Stapleton Cotton of Peninsula days, inspected the regiment prior to leaving. The majority of the horses were to be left in France, 151 going to the 7th Hussars and eighteen to the 11th Light Dragoons, leaving about seventy-six horses with the regiment.

The 15th accompanied by the 13th marched on foot to Calais on 7 May but some of the transports were delayed by contrary winds until 14 May. The regiment landed at Dover and proceeded immediately to Canterbury where they joined the depot. While stationed here, the officers and men were awarded the Waterloo medal and it was announced that all ranks could count two years additional service for the battle. Colonel Dalrymple was made a Companion of the Bath; Captain Thackwell was made major replacing poor Edwin, and Captain Hancox was made brevet major.

With the end of the regiment's foreign deployment, we draw this narrative to a close.

---

* Lieutenant Colonel Patrick Doherty was laid up at Brussels sick with fever on 18 June but was awarded a Waterloo Medal. He quit the service in 1818 and died at Bath in 1837.

EPILOGUE

The regiment was quickly reduced and settled back into the routines of life on home service, moving around the country to the various seats of unrest and parcelled out in small detachments across vast swathes of countryside. In 1820 Lieutenant Colonel Dalrymple died and Thackwell took command of the regiment, Frederick becoming the major by purchase on 11 July 1822. In 1824 the regiment moved to Ireland when Frederick decided to retire on half pay as a lieutenant colonel 14 January 1826. He also took a wife, one Margaret Palliser, who bore him three children, Grace, Frederick (died young) and rather poignantly an Edwin.

With regard to Edwin's two sisters still at Rhual, Charlotte and Caroline, Charlotte was to marry a Wynne-Eyton of Leeswood and set up home at the vicarage at Llangollen; Caroline does not appear to have married. All four of the sisters wanted their share of the inheritance and it was finally decided to sell Rhual. It had sold within three months to a Mr Samuel Knight, a wealthy banker and speculator for the vast sum of £24,500.

In 1830, on the coronation of William IV, the new sovereign decided to promote the two oldest general officers in the army to the rank of field marshal. Sir Alured Clarke, now eighty-five, was one of those so honoured. At the same moment, chance would have it that Mr Knight lost his fortune and Rhual was put up for sale. Sir Alured made the decision to buy back the house for the family and his portrait and marshal's baton of crimson velvet with a massive gold figure of St George and the Dragon atop still adorn the dining room of Rhual. Family history relates that Frederick danced for joy in the great hall on entering the house for the first time after his great uncle had bought it.

Unfortunately Sir Alured died soon after in 1832, when on a visit to his niece Charlotte in Llangollen. The contents of his house in Mansfield Place, London, were auctioned off including some 6,580 bottles of wine in the cellar!

Frederick inherited Rhual where his family now lived and his army career terminated when he transferred to the 82nd Foot on 5 April 1833 and retired by the sale of his commission on 5 July 1833.

Epilogue

Frederick also became deputy lieutenant for the county of Flint and survived until 13 July 1852, when at the age of fifty-nine he died while on a tour of Italy at Bagni di Lucca, Toscano, near Florence, where he lies buried in the English cemetery.

So ends the story of two
King's Hussars

BIBLIOGRAPHY

Unpublished Sources

The Rhual papers: D/HE/ 439 to 554; the military letters and journals of Major Edwin Griffith and Captain Frederick Philips. County Record Office, Hawarden, Flint.
Army records: The National Archives, Kew.

Published Sources

Anglesey, Marquess of, *One-Leg, the Life and Letters of Henry William Paget, First Marquess of Anglesey 1768–1854.* Jonathan Cape, London, 1961.
Anonymous, *Jottings from my Sabretasch*. R. Bentley, London, 1847. (Reprinted Ken Trotman, Cambridge, 2006.)
Anonymous, *The British Cavalry on the Peninsula; USJ 1831–33.* (Reprinted in book form Thompson, Sunderland, 1996–7.)*
Carnock, Maj. Ld, *Cavalry in the Corunna Campaign; extracts from the diary of the adjutant of the 15th Hussars.* The Journal for Army Historical Research, Special Publication No. 4, 1936.
Chandler, D. G., *A Dictionary of the Napoleonic Wars.* Arms & Armour Press, London, 1979.
Dalton, C., *The Waterloo Roll Call 2nd edition.* Eyre & Spottiswoode, London, 1904. (Reprinted Naval & Military Press, Uckfield, 1992.)
Fletcher, I. *Galloping at Everything.* Spellmount, Staplehurst, 1999.
Gibney, Major R. D., *Eighty Years Ago or the Recollections of an Old Army Officer.* John Murray, London, 1896.
Glover, G. [Ed.], *Letters from the Battle of Waterloo.* Greenhill Books, London, 2004.

---

* The anonymous writer of these articles, originally published in the United Service Journal in 1831, can be identified clearly by a little bit of detective work, as one Captain Thomas Dundas of the 15th Light Dragoons.

Bibliography

Gordon, Capt. Alexander, *A Cavalry Officer in the Corunna Campaign 1808–1809*. John Murray, London, 1913. (Reprinted Worley, Tyne and Wear, 1990.)

Gurwood, Lt Colonel, *Duke of Wellington's Dispatches 1799–1815*. John Murray, London, 1837–8.

Hall, J. A., *History of the Peninsular War Vol. VIII*. Greenhill Books, London, 1998.

Haythornthwaite, P., *Wellington's Military Machine*. Guild, London, 1989.

Heaton, Major B., *A Short History of Rhual*. Livesey, Shrewsbury, 1987.

Hunt, E., *Charging against Napoleon*. Pen & Sword, Barnsley, 2001.

Mollo, J., *The Prince's Dolls*. Pen & Sword, Barnsley, 1997.

Nafziger, G. and Park, S., *The British Military, Its System and Organization 1803–1825*. Rafm, Canada, 1983.

Oman, Sir C., *Wellington's Army 1809–1814*. Edward Arnold, London, 1913. (Reprinted Greenhill Books, London, 1986.)

Oman, Sir C., *Sir John Moore*. Hodder & Stoughton, London, 1953.

Oman, Sir C., *A History of the Peninsular War*. OUP, Oxford, 1914. (Reprinted Greenhill Books, London, 1996.)

Robertson, I. C., *Wellington at War in the Peninsula*. Pen & Sword, Barnsley, 2000.

Siborne, H. T., *The Waterloo Letters*. Cassell, London, 1891. (Reprinted Greenhill Books, London, 1983.)

Siborne, W., *History of the Waterloo Campaign 3rd Edition*. T & W Boone, London, 1848. (Reprinted Greenhill Books, London, 1990.)

Smith, D., *Napoleon's Regiments*. Greenhill Books, London, 2000.

Thoumine, R. H., *Scientific Soldier, a Life of General le Marchant 1766–1812*. OUP, London, 1968.

Tucker, N., *Peninsular War Letters*. National Library of Wales Journal XII, No. 2. Aberystwyth, 1961.

Vivian, Hon. C., *Richard Hussey Vivian, First Lord Vivian, a Memoir*. Isbister, London, 1897. (Reprinted Ken Trotman, Cambridge, 2004.)

War Office, *A List of all the Officers of the Army and Royal Marines*, 1815. (Reprinted Naval & Military Press, Uckfield, 2005.)

Wood, Gen. Sir E., *Cavalry in the Waterloo Campaign*. Pall Mall Magazine Library, London, 1895. (Reprinted Worley, Tyne and Wear, 1998.)

Wylly, Col. H. C., *The Military Memoirs of Lieut-General Sir Joseph Thackwell*. John Murray, London, 1908. (Reprinted Naval & Military Press, Uckfield, 2003.)

Wylly, Col. H. C., *XVth (The King's) Hussars 1759 to 1913*. Caxton, London, 1914.

The Royal Military Calendar, 3rd Edition. London, 1820. (Reprinted Naval & Military Press, Uckfield, 2003.)

INDEX

Index

Index

Index

Index

Index

Index

Letters from the
Battle of Waterloo
The Unpublished Correspondence
by Allied Officers from the Siborne Papers
edited by
Gareth Glover

'Unprecedented new information for historians.'
The Guardian

'An extraordinarily valuable contribution to our
understanding of the battle . . . These letters show
just how formidable Siborne's task was, even
without the opposition of great men.'
Richard Holmes in *History*

Waterloo is probably the most famous battle in military history. Thousands of books have been written on the subject and yet so many mysteries remain, so much controversy abounds.

Letters from the Battle of Waterloo, by presenting more than 200 previously unpublished accounts by Allied officers who fought at the battle, goes right back to primary source material. In the letters the Allied officers recount where they were and what they saw. Gareth Glover has provided background historical information but lets the officers speak for themselves as they reveal exactly what happened on the 16, 17 and 18 June 1815.

Originally sent to, and at the request of, Captain W. Siborne, then in the process of building his famous model of the battle, these letters have remained unread in the Siborne papers in the British Library. A selection of material was published in Waterloo Letters in 1891 but much of vast historical significance did not see the light then and has remained inaccessible until now.

Gareth Glover now presents this collection of revelatory correspondence for the first time. There are letters here by Major Baring, George Bowles, Edward Whinyates, John Gurwood and Edward Cotton as well as letters by Hanoverian and King's German Legion officers.

This is a veritable treasure trove of new material on the battle and one which will mean that every historian's view of the battle will need correcting.

Gareth Glover is a historian specialising in the Waterloo campaign and the Peninsular War.

Available now
Hardback
240 x 159 mm
pp. 320
ISBN 1-85367-597-0
£25.00
Greenhill Books